THE ART
OF JAZZ

THE ART

OF JAZZ

RAGTIME TO BEBOP

Edited by
MARTIN T. WILLIAMS

A DACAPO PAPERBACK

Library of Congress Cataloging in Publication Data

Williams, Martin T ed.
  The art of jazz.

  (A Da Capo paperback)
  Reprint of the ed. published by Oxford University
Press, New York.
  Includes index.
  1. Jazz music. 2. Jazz musicians. I. Title.
[ML3506.W53 1981] 781'.57   80-29197
ISBN 0-306-80134-5 (pbk.)

This Da Capo Press paperback edition of
The Art of Jazz: Ragtime to Bebop
is an unabridged republication of the first
edition, originally entitled *The Art of Jazz:
Essays in the Nature and Development of Jazz*
and published in New York in 1959, here supplemented
with an Afterword by Gunter Schuller. It is reprinted
by arrangement with Oxford University Press, Inc.

Published by Da Capo Press, Inc.
A Subsidiary of Plenum Publishing Corporation
227 West 17th Street, New York, N.Y. 10011

CONTENTS

Any anthology probably needs some introduction, but perhaps for some of us what an anthology of essays on jazz needs is an excuse.

As they have been telling us for a long time now, jazz is "America's contribution to the arts," but, from the way it is most often discussed, one would hardly think so. And if it had inspired only the kind of enthusiasm we are all too familiar with, one might conclude that the "art" of jazz did not exist but that it was some sort of intriguing emotional outburst that happened to be expressed on musical instruments, a pseudo-musical track meet, or a strange branch of big-time show biz that interests adolescents of all ages.

The answer is that jazz has inspired, besides the enthusiasm and the sometimes valuable, but naïvely dogmatic, sifting of names, a small but respectable body of criticism—the kind that only an art can inspire and that only an art deserves.

The most honest way for me to put it is, of course, the most subjective. My own contributions excepted, I have learned most from these essays on jazz. I had my enthusiasm to begin with, and, although the enthusiasms of others may have made it a bit more selective, it was writings like these which made me listen more carefully and I hope more perceptively. And it was writings such as these which were respectable enough so that I would be willing to recommend them to another who was curious but perhaps did not share my enthusiasm.

There is a healthy disagreement among the contributors, of course, and there is a variety of approaches from biography through modified musicology, from the "absolute" impressionistic tribute to an evolutionary relativism.

When the essays are placed in the order in which they appear here, they do make up a critical examination of the evolution of jazz music, a kind of handbook for listeners and critics. Inevitably there are gaps. Here, for example, there is no comprehensive essay on one of the few figures in jazz that one would be tempted to call a "genius", Louis Armstrong—none here, because none exists. And we need comprehensive examinations of Fletcher Henderson, Jack Teagarden, Baby Dodds, Blind Lemon Jefferson, Fats Waller, Earl Hines, Jimmie Lunceford, Benny Carter, Red Allen, Roy Eldridge—and many others. But this collection suffers from a certain imbalance; for example, William Russell's reviews of boogie woogie pianists were exceptional jazz criticism and had to be included. But knowing how Yancey did it, we understand more about how a Monk does it; understanding how a Max Roach does it, we hear a Sonny Greer with more understanding.

I think that in one sense the collection may also stand (my own contributions again excepted) as a kind of summary of what we know and of the various constructive ways of looking at what we know. Such work has laid some bases on which to proceed, a summation and point of departure for comment on jazz in the future, and a degree of critical respectability on which those of us who love jazz should be willing to present it to others for their understanding of its methods and achievements.

In preparing this volume, I have received assistance and advice especially from Nat Hentoff, Whitney Balliett, Marshall Stearns, Max Harrison, Albert J. McCarthy, and Peter Gammond. I might also thank the writers and their first publishers for their permission to use their essays, but what I should really thank them for is having helped me hear jazz with a greater understanding and having put me in closer touch with its art.

MARTIN WILLIAMS

New York
April 1959

THE ART
OF JAZZ

Jelly Roll Morton. (Photo courtesy of the New York Jazz Museum.)

Scott Joplin. (Photo courtesy of the New York Jazz Museum.)

Sidney Bechet. (Photo courtesy of the Institute for Jazz Studies.)

Meade "Lux" Lewis. (Photo courtesy of the Institute for Jazz Studies.)

Charlie Christian. (Photo courtesy of the Institute for Jazz Studies.)

The Modern Jazz Quartet. Forward, left to right: **Milt Jackson, John Lewis;** behind, left to right: **Connie Kay, Percy Heath.** (Photo courtesy of the Institute for Jazz Studies.)

Art Tatum. (Photo courtesy of the Institute for Jazz Studies.)

Billie Holiday. (Photo courtesy of the Institute for Jazz Studies.)

*The recognition of ragtime and jazz in one or another of their forms
by European intellectuals, artists, and enthusiasts is, as we know, at least
as old as Brahms—and we have long been told that real critical discussion
of jazz began in Europe.*

*Ernest Ansermet's essay on Will Marion Cook first appeared in 1918
in the Swiss Revue Romande. Although in some parts of his discussion,
M. Ansermet confused American popular music and the pseudo-ragtime
of Tin Pan Alley with the kind of music that Bechet stood for (an
entirely natural and even inevitable mistake), his perception about jazz
and Bechet's playing was significant and has proved enduring,
complemented only by Ernest Borneman's appreciation of Bechet
(Melody Maker, November 19, 1955).*

*The following extracts are used with the kind permission of M.
Ansermet and their translator, Walter E. Schapp.*

ERNEST ANSERMET

Prologue: Sidney Bechet in Europe, 1919

The first thing that strikes one about the Southern Syncopated Orchestra is the astonishing perfection, the superb taste,
and the fervor of its playing. I couldn't tell whether these artists feel it is their duty to be sincere, or whether they are driven
by the idea that they have a "mission" to fulfill, or whether they
are convinced of the "nobility" of their task, or have that holy
"audacity" and that sacred "valor" which the musical code requires of our European musicians, nor indeed whether they are
animated by any "idea" whatsoever. But I can see they have a
very keen sense of the music they love, and a pleasure in making it which they communicate to the hearer with irresistible
force—a pleasure which pushes them to outdo themselves all
the time, to constantly enrich and refine their medium. They
play generally without written music, and even when they have

it, the score only serves to indicate the general line, for there are very few numbers I have heard them execute twice with exactly the same effects. I imagine that, knowing the voice attributed to them in the harmonic ensemble and conscious of the role their instrument is to play, they can let themselves go, in a certain direction and within certain limits, as their hearts desire. They are so entirely possessed by the music they play that they can't stop themselves from dancing inwardly to it in such a way that their playing is a real show. When they indulge in one of their favorite effects, which is to take up the refrain of a dance in a tempo suddenly twice as slow and with redoubled intensity and figuration, a truly gripping thing takes place: it seems as if a great wind is passing over a forest or as if a door is suddenly opened on a wild orgy.

The musician who directs them and who is responsible for creating the ensemble, Mr. Will Marion Cook, is, moreover, a master in every respect, and there is no orchestra leader I so delight in seeing conduct. As for the music which makes up their repertory, it is purely vocal,—or for one voice, a vocal quartet, or a choir accompanied by instruments,—or again purely instrumental; it bears the names of the composers (all unknown to our world) or is simply marked *Traditional*. This traditional music is religious in inspiration. It is the index of a whole mode of religion and of a veritable religious art which merits a study of its own. The whole Old Testament is related with a very touching realism and familiarity. There is much about Moses, Gideon, the Jordan, and Pharaoh. In an immense unison, the voices intone: "Go down, Moses, way down in Egypt land. Tell old Pharaoh: Let my people go." And suddenly, there they are clapping their hands and beating their feet with the joy of a schoolboy told that the teacher is sick: "Good news! Good news! Sweet Chariot's coming."

Or else a singer gets up, "I got a shoes [pronouncing the *s* to make it sound nice], you got a shoes, all God's children got a shoes. When I get to heaven, gonna put on my shoes, gonna walk all over God's heaven." And the word *heaven* they pronounce in one syllable as *he'm*, which makes a long resonance in their closed mouths, like a gong. Another time, a deep bass points out the empty platform to one of his companions and invites him to come and relate the battle of Jericho, and it's a terrible story which begins, with the mighty deeds of King Joshua and all sorts of menacing fists and martial treads; their hands are raised and then lowered, and the walls come tumbling down. In a lower tone, but with such a tender accent, the quartet also sings "Give me your hand" or sometimes "Brother, give me your hand." There is another very beautiful part in which a female voice sings the ample sweeping melody (wavering between the major and minor) about those who are going away toward the valley of the Jordan to cross the river, while the choir scans with an ever more vehement motif, "Nobody was heard praying."

Of the nonanonymous works, some are related to a greater or lesser extent to these religiously inspired works, others sing of the sweetness of Georgia peaches, or of the perfume of flowers, or of country, mother, or sweetheart; the instrumental works are rags or even European dances. Among the authors, some are Negroes, but these are the exceptions. Even though the author does not have a European origin, the music does, for most ragtime, for example, is founded on well-known motifs or on formulas peculiar to our art—there is one on the *Wedding March* from *Midsummer Night's Dream,* another on Rachmaninoff's celebrated *Prelude,* another on typical Debussy chords, another simply on the major scale.

The aforementioned traditional music itself has its source, as could doubtless be easily rediscovered, in the songs the Negroes learned from the English missionaries. Thus, all, or nearly all, the music of the Southern Syncopated Orchestra is in origin foreign to these Negroes. How is this possible? Because it is not the material that makes Negro music, it is the spirit. . . .

Nevertheless, some works in the repertory of the Southern Syncopated Orchestra mark the passage from oral tradition to written tradition, or, if you choose, from popular art to learned art. First, we have a number for choir, soprano, and orchestra, inspired by the traditional works, and signed Dett.

On a Biblical text, *Listen to the Lambs,* which Handel too has treated in the *Messiah,* this musician has written a work which is very simple yet very pure and has a beautiful rapturous quality. Or we have some works of Will Marion Cook, including a very fine vocal scene entitled *Rainsong.* Perhaps one of these days we shall see the Glinka of Negro music. But I am inclined to think that the strongest manifestation of the racial genius lies in the *Blues.*

The blues occurs when the Negro is sad, when he is far from his home, his mother, or his sweetheart. Then he thinks of a motif or a preferred rhythm and takes his trombone, or his violin, or his banjo, or his clarinet, or his drum, or else he sings, or simply dances. And on the chosen motif, he plumbs the depths of his imagination. This makes his sadness pass away—it is the Blues.

There is in the Southern Syncopated Orchestra an extraordinary clarinet virtuoso who is, so it seems, the first of his race to have composed perfectly formed blues on the clarinet. I've heard two of them which he elaborated at great length. They are admirable equally for their richness of invention, their force of accent, and their daring novelty and unexpected turns. These solos already show the germ of a new style. Their form is gripping, abrupt, harsh, with a brusque and pitiless ending like that of Bach's Second Brandenburg Concerto. I wish to set down the name of this artist of genius; as for myself, I shall never forget it—it is Sidney Bechet. When one has tried so often to find in the past one of those figures to whom we owe the creation of our art as we know it today—those men of the 17th and 18th centuries, for example, who wrote the expressive works of dance airs which cleared the way for Haydn and Mozart—what a moving thing it is to meet this black, fat boy with white teeth and narrow forehead, who is very glad one likes what he does, but can say nothing of his art, except that he follows his "own way"—and then one considers that perhaps his "own way" is the highway along which the whole world will swing tomorrow.

When Marshall Stearns undertook to notate a Sonny Terry LP, he wrote (with the acknowledged help of the work of Frederic Ramsey, Jr.) one of the most useful brief accounts of what went into the blues and of the variety of regional styles—a kind of summary of some of the work which had been going on since the appearance of Abbe Niles's introductory essay to the W. C. Handy anthology, The Blues, in 1926.

His remarks, here slightly condensed, are used by permission of Riverside Records (on whose 12-644 they now appear) and Dr. Stearns.

MARSHALL STEARNS

Sonny Terry and His Blues

Blind Sonny Terry can "play more blues than a peg-leg man" —to quote Sonny's own definition of a fine performance. This is authentic Negro folk music, handed down by word of mouth and, later, recordings, blues in a style that probably predates the Civil War, and a rare example of an early stage in the blending of European and West African music in the U.S.A. that evolved into jazz.

The blues are almost as old as America. Pioneer jazzmen in New Orleans, born in the late 1860s, scratch their heads and recall: "The blues was here when I come."

The tradition began when the first Negro American accompanied his own thoughts on an improvised instrument. He translated the facts of his own life into terms of intimate inconvenience. A documentary mixture of salty humor and Stoicism which implied a deep distrust of the florid emotionalism of his masters. A wry, matter-of-fact philosophy that laughed to keep from crying. And an appeal that was to prove world-wide.

The general public heard about it much later—and indirectly

—if at all. At the turn of the century, our popular music ran to
the sad and sentimental *(Bird in a Gilded Cage)* or the gay and
boisterous *(The Gang's All Here)*. By 1912, when W. C. Handy's
Memphis Blues appeared, a gradual change was taking place.
Music publishing houses wanted danceable music and the bit-
tersweet blues lyrics were becoming the rage. The public was
deluged with synthetic blues, near-blues, and non-blues-called-
blues.

By 1920, the first authentic blues was recorded (Mamie
Smith's *Crazy Blues)* when the companies became aware of a
Negro market. But only for the "race" trade. Throughout the
'twenties and 'thirties, the system of distribution itself kept
most of these recordings from falling into white hands—as it
does today—except for the fanatic *aficionado* and a few musicians who adopted and adapted and sometimes profited hand-
somely.

Eventually it became clear that a Tin Pan Alley hit such as
Blues in the Night was a dilution of a rural folk tradition that
still miraculously survived in the nooks and crannies of the
deep South, and which appeared in the Negro sections of big
Northern cities. It appeared once more on the "rhythm and
blues" series of the record companies in answer to a growing
demand. An ancient and durable tradition.

As we hear it today, the blues originated in a fluid combination of the field-holler, the work-song, and the spiritual. Perhaps the best way to date a blues is by the amount of harmony
it employs. Most of the harmony, which was probably taken
from a hymn or spiritual, is European, and its use represents
a later and more sophisticated stage. In these blues, the chord
progression is decidedly secondary. Rhythm—and then melody
—comes first, with the emphasis upon the mood that the words
convey.

Sonny Terry's harmonica, an instrument invented in 1829
and capable of but two chords, switches back and forth in a
virtuoso but eminently non-European style as he carves out the
mood. His close friend of a decade, Alec Stewart, whose subtle
accompaniments may be heard on this record, simply waits

for the end of the second verse before changing the chord on the guitar—a shifting but synchronized tonality that characterizes folk blues, and a sign of the survival of West African musical elements.

At a much later stage, when blues became an ensemble performance, the chord progression necessarily became set. The standard twelve-bar blues is divided into three parts with a different chord for each: the tonic, subdominant, and dominant —in that order. These are the simplest chords in the European musical language, complicated according to the sophistication of the musician. Along with the tripartite lyrics, this division of the stanza is rarely found in English prosody.

Sonny Terry's cries, or "whoops" as he calls them (listen to *The Fox Chase*), are closely related to the field-holler and employ a falsetto that is found throughout West Africa (the Swiss yodel seems a doubtful model for the antebellum plantation slave). And the call-and-response pattern, heard in the alternate singing and harmonica reply, is the basis of the work-song universal in West Africa. The over-all combination is a mixture of mixtures, a marvelous hybrid in a musical melting pot.

There are many archaic blues styles associated with various localities: Texas, Alabama, Florida, and Georgia. The Texas style has echoes of the cowboy, the Alabama style sounds more atonal and "primitive." The blues of Sonny Terry and Alec Stewart are slightly flavored with reels and jigs—breakdown music for transformed European social dances—the mountain music tradition, Georgia style. Sonny's parents were from Georgia, where his grandparents were slaves.

So young Sonny Terry listened to his father's harmonica and "juice" harp, attended Baptist revivals and tent shows, and played for "bug" (buck) dances. An itinerant hill-billy named Defoe Bailey from Tennessee, who recorded *Alcoholic Blues* in the early days, made a deep impression. In 1924 his father bought a hand-wound phonograph, and Sonny heard Ma Rainey, Lemon Jefferson, Bessie Smith, Blind Blake, Willie Johnson, and a host of others.

With the exception of *The Fox Chase, Red River, John Henry,*

and *Moanin' and Mournin'* (all excellent examples of Sonny
Terry's artistry as a folk performer), the tunes on this record
are all traditional blues—traditional in the sense that they are
improvised on the spot and never sung the same way twice.
Their most distinguishing feature perhaps is the words, which
represent a similarly old but less various tradition. *Old Woman
Blues* suggests the West African tradition of songs of recrimina-
tion and ridicule. The rest deal with classic blues situations and
the wry realities of Negro life: the awful fact of infidelity and
the inadequate threat of departure—the conflict between the
drive to escape and the shackles of sharecropping. No wonder
this music has circled the globe, for we all have blue moods
and, in a fundamental sense, none of us is wholly free.

When it became obvious that the "little" American jazz magazines of the late 'thirties and 'forties were open to explorations of past styles, comments on ragtime (chiefly by Roy Carew, S. Brunson Campbell, and Kay C. Thompson) began to appear. Then came the very useful history by Rudi Blesh and Harriet Janis, They All Played Ragtime. *But it was not until the mid-'fifties that Guy Waterman, in this two-part series which appeared in* The Record Changer, *began the valuable work of characterizing and evaluating this music and establishing its relationship to jazz. These essays are used by permission of* Record Changer *editors Bill Grauer and Orrin Keepnews.*

Musical examples from Scott Joplin's Magnetic Rag *and* Euphonic Sounds *will be found at the end of this article.*

GUY WATERMAN

Ragtime

I—A SURVEY

Ragtime occupies a peculiar place in the development of jazz. We often think of jazz originating in New Orleans and trace its evolution from there. We have a reasonably clear picture of New Orleans music developing out of nineteenth-century folk music, collecting a variety of material from external sources and synthesizing it into a new body of music distinguished by the label "jazz," a music which then develops in many directions, geographic and musical, after World War I. But ragtime was a contemporary of the earliest jazz and to some extent isolated from it. Furthermore, it is not sufficient to treat it merely as one external influence on jazz. It is a separate body of music and needs separate attention.

The period of ragtime composition ended more than thirty years ago. Jazz, since an improvised music exists for posterity only on records, has an observable life of not much more than thirty years—years packed with rapid and drastic development in many directions. We are therefore in a position to make conclusions and generalizations about ragtime which we cannot yet hope to make with certainty about jazz.

Nearly ten years ago, Roy J. Carew and Don E. Fowler, writing in *The Record Changer* (Sept., Oct., Dec., 1944), called attention to the "overlooked genius," Scott Joplin. Carew and Fowler pleaded for more attention to ragtime, basing their case on its importance as a contribution to early jazz. Since then that importance has been increasingly recognized. Rudi Blesh and Harriet Janis's *They All Played Ragtime* has told the "story" of ragtime in full, without, however, any musical analysis. What is now needed is a more intensive study of the music itself. This article attempts to point out some fundamental facts that have been sometimes overlooked and to provide a general outline of ragtime's evolution as a style—its growth, development, and decline.

One fundamental consideration bears immediate examination, since it has already been implied—that is, that ragtime is a composed, not an improvised or arranged, music. There is an essential difference here between ragtime and jazz. Improvisation and arrangement are fundamentally the same. They are opposite ends of a continuum, and no performance really falls entirely at either extreme. The process of arrangement (or improvisation) consists of expanding on a given theme and its harmony. The starting point is the theme and the "chords" that accompany that theme; the end product depends entirely on the improvisors and/or arrangers. Jelly Roll's piano solo of *King Porter Stomp* and Fletcher Henderson's arrangement for Benny Goodman's orchestra are both *King Porter Stomp,* but the results are poles apart. The fact that each "school" of jazz tends to create its own repertoire of tunes modifies this proposition, but basically the process of creation still starts at the melody and chords.

On the other hand, ragtime is a composed music. Composition consists of writing a piece of music, a complete piece of music, intended to stand alone. The composer does not start with any preconceived melody; nor does he first write a melody and then set about arranging it. He conceives the whole composition with all its parts. This is the method of concert composers. And, in this sense, ragtime is closer to the world of legitimate music than it is to jazz.

Another point to bear in mind is that our study of ragtime is to be concerned almost exclusively with the published compositions. Jazz critics early discovered that the quest for "influences," "sources," and "origins" is a delightful exercise. Such research is unquestionably very useful in all branches of music. The center of attention, however, must remain on the music itself. It is probably true that ragtime pianists indulged in improvisation. It is equally true that we have no record of the manner in which it was done. Perhaps it is only necessity that compels us to view ragtime *solely* as a composed music, but it is a very practical necessity and one that we can easily accept.

The vast flood of sheet music which was published during the first two decades of the century presents us with a problem of selection that may at first seem almost insurmountable. We are helped here if we recognize a distinction between popular music and art-music. This distinction is very fuzzy, particularly since it rests largely on the motives of the composer. The writer of popular music has as his *first* concern the satisfaction of a wide audience; his technique is essentially that of a craft. The writer of art-music attends *first* to the expression of his personal artistic inclinations. Notice that I emphasize that these divergent aims are only the primary considerations of the approaches. Cole Porter, a truly remarkable craftsman, allows much room for personal expression within the limits of that which can be sold. Furthermore, Scott Joplin was presumably pleased with the financial success of *Maple Leaf Rag*. (Notice also that I have not attached relative value to either approach.)

Needless to say, we do not have to analyze the composer's motives in each case. We can safely say that most of the rags

were turned out strictly for popular consumption, especially
as the style gained national popularity. But certain composers
have recently been recognized as serious musicians, and further
research will probably bring out a few more. At the present, only
about half a dozen figures stand in the front rank as consistently capable of writing ragtime on the level of art.

The appearance of William Krell's *Mississippi Rag* in 1897
has given that year acceptance as the beginning date of ragtime publication. In the next few years, Tom Turpin, Scott
Joplin, and others produced rags which incorporated certain
characteristics that govern the style throughout its history—the
familiar multi-theme structure, key change, and of course, the
familiar rhythm of two-beat plus simple syncopation. The early
rags are among the best known and most played—Turpin's
Harlem Rag and *St. Louis Rag*, Joplin's *Maple Leaf Rag* and
The Entertainer, and the Joplin-Scott Hayden collaboration
Sunflower Slow Drag. Their charm rests on the novelty of
simple syncopation and the grace of the four-square melodic
lines. They form the basis of the style.

James Scott administered the first shock to ragtime composition. *Frog Legs Rag*, published in 1906, displayed a vigor and
brilliance not found in the placid two-beat of Turpin and Joplin.
He gave the music richness and power, symbolized by his selection of the deeper flatted keys of the piano (A and D principally), with a crisper attack, sometimes built entirely on a one-
bar splash of syncopation, as, for example, in the second theme
of *Grace and Beauty.*

In 1907 and 1908, Joplin produced several rags which show
a definite advance over his simpler models. His development is
independent of and contrasts with Scott's. Where Scott tended
to reduce the phrase to startling brevity, Joplin tended to
lengthen it, giving his line a more serene legato effect. Scott swept
away all problems by the sheer force of his energy; Joplin attacked his problems head on, striving to subdue the essentially
bouncy spirit of ragtime. *Rose Leaf Rag* is a masterpiece for
this period. In *Pineapple Rag, Searchlight Rag,* and *Fig Leaf*

Rag, the fluid phrasing increasingly leads to something like grandeur, *Fig Leaf Rag* achieving incredible dignity, especially at the final theme.

Joseph Lamb is the third composer of importance in this movement. Lamb strives for the same two-fisted exuberance of Scott, but he loses the impetuous spontaneity. Devices, such as four-note chords in the treble and kaleidoscopic register changes, nevertheless frequently meet with artistic success and are always interesting. The third theme of *American Beauty Rag,* for example, is carefully, almost mathematically, constructed, but is still effective in context. Lamb saw more clearly than Scott the potential depths of ragtime, but in execution he had no achievement to match either Scott's fire or Joplin's serenity.

Joplin, Scott, and Lamb brought ragtime, in these years, to what may probably be called its heights. Against their principles of strict musicianship—and all three consciously strove for a place as respectable composers—arose two threats. The first, which grew up with Scott and Lamb, was the tendency within ragtime to increased tempo and sensational exploits. Throughout their careers they opposed this tendency without being able to arrest it. Eventually it developed into a national fad, making hits of Christensen's *Instruction Book for Rag-Time Piano Playing* and Irving Berlin's *Alexander's Ragtime Band.* Like all fads, this declined before another: jazz.

Jazz, the second threat to the ragtime composers, proved more destructive. The rougher syncopation and more flexible harmonies of jazz moved in and absorbed the younger musicians. In the hands of jazz pianists, ragtime was so transformed as to lose its identity.

We have said before that an improvised music is essentially different from a composed. A clear illustration of jazz's adaptation of ragtime to the requirements of improvisation lies in the new treatment of form. In ragtime there are four equal themes; each is as important as the others. Such a structure is not suitable for improvisation. Which melody shall be used as the basepoint? We see, therefore, a gradual alteration, with the final theme assuming greater importance and the earlier themes reduced in number and in influence. Eventually the opening melodies serve obviously as verse, the last exalted to a chorus on which all the ideas of the musicians are brought to bear. To illustrate this process, we could trace a direct line through *Grace and Beauty* (four equally important themes); *King Porter Stomp,* played by Jelly Roll Morton (two carefully handled themes plus a third on which the tune and most of the improvisation are based); *Squeeze Me,* on the Fats Waller piano roll (a verse, stated at the beginning and once in the middle, with all attention fixed on the chorus); and *Monday Date,* Earl Hines's classic (one chorus repeated throughout). Never again in jazz did structure revert to the form of ragtime, since improvisation has been at the root of jazz throughout its subsequent history.

From a historical viewpoint, the absorption of ragtime by jazz is the most important change that occurred after the period of Scott, Lamb, and Joplin's 1907-08 rags. Scott and Lamb did not have flexible minds. There is essentially no difference in style between *Frog Legs Rag* (1906) and *Peace and Plenty Rag* (1919), between *Ethiopia Rag* (1909) and *Top Liner Rag* (1916). No art, however, may remain static. The triumph of jazz over ragtime stems not only from the tremendous possibilities of jazz, but also from ragtime's failure to develop.

Two men offered possible solutions to ragtime's problem, Artie Matthews and the ever-resilient Joplin. Matthews's five *Pastimes,* written between 1913 and 1916, introduced a charming assortment of contrivances—breaks, Spanish beats, walking basses—on an essentially simple ragtime style. Joplin's efforts from 1909 until shortly before his death in 1917 were more fundamental.

Joplin's "last period" is a strange collection of contradictions. Some of his rags reach more toward concert music than did any jazz up to Lennie Tristano's, while others seem to revert to his 1900 style. Profoundly ambitious passages lie side by side with meaningless, mechanical ditties. It is not hard to find in these compositions a reflection of his approaching derangement—he lost his mind in 1916.

The daring of Joplin's last period, however, is only the last chapter of a very interesting book. There is a wealth of music in ragtime, and it may, with profit, be approached from many directions.

For the serious composer, ragtime does not represent jazz's greatest achievements, which are essentially rhythmic, since ragtime's rhythmic importance is solely historical. But, ragtime approaches the problems of composition in the same way as does very modern jazz (that of Gerry Mulligan, Milt Jackson, Hall Overton, and others), and alone uses its method. And if, as Aaron Copland found, "the general spirit of jazz was much too limited to be used as the basis for a fully-rounded music," then the general spirit of ragtime is worth a look, since it is a compromise. For the serious composer, however, most important are the efforts by Joplin and perhaps Artie Matthews to set a framework of free composition on an integrated but insistent beat.

For the jazz musician—jazz's counterpart to the serious composer—ragtime has little but historical significance. The devices of ragtime leave jazz piano once one passes Jelly Roll Morton. Resemblances to the Harlem style of James P. Johnson and Fats Waller are superficial. The ultra-moderns of today, however, would find at least two passages in the literature of ragtime worth attention—the second theme of *Euphonic Sounds,* for its shifting tonality and for its maintenance of a rhythmic pulse without explicit delineation, and the third theme of *Magnetic Rag,* for its successful passing of the sixteenth bar.

Ragtime performance presents a challenge to interpretive abilities. Interpretation of this sort is not easy for jazz pianists. In distinguishing between composition and improvisation, I pointed out that the process of improvisation starts with a melody and its chords. There are two points to note here. First, the melody and chords are not self-sufficient. They do not, by themselves, constitute a work of jazz. They are merely the raw materials with which every jazz musician works. The second point is that, if the creative act starts with the melody and the chords given, no two jazz musicians will play the same tune in the same way. If a pianist were to use precisely the same arrangement as someone who had come before, he would be creating nothing. Jazz has never honored musicians who merely interpret the work of others, as legitimate performers do.

The pianists of the revival have come closest to the strictly interpretive approach. They accept a general framework that was laid down years ago. Excessive originality is censured. Yet even here a premium is placed on not being a "carbon copy" of anyone who came before. The revival has created a new standard of value for musicians: originality within an established framework. All critical praise of Don Ewell, for example, rests on this standard. In *Shining Trumpets*, Rudi Blesh refers to Ewell's "style based on that of Jelly Roll Morton but so completely assimilated that he is able to create individually within it." I should add that I thoroughly accept this standard for judging jazz revival piano (and that I consider Ewell the best of the revivalists).

Ragtime, however, is not an improvised music. The revivalists have not yet realized this. Those who profess to "revive" rags use the same technique they would in reviving an old jazz tune. They are not playing ragtime; they are using rags as points of departure. This observation does not condemn their work; it merely insists that jazz's standards, not ragtime's, inform their playing.

For the listener, ragtime offers music of lasting interest. At present, things are still subject to the tyranny of jazz standards; the average listener is disappointed in anything played "straight." If faithful performance, approached by at least one pianist, the late Lee Stafford, is increasingly heard in the future, this difficulty may be overcome. Many of the best rags have not yet been heard. With these and with a sharpened understanding of already familiar composition, ragtime offers what may almost be called undiscovered musical riches.

II—JOPLIN'S LATE RAGS

John Stark, the ragtime publisher, wrote in his famous obituary on Scott Joplin, "he left his mark on American music." Joplin was unquestionably the foremost figure in the story of ragtime. Historians have usually counted Joplin and Tom Turpin as the most important influences on the composers of the 1900-10 period. If their work is taken as a whole, he and James Scott were probably the greatest writers in the idiom. And, since ragtime contributed much to jazz of its time and later, Stark's generosity is well founded.

But there is another part of Joplin's legacy which is equally important—his effort late in life to synthesize the ragtime he helped to create with certain methods and devices of concert composition. This part of Joplin's work left no mark on American music—it has been almost completely ignored. Indeed, its only publicity has been a handful of recordings, none of which has received much notice.

Before we begin to examine his efforts, we should have a clear picture of his previous career and, to see things in perspective, of the contemporary developments in his musical environment.

Back at the turn of the century, Joplin had been one of the founding fathers of written ragtime. The early rags established the basic principles of the style—multi-theme structure, harmonic orthodoxy, simple syncopation, and the other elements usually associated with the term "ragtime." It is difficult to single out particular tunes as typical, but these include most of the more familiar rags, like Turpin's *St. Louis Rag*, Joplin's *Maple Leaf Rag*, and the Joplin-Scott Hayden collaboration, *Sunflower Slow Drag*.

In the years just preceding 1909 (when Joplin was to embark on his great experimentation), ragtime was raised to a somewhat higher plane than that of melodious Turpin two-beat. James Scott published his first rag in 1903. In 1906 his electric *Frog Legs Rag* appeared, and was followed immediately by such classics as *The Ragtime Betty, Grace and Beauty,* and *Hilarity Rag.* Joseph Lamb started in 1908 with *Sensation.* Joplin himself had a banner year in 1907 with six of his best rags (including the Chauvin collaboration, *Heliotrope Bouquet*), each of which reveals greater powers of expression than those of his earlier years. Three more followed in 1908, including the monumental *Fig Leaf Rag.* This was the golden age of ragtime proper.

Another trend was developing simultaneously. This was the so-called "St. Louis school" of sensationalistic, showy display. This trend proved stronger than the work of Scott and Joplin's 1907-08 period, since its appeal was infectious and immediate.

Scott and Lamb had established themselves as writers of "classic" ragtime. Joplin had written some of the greatest rags —*Rose Leaf Rag, Gladiolus Rag, Fig Leaf Rag.* Scott and Lamb continued to write in much the same way. They wrote uniformly fine rags, but no first-rate composer will stay long in one groove. Joplin's position was that great things had been said in the ragtime style of the time, and that truly fresh creation required new resources.

No art may remain static. Internal development is necessary if it is to continue vital. Joplin had already participated in one great transformation of rag style, that which occurs between his works of 1904 and 1907, between Turpin and Scott. He now embarked on a new course, that which begins with the five 1909 rags and continues until his death in 1917.

What one first notices about late Joplin rags is the "serious" cast. Syncopation, while remaining an essential part of his musical equipment, is almost deliberately toned down, phrasing is longer, harmonies more complex. Modulation is more extensive and foreign keys are occasionally established within the sixteen-bar framework. Specifically, three main features of the style stand out: increased freedom in the left hand; the attempt to keep rhythmic momentum implicit rather than explicit; and a new, or at least increased, concern with structure.

One of the chief weaknesses of strict ragtime (though probably one of its strong points as well) was its reliance on the oom-pah left-hand pattern. From this strait jacket Joplin now sought emancipation. The left hand assumed a more independent character, carrying melodic passages and delineating harmonies more specifically. A good contrast between the earlier role of the left hand and its new importance is provided in the opening bars of *Rose Leaf Rag* (1907) and *Euphonic Sounds* (1909). The former is one of the most contrapuntal of the pre-1909 rags, yet, after four bars of sixteenth-note runs, the left hand lapses into the safe and sane oom-pah. *Euphonic Sounds* opens with an equally moving left hand, but at the fifth bar, and again at the thirteenth, the oom-pah is not required. It should be stressed that in the majority of late rags, Joplin retained the crutch, and in the Hayden collaborations, *Kismet* and *Felicity*, used it almost exclusively. It should also be pointed out that in some cases, other devices were used as rather lame substitutes— the straight chords of the trios in *Paragon* and *Euphonic Sounds*, and the arpeggios that too often passed for Joplin counterpoint. Nevertheless, the problem is squarely faced in enough passages to make the point.

The attempt to maintain rhythmic momentum without explicit delineation is not peculiarly Joplin's. The same problems confront the ultra-moderns of today—Gerry Mulligan, the Modern Jazz Quartet, Hall Overton's group. The beat was central to ragtime as it has been to jazz. In both, of course, it has been used as a positive force. Nevertheless, it is significant that in both cases musicians have appeared who felt its obvious statement to be a restriction. Aside from isolated passages in *Solace*, *Wall Street Rag*, and *Reflection Rag*, Joplin's most basic efforts in this line occur in the first two strains of *Euphonic Sounds* and the last of *Magnetic Rag*. The usual procedure is to curve the moving voice so that it syncopates the third beat. Typical examples are from the trio of *Solace* and the opening of *Wall Street Rag*. I shall discuss the second theme of *Euphonic Sounds* at greater length below. (It should be mentioned that Hines and almost all modern jazz since Thelonious Monk is also concerned with making the beat implicit—but with a view to heightening the rhythmic sense, not subduing it, as in Joplin.)

The structure of a rag had been one of the most firmly entrenched traditions. There were two accepted formulas: ABACD and ABCD. In his last period, Joplin became aware of structure as an end in itself and used it with more care than it has ever received in jazz. (By structure I simply mean the large-scale organization of a tune—as opposed, perhaps, to "phrasing," on a smaller scale.) *Euphonic Sounds* is the first rag, so far as I know, to be cast in truly cyclical form. Earlier rags had used phrases that repeated through several themes—in *Sunflower Slow Drag*, for example. In *The Entertainer*, he inserted a section of the second theme just before the last. But *Euphonic Sounds* is a full-blown model rondo: ABACA. Three other rags used the cyclical technique—*Kismet, Scott Joplin's New Rag*, and *Magnetic Rag*. Since *Kismet* and *Magnetic Rag* state the theme only at the beginning and the end they are not authentic rondos. The *New Rag* is a special case. The form would seem to be ABACDA. But the "D" theme has the quality of an interlude, since it is entered by a three-bar fragment in the dominant of the new key and since it ends with an irreversible lead into the recapitulation of "A". It is the only theme in Joplin's work which is not repeated. One might therefore characterize the *New Rag* either as a standard rag with recapitulation added or as a rondo with extended second interlude. Another structural innovation of late Joplin is the coda. It cannot be said that Joplin ever learned to use this device effectively. The only purpose it seems to serve—in *Euphonic Sounds, New Rag*, and *Magnetic Rag*—is the avoidance of too abrupt an ending. A corollary of this attention to structure was an interest in key relationships: in tonal music the two usually go together.

Notice that Joplin's change of rag form is directly opposed to the transformation wrought by jazz pianists. Jazz, seeking one theme as a center for improvisation, tended to weaken the sense of form that it inherited from ragtime. Jelly Roll Morton was the last pianist to make a serious thing of it. Joplin's efforts obviously strengthen this sense of form. One has only to hear the blazing return of the first theme of *Magnetic Rag*—the restoration of major tonality, the momentum of the renewed beat —to recognize the power of recapitulation in ragtime.

Joplin's struggles were not all successful. There are several aspects of his late writing which betray something less than finished artisanship. I have mentioned that he never really found what to do with the beat. A similar question he raised concerned the sixteen-bar limit, and this also remained unanswered. Only once did Joplin break through that barrier—in the third theme of *Magnetic Rag*—although portions of *Magnetic Rag, Euphonic Sounds,* and the *New Rag* do not sound tied down. In general, one might say that the various ideas with which Joplin was working were not sufficiently synthesized into a unified style. Perhaps the enormity of the task required more time than he was permitted (only seven active years followed 1909 before he was committed to an asylum). One might also notice a loss of drive, a running down of energy in the late rags as compared with *Maple Leaf, Sunflower Slow Drag,* and *Gladiolus Rag.*

Perhaps the most unfortunate aspect of the late period is the uneven quality of the rags. This is in striking contrast with the Joplin of earlier days who turned out quality rags as effortlessly as Bach his 371 chorales or Haydn his symphonies. Any specific comment along these lines, of course, is partly subjective. I would say that only *Euphonic Sounds* and Scott Joplin's *New Rag* are real *tours de force. Magnetic Rag,* his most ambitious in conception, falls a little short in execution. *Solace* is frankly experimental. Some of the less pretentious rags, like *Paragon* and *Kismet,* are thoroughly enjoyable, but they are colorless next to *Euphonic Sounds* and *Magnetic Rag* on the one side and *Rose Leaf Rag* and *Fig Leaf Rag,* or even the earlier rags, on the other.

The reader will notice that I am omitting the opera *Treemonisha* from my discussion. This gigantic thing is almost completely unexplored territory. Doubtless there is much of both grain and chaff therein—it is an inviting task for the adventurous—but until it is more familiar to both the reader and this writer it is best left alone.

An intensive study of *Euphonic Sounds* shows what heights Joplin achieved in his last period. Perhaps it would be more accurate to say it shows what potentialities his new ideas suggested, since it cannot be said that he fully realized these thoughts in his lifetime. Since *Euphonic Sounds* has received some notice in recent years, it has been attacked in some quarters, just as Louis Armstrong and, more recently, Jelly Roll Morton have been subjected to excessive counterattack after years of unqualified critical praise. It is damned with the faint praise of such terms as "interesting," with the implication that it is not really very profound. Nevertheless, as with Louis and Jelly, realistic examination of the music itself reaffirms the more generous appraisal.

As I pointed out above, *Euphonic Sounds* is cast in rondo form. The principal theme is stated three times with two subordinate sections sandwiched between. It is interesting to notice the ways the composer contrasts this theme with the other two. The home tonic is B♭ major, and no real modulation takes place within the first theme. Throughout the other two this key is never established—they pass through several others, mostly minor. The interludes are themes of conflict, of disturbance. The main theme is one of resolution, of redemption. The returns from the middle themes to the main one use this contrast to great artistic effect.

A further contrast lies in the internal structure of the themes. The first is the only one of the three that can be subdivided into the two traditional eight-bar sentences. The second works through an uninterrupted climax to the twelfth bar, then settles down, builds up through the repeat and returns once again to the opening theme. The third works to a climax earlier, in bar 7, then works its way into position for the return. These asymmetrical frames heighten the feeling of restlessness, the regular composition of the home theme strengthening its calm.

Internally, the first theme is a masterpiece. Each of the two sentences opens with a flowing contrapuntal phrase. The first time this is followed by a quiet four-bar phrase suggesting a modulation to the relative minor, a suggestion quickly rejected by the reappearance of the opening bars. After the second statement, a two-bar outburst vindicates the tonality beyond question, ending on the cadential six-four chord, which is easily resolved to the end.

The second theme has no such supreme confidence. It is important to follow the tonality through this section, for it is extremely well worked out to give great emotional effect.

The theme is introduced by a descending passage which leads to a low B♭ on the first note. From here until the climactic twelfth bar is a constant ascent in the treble and, most of the way, an equally towering descent in the bass. Almost immediately a minor key (B minor) is established. In bar five, C minor appears, in a magnificent modulation designed to suit the nature of the climax. Technically the six-four chord of B minor becomes, by a chromatic alteration as simple as it is effective, the dominant ninth of the new key, flatted and with root omitted. (Joplin always approaches a key through its dominant, after the fashion of the great tonal composers and Beethoven in particular.) The change into G minor in bar nine is accomplished by the dramatic augmented six-four-three chord leading to the dominant—notice that each new modulation is increasingly imperative, driving the motion to its apex in bar twelve.

Up to bar eleven, each new key had been minor. Bar thirteen asserts D♭ major, next to G♭ the richest and deepest of all keys, although the theme is not yet home. Bar twelve is a brilliant stroke. Besides the tonal changes, it is the focal point in two other ways—up to that point the melody rises, thereafter it descends, and up to that point is a constant crescendo, thereafter diminuendo. It is therefore a crucial measure, and the composer is equal to the task. Such a touch as this is not susceptible to cold analysis. The reader should notice two things, however, with reference to the passages on either side—the dynamics indicated for that measure, and the position of the two notes in the chords that immediately precede and follow. It is not too much to say that this one measure, in context, is sufficient evidence of Joplin's claim to greatness.

The third theme is not so successful. Again the modulations

are interesting, rotating around F major, which ultimately serves as the dominant of the home key for the final return. But the construction is not so dramatic, and in places, bars seven and eight in particular, the conception seems to presuppose a fuller treatment (more notes) than Joplin was prepared to introduce.

Incidentally, examination of rags like this explodes two theories which unfortunately still claim adherents: (a) that early ragtime and jazz were very simple affairs devoid of subtlety; and (b) that Joplin was a tune thief, not responsible for all the compositions that bear his name. The first contention appears for example, in Barry Ulanov's recent history: "Nothing especially important musically happened to jazz on the piano until the music got to Chicago and Earl Hines. . . ." Such a judgment seems rather blind when we realize that by itself even such a masterpiece as *Euphonic Sounds* does not measure up to the great rags of Joplin's earlier years or those of Scott at his best, and, further, that no ragtime composer crammed such towering musical logic into his work as did the purportedly uncomplicated Jelly Roll Morton. In saying this, one takes nothing away from the standing of the great revolutionist Hines or his successors.

The second contention, based mostly on some undocumented claims of one Otis Saunders, has been backed by the English historian Rex Harris, among others. The only answer is that if Saunders is to take Joplin's place, he, Saunders, must prove he wrote practically all Joplin's work. Not only are they all fine rags, but the development from *Original Rags* in 1899 to *Reflection Rag* in 1917 is clearly that of one man working out his musical ideas. If this man's name was not Joplin, that is a matter of semantics.

It is obvious from such analysis as I have suggested that Joplin's late work was a tremendous undertaking. *Euphonic Sounds* is his biggest achievement after 1908, but *Magnetic Rag* is even more ambitious, and *Scott Joplin's New Rag, Solace,* and the posthumous *Reflection Rag* reward study.

When we remember that Joplin was established as "King of Ragtime Writers" when he *began* this experimentation, we realize that it was more than a whim which led to the development. Scott continued to the end in the same pattern. This dynamic quality of Joplin's musical personality is the true measure of his stature. Every outstanding composer of the Western world maintained a fresh outlook throughout his career—from Bach and Haydn to the twentieth-century leaders, Schoenberg, Stravinsky, Hindemith. It is this quality more than the merits of *Maple Leaf Rag* or any other rag that sets Joplin above his contemporaries.

Unfortunately, jazz musicians seem to die at the wrong time. Bix Beiderbecke, Fats Waller, and Tony Jackson, as well as half a dozen modernists, all died much too soon. On the other hand, from musical considerations alone, many would say that Louis Armstrong, Sidney Bechet, and some others are long overdue. Joplin belongs in the former category. He was almost fifty when he died—not young perhaps, but he had barely started on a line of development which required much time and experimentation to complete. More important, Joplin alone was equipped to work it out. The musical trends of his time and later were such that no one could follow in his path. The course which he blazed resulted from his own mind, and it diverged from the main road—jazz—which caught up the younger musicians in its headlong course. The discipline of ragtime was too sophisticated for the new jazz; it was not sophisticated enough for Joplin. He was a true prophet in the wilderness, but where in 1899 and 1907 others had followed, in 1909 he set out on a course which had no attraction for anyone save himself. He was Wrong-way Corrigan, except that he did not turn out a hero to anyone but himself.

For us, looking back at him today, however, this music is meaningful. It is unlikely that anyone will continue in the directions he indicated, but that does not matter. The less radical rags—*Paragon, Kismet, Felicity*—are enough like orthodox ragtime to suit anyone for whom Turpin or Matthews has appeal. And the real achievement of his last years, while pregnant with suggestion of what might have been, still stands among the finest in ragtime and jazz.

RECORD NOTE

The best versions of ragtime currently available on records are those transcribed from mechanical piano rolls. Take warning that the record companies often run them too fast when transcribing:

Riverside 12–110 includes Scott Joplin's *Pineapple Rag, Euphonic Sounds,* and (unlisted on label or liner) *Cascades.* Riverside 12–126 James Scott's *Grace and Beauty,* Joplin's *New Rag, Original Rags,* and *Fig Leaf Rag.*

Previous ten-inch collections had included Scott's *Frog Legs Rag* and Joplin's *Magnetic Rag* (on RLP–1049), Joplin's *Maple Leaf Rag* and *Cascades* (on RLP–1025).

RAGTIME EXAMPLES:

Magnetic Rag by Scott Joplin

Third theme:

Euphonic Sounds by Scott Joplin

Excerpt from first theme:

Second theme:

Mr. Russell's essay appeared in The Needle *in 1944. Its occasion was the first issue of a previously unknown Morton solo found in a "test pressing" on a junk pile. Its achievement was in its understanding of Morton's music, of his sense of form, and even, by implication, of his fine orchestral recordings. Russell has been one American commentator on jazz who could be called a critic. His academic musical training and experience as a composer of concert works only partly account for his eminence in this field.*

Morton's real reputation depends, of course, on the series of records he made for the Victor company between 1926 and 1928, leading the "Red Hot Peppers." This series fulfills and enlarges the promise which his piano solos had shown a few years earlier. Russell's essay gets to the essentials of Morton's music so well that it may serve, I think, as an excellent introduction to those brilliant "Peppers" records as well.

Musical examples of the theme, trio, and variation from the Frog-i-more *Rag are at the end of this article.*

WILLIAM RUSSELL

Jelly Roll Morton and the Frog-i-more Rag

The release of a new Jelly Roll Morton solo at this late date is a most welcome surprise. Thanks to John Steiner, who discovered the test in a Chicago junk shop four years ago, and to his partner Hugh Davis, who is applying the most advanced sound engineering techniques to their excellent series of reissues, another Jelly Roll gem is now available to all.

According to some of Jelly's West Coast friends, *Frog-i-more Rag* was composed during his second California visit (1917-22), when he was associated with the Spikes Bros. Publishing Co. in Los Angeles. When Jelly Roll came to California from Chicago in 1917, he had as always a variety of interests. He worked at first in various Central Avenue resorts—the Cadillac Cafe, the Newport Bar, and the upstairs Penny Dance Hall at 9th Street. There was also the band with Buddy Petit and Frankie Duson down at Baron Long's in Watts, and later a six-piece band at Leek's Lake and Wayside Park (where he entertained King Oliver as guest star one night in April 1922). The period was one of Jelly's happiest and most prosperous. He could have his big car, his diamonds, and could keep his music just as a sideline for special kicks while he made his real money from the Pacific Coast "Line." As one friend put it, "You don't think Jelly got all those diamonds he wore on his garters with the $35 a week he made in music." But whether Jelly was really "one of the higher ups," as he claimed, or just a procurer is immaterial, for Jelly's real interest undeniably was always music. On the Gulf Coast they'd called him a pool shark and gambler, with music as a "decoy." But the important point is that to his dying day Jelly loved music and played his blues, rags, and stomps not because he had to, but because of the immeasurable pleasure he received.

So up and down the Coast from Vancouver, Canada, to Tampico, Mexico, Jelly went, always carrying with him, among the other commodities of "good time," the *new music* of New Orleans. In San Diego, at the U.S. Grant Hotel, he had an orchestra with Wade Waley, Dink Johnson, Paul Howard, and Baron Morehead. When someone told Jelly the hotel paid their white musicians $75 a week, he pulled his band out without notice. In San Francisco Jelly even participated in the final days of the notorious Barbary Coast and played for a while at the Jupiter on Columbus Avenue at Pacific.

Just as the exact date of the composition of *Frog-i-more* is unknown, the spelling and meaning of the title are disputed. In 1938, speaking of the Oliver record of *Froggie Moore*, Jelly told me the name meant nothing at all—just something he'd thought up. But Harrison Smith, once Jelly's New York representative, claims the piece was named after a vaudeville contortionist known as Moore, The Frog Man. A title so unusual might be expected to have some significance, and possibly Jelly had no desire to go into an explanation of who Froggie Moore was, although to pass up an opportunity to talk would be most unusual for Jelly. Roy Carew, close friend of Jelly Roll and a publisher of his music, says the real title is *Frog-i-more Rag*, this being the spelling exactly as written in Jelly's own handwriting. In any case the significance of the title is of infinitesimal importance compared to the music and the performance itself, which fortunately we have preserved just as full of life as the day Jelly left it for us.

The date of this recording also remains unknown. However, it was most likely made in the mid 'twenties, after Jelly's return to Chicago, and probably before 1926. Since Jelly Roll's style remained unchanged, and his artistry showed no decline whatever during the twenty years of his recording activity, the exact date of any Morton recording is of little consequence.

The 1923 Oliver Gennett 5135 of *Froggie Moore* was probably the first recording of this tune. In form it follows the piano solo version very closely except that the first strain is repeated. Jelly intimated that this tune which Oliver obtained from him in Los Angeles helped make Joe "King," although at another time he claimed that the Oliver band never really went over big until they recorded his *Dead Man Blues*. (Actually *Dead Man Blues* was Oliver's best seller.)

In 1926 Jelly revised *Frog-i-more*, using a new first section. Walter Melrose added some lyrics and published the new arrangement under the title *Sweetheart O' Mine*, much to Jelly's disgust. His displeasure is more understandable when we consider the lyrics; nevertheless, a new arrangement using the entire trio and ideas from the original second strain of *Frog-i-more* was recorded as *Sweetheart O' Mine* when Jelly Roll had his solo date for Vocalion in April 1926. A still further revision of the stomp was published soon afterward in a new orchestration by Charlie Cooke.

Jelly Roll's piano style and musical greatness are nowhere better demonstrated than in this early recording of *Frog-i-more*. All the most typical features of Jelly's style are abundantly evident: his wealth of melodic invention and skill in variation; the tremendous swing, which made him a veritable one-man band; his feeling for formal design and attention to detail; his effective use of pianistic resources; the contrasts of subtle elegance with hard hitting drive; the variety of harmony, and yet freedom from complication and superficial display that might have brought him more popularity.

Jelly's chosen instrument is one that in many ways seems less suitable for expressing personal warmth and the various tonal qualities generally considered essential in the performance of both vocal and instrumental jazz. Yet such was Jelly's ability that he was able to surmount the intrinsic limitations of the piano as a jazz instrument. In his music may be found to a remarkable degree the self-same qualities that constitute the ultimate in instrumental jazz, as exemplified, for instance, in Bunk Johnson's music. Somehow Jelly Roll had the *touch* to transmit the warmth of his rich personality into piano tone. He was master of those devices that gave a feeling of blueness to his harmony, the illusion of smear and roughness to his tone, and the characteristic turns of melodic pattern peculiar to Negro music. Most important of all, however, was his feeling for a joyful, raggy, and stompy rhythm—a beat that really moved, a swing that "rocked the joint."

Jelly Roll had a more formal musical training and background than many New Orleans musicians. Perhaps this fact is reflected in the formal construction of his compositions. At times the close-knit design is marked by an economy of means that amounts to understatement. *Frog-i-more* follows the usual form of Morton's stomps—introduction, a short three-part song form, and a trio selection. A definite musical idea is used for each new part. Since the opening idea of the first strain, an ascending succession of seventh chords, does not immediately establish the tonality, a curious effect of an extension of the introduction is created. The contrasting second strain is unusually forceful, employing a repeated-note motive and powerful left-hand bass figures in Jelly's full *two-handed* style. After a modified return of the first strain a characteristic Morton trill bridges over to the trio.

To find a more resourceful imagination and greater skill in

melodic variation than Jelly Roll Morton possessed, one can
go only to Bunk Johnson. Jelly took great pride in his "improvisations." I was aware that Jelly Roll was not an unqualified admirer of Louis Armstrong, but being particularly an
Armstrong fanatic and unable to understand his lack of enthusiasm, I always avoided any argument whenever Jelly
brought up the subject of Armstrong. However, Jelly explained
to Ken Hulsizer that he thought Louis lacked ability to "improvise *on the theme.*" If anyone should think Jelly's attitude
unduly presumptuous let him but listen to the trio section of
Frog-i-more to discover Jelly's own phenomenal skill in variation. And if one were to study the four different versions of
The Pearls or the half a dozen recordings of *Mr. Jelly Lord,*
and perhaps also take time to compare some of these variations
with the published versions, he would begin to get an idea of
Jelly's unlimited imagination and mastery of motival variation,
and possibly understand why Jelly Roll had a right to say
something on the subject of "improvisation."

The beautiful chorale-like melody of the *Frog-i-more* trio is
first played very simply, in a style reminiscent of the sustained
trio of *Wolverine Blues.* This first statement, marked "organ
chorus" in the Melrose publication, is played entirely in the
treble range. On paper the tune, with its constantly repeated
motive, presents a singularly four-square appearance, but
Jelly's performance is a revelation of rhythmic variety by
means of such devices as shifted accents, slight delays, and
anticipations. Of course, to some of our European trained
"critics" this is only a bad performance, by a pianist unable
to keep correct time, of a piece any third grade conservatory
pupil could play right off at sight. Curiously, as raggy as Jelly's
performance of this chorale is, it nevertheless is in perfect
time; the regular pulse can be felt throughout with no loss at
all in momentum.

The real marvel of this record, however, is the final trio
chorus. The left hand resumes its regular beat—and how Jelly
makes his old piano rock! Such final choruses are usually
labeled "stomp" in his published solos, and that is certainly

an apt though almost tame term for the manner in which Jelly bears down and rides on out.

The melodic invention of this finale is as notable as its immense rhythmic vitality. Although the melodic developments of the stomp version follow closely the simple lines of the "organ chorus," Jelly's rhythmic impetus and melodic embellishment give the effect of fantastic and frenzied variation. Actually each bar is directly related to its counterpart in the first simple statement, and all of Jelly's most characteristic and fanciful "figurations" are fused with the basic idea as though they belonged there originally.

What a contrast to the final choruses of the jumping-jive Harlem musicians who think that to obtain any semblance to rhythmic excitement they must leave the theme and thus become lost altogether. But with Jelly Roll, no matter how exuberant rhythmically or varied melodically the final choruses become, there never is any doubt of their musical logic and that each note grows out of the original motive. Nor is the typical flavor of the unique Morton style ever for a second lost. *Frog-i-more Rag* offers new and most striking testimony of the mastery that placed Jelly Roll in the very vanguard of jazz composers and pianists.

RECORD NOTE

Morton's *Frog-i-more Rag* solo was last available on Riverside RLP-1041 and has somehow not been included in the current twelve-inch collections. *Sweetheart O'Mine* is on Brunswick 54015.

A generally excellent collection of the Gennett-Paramount-Rialto solos is on Riverside 12–111. RCA Victor LPM-1649 collects fourteen of the great orchestral series, but several of the alternate "takes" used on that LP were decidedly inferior ones, particularly the version of the superb *Dead Man Blues*.

EXCERPTS FROM *FROG-I-MORE RAG*

Introduction and beginning of first theme (all excerpts transcribed by J. Lawrence Cook):

Beginning of trio theme:

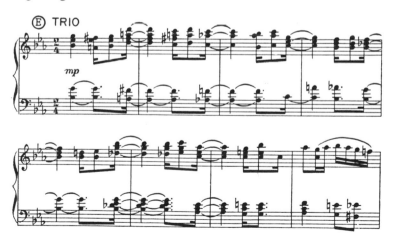

Variation on trio:

The following review of Riverside LP–12–122 appeared in the first issue of The Jazz Review. *When I asked Larry Gushee to review the recording, he muttered something about "going over that ground again." He undoubtedly profited by previous comments on the Creole Band, but I think he swept them before him. As a co-editor of the magazine I had little trouble obtaining permission for its use here.*

LARRY GUSHEE

King Oliver's Creole Jazz Band

The title of this album—"Louis Armstrong 1923: with King Oliver's Creole Jazz Band"—may be commercial good sense; musically, however, it is simply nonsense. There have been blessed few bands that have ever played together like Joe Oliver's, and Louis' presence is but one of many elements responsible. And his contribution is, in a sense, a negative one, for he is rarely heard in the role in which he found real greatness, that of genial, poignant, triumphant soloist, set off by subordinate, if not run-of-the-mill, musicians. Here and there we hear a phrase, sometimes only a single tone, played with the warm, slightly irregular vibrato so different from Joe Oliver's. We know it is Louis and are thankful for that knowledge.

If a band can be said to have a clearly recognizable and highly original sound, it must consist of something more than the arithmetic sum of a certain number of individual styles. I suspect that the *sine qua non* is discipline, which chiefly finds expression as consistency and limitation. Individual talent and skill do not even come into question here, at least as they are generally thought of, for one of the paradoxes of style is that poor musicians can create a fine sound ("Unconscious Poetry of the People," as they used to call it). Begin with a group of musicians out of the common run, who are guided by some dominant principle or personality, and the resultant sound will be truly unique, pleasing to the ears because it is musical, to the soul because it is integral. This is what makes the first records of Parker with Gillespie, the Mulligan Quartet, the Original Dixieland Jazz Band, stylistically great, as well as musically pleasing.

And so these recordings, in their way, are a norm, and object lessons of what a jazz band needs to be great. Unfortunately, it is not quite possible to say to the infidel, "Listen and believe," for so much of the music escaped the acoustical recording technique. Happily, the imagination will gradually supply much of what the ear cannot perceive, much as it can fill in (indeed, is expected to fill in) the gaps in a figure incompletely sketched.

Our idea of how this band *really* sounded, however, will always contain one element of uncertainty, barring the discovery of time travel, since the recorded sound of the Creole Band depended to so great an extent on the company that recorded it. On this re-issue the sides made for Gennett (all except 3 on side 2) must have been cut in marshmallow—with Johnny Dodds crouched inside the recording horn. It seems to me that the Paramounts (the above-mentioned exceptions) must sound more like actuality: clarinet is toned down, cornets are strong, with the second part actually being heard, the piano chording does not run together in an amorphous droning, and the bass line is generally clearer, the more so since it is re-inforced by bass sax.

Still, the Gennetts are in the majority here, and assisted by Riverside's remastering, they sound fine. Chiefly they sound fine because Oliver, like Jelly Roll in his happiest days, knew the sound he wanted, and had the brass and the guts and the prestige to run a band his way. Whether the tempos, so often felicitous, were Joe Oliver's independent choice, or determined by prevailing dance style, I cannot know. The fact remains that the Creole Band (and the New Orleans Rhythm Kings) played a good deal slower than bands like the Wolverines and the Bucktown 5, which recorded only a year later. The tempos they chose never exceeded their technical limitations, while, for instance, the Wolverines and, especially, the later Chicagoans, often played too fast for comfort (theirs and ours). I am sure that this accounts for much of the superb swing of the Creole Band.

But even more important is the manner in which the separate beats of the measure are accented. Here we tread on thin ice, the subjective conditions of hearing being difficult to verify objectively. Different people must hear the relative amplitudes of the beats differently—how else to account for the fact that many contemporary emulators of this style seem, to my ears, to accentuate the secondary beats far too much, rather than playing a truly flat four-four as did Oliver's rhythm section? You see, though, that I already beg the question. On the other hand, some of the so-called revival bands manage to reproduce the effect of the Creole Band's rhythm, while failing in other respects. The trouble is, I suspect, that the horns sound as if they are working too hard, and any suggestion of laboriousness immediately sets a band apart from the relaxed assurance and ease of the older group.

The truly phenomenal rhythmic momentum generated by Oliver is just as much dependent on *continuity* of rhythmic pulse—only reinforced by uniformity of accentuation in the rhythm section and relaxed playing. One never hears the vertiginous excitement of Bix Beiderbecke or Frank Teschemacher; one never feels that, with a little less control, a break or an entire chorus would fall into irrationality or musical *bizarrerie*. Oliver's swing is exciting after a different fashion: it is predictable, positive, and consistent. Only rarely is the total effect *manque*, as in *Froggie Moore*, where the stop-and-go character of the tune makes consistency more difficult to achieve.

Its consistency is, as I have said, largely the result of Oliver's personal conception of a band sound. How much he molded the musicians to fit the ideal pattern of his own imagination, or how much he chose them with the knowledge that they would fit in, without trying to change their personal styles, is something we can't determine since we lack recordings by New Orleans bands before 1923. We have no record of how Louis sounded before he came to Chicago—we know he is full of the spirit of King Joe, although their ideas of instrumental tone were divergent. Johnny Dodds's rare gift of phrasing, his ability to use his clarinet to bridge the gap between trumpet phrases (generally those of the tune itself) and to place the final note of his own phrase on the beginning of a trumpet phrase, we know from many other records, but none of them antedate these sides. And the rhythmic approach, too, is initiated by the Creole Band, with due note taken of Kid Ory's 1921 *Sunshine* date; we hear it again but infrequently, perhaps a bit in the New Orleans Rhythm Kings, certainly in the Tuxedo Band, in Sam Morgan's Band, and in many of Bunk Johnson's records, and other more recent ones in that tradition.

The impression of consistency is made all the stronger by the refusal of the musicians to permit themselves too much freedom. In successive choruses of a tune Oliver's sidemen often play the same part note for note, or with only slight variation —notice trombonist Honore Dutray in *Froggie Moore*, especially; Dodds in the same tune and in *Snake Rag*. The Original Dixieland Jazz Band did this too, but there is always an undertone (overtone to some) of the ludicrous—visions of tiny mechanical men playing chorus after chorus identically come to us, and one wonders how or why they go on. . . . Dutray, to be sure, often plays a pretty strict harmony part, as if from an orchestration, but there is a good deal more besides, and his mannerisms, his agility and grace, are strictly his own and not from the public domain.

A riff produces somewhat the same kind of excitement as does Oliver's "consistency," stemming ultimately from the irritation born of sameness, and expectation of change unfulfilled by the riff itself, but heard in a superimposed solo. The excitement of riffs, however, is bought too cheap, and works best in the immediacy of ecstatic suspension of our normal listening habits, most effective in the physical presence of a band. The Creole Band's way is less obvious, more complex, and, in the long run, makes a *record* that remains satisfying for year after year.

All these words will never convince someone against his will, and perhaps some will never feel or know why the Creole Jazz Band is so great and sets the standard (possibly, who knows, only because of an historical accident) for all kinds of jazz that do not base their excellence on individual expressiveness, but on form and *shape* achieved through control and balance.

My panegyric tone admits of modification in some instances. The Paramount *Mabel's Dream* is too slow—in fact, the tempo is an exception in the group of tunes on this record, neither as slow as the *andante Southern Stomps* and *Riverside Blues*, nor as fast as the rather relaxed *Chimes Blues*. The latter is too relaxed for its own good, the tricky chimes effects are dated and special, and Louis solos better elsewhere *(Riverside Blues* and *Froggie Moore)*.

But all of this is trivial. I love this band and its myth, the perfection it stands for and almost is, its affirmation and integrity, the somber stride of *Riverside Blues*, the steady roll of *Southern Stomps*, the rock of *Canal Street Blues*, the headlong sprint of *Weather Bird;* I love the musicians in this band, too, although my affection is tinged with sadness to think that, with the exception of young Louis, already himself but not yet complete, none of them ever again realized himself so well within a band. This is no reproach to them; it is only the result of the paradoxical fact that this band, recorded only a generation ago and marking the beginning of consistent recording of jazz, was one of the very best that jazz has ever known.

RECORD NOTE

The best Oliver collection is the one reviewed here, Riverside 12–122. Epic LN–3209 contains excellent music but on some tracks is poorly dubbed. Riverside 12–101 includes three tracks by Oliver's Creole Jazz Band.

When Jazz Information, *edited by Eugene Williams and Ralph J. Gleason, began appearing in the late 'thirties, it became a kind of center for discographical and historical research in jazz. It did not last long by the standards of fan or trade magazines, but its influence is still with us both here and abroad. Russell's essay on James P. Johnson, used here with the author's permission, appeared in its last issue. Subsequent researchers have added more names and influences to the hierarchy of Harlem "stride" piano, established a more exact relationship between it and ragtime, and confirmed a major source of inspiration in a highly schooled group of pianists centered in Baltimore. But Russell's comments on Johnson's life and piano stand and have received supplements only in John Hammond's tribute on James P.'s death in a November 1955* Down Beat, *a closer critical examination of his style by Dick Wellstood in* The Jazz Review *for December 1958, and the series of autobiographical transcriptions made by Tom Davin which began in* The Jazz Review *in 1959.*

ROSS RUSSELL

James P. Johnson

James P. Johnson, often called the "grandfather of hot piano," is a discouraging subject for a biographer, which may explain why he has been overlooked so often by critics and historians of jazz. *Jazzmen* failed to mention James P. once in its three hundred-odd pages; and this could hardly have been the intent of the editors of that excellent book, but rather the difficulty of tying him in with the tradition. Unfortunately Johnson never rode a coal cart in his life. He never played piano in a whorehouse, got expelled from Austin High, experimented with cigarbox guitars, purloined a beat-up trumpet from a

pawn shop, or even fiddled with the instruments on a riverboat. The facts are definitely against him.

Johnson was born and grew up in New Brunswick, New
Jersey, and that is a far cry from Storyville. For his first instrument he had to go no farther than the parlor of his own home,
and for a first teacher, his mother. He came by his music and
his medium of expressing this music logically, naturally, almost
casually. That he achieved his success with a minimum of frustration and deviation is perhaps a tribute to his innate genius;
and the fact is yet more amazing when we see that his creative
talents were constantly being threatened with complete obscurity by a tremendously active and successful career in the field of
Negro commercial music.

He was born February 1, 1891, a contemporary of the New
Orleans giants who were to fashion first principles of jazz
just after the turn of the century. His mother, a fair amateur
musician, taught him to play a rag on the parlor upright as soon
as he was old enough to manipulate the keys. When that had
been committed to memory she taught him another, and after
that stomps, more rags, and a few blues. At the age of nine
James P. was apprenticed to a local piano teacher for regular
lessons. Here Johnson got a real break. The teacher, one Bruto
Giannini, was an old-country musician, a strict disciplinarian,
a man of scales and exercise books. Somehow this Giannini
possessed the good judgment not to meddle with his new
pupil's natural bent. James P. was allowed to play his rags
and stomps, but with an important innovation—only after the
fingering had been corrected.

Looking back, Johnson is happy about this strange apprenticeship with the old-school maestro who helped him give
form to the still crude material. Along with correct fingering,
Giannini taught the boy harmony; enough at least to augment
a splendid natural ear and unlock the technical mysteries
which popular music might hold. So equipped, James P., just
entering his teens, took the cold plunge into the sea of professional music that was then beginning to lap at the shores of
Manhattan.

His first full-time job was that of "piano kid" at Barron Wilkins's cabaret in New York. Here he played the popular stuff of the day, seasoned with liberal doses of ragtime. Here he met and became intimate with one Charles "Luckey" Roberts. Roberts, a whimsical maniac, had a considerable reputation as an entertainer and "eccentric pianist."

Roberts's influence made itself felt during Johnson's formative period, leaving its deepest impression in the brilliant right hand which marks the grandfather's style even now. But this was mere keyboard showmanship, a fact which Johnson recognized and wished to remedy. He wanted a solider, more two-fisted style than Roberts's and, gigging around the big town, he found his answer in the work of one Abbalaba, a bordello "professor" who, according to James P., had a left hand like a "walking beam." This was the inspiration for James P.'s walking bass.

During the 'teen years Johnson worked steadily at various bright spots, satisfying the patrons, and at his own style, expanding and tightening it so that by the time of the great jazz boom he was able to emerge a full-fledged virtuoso. Immediately following the epoch-making Reisenweber stand at the Original Dixieland Jazz Band, Johnson took advantage of the boom. With Shrimp Jones, Nelson Kincaid, Ford Dabney, and others, he formed a band and bid successfully on the Clef Club job. This combination, fronted by and featuring Johnson at the keyboard, made a long stand at the Clef and helped establish the reputations of most of the men in it.

When the date finally expired, and the musicians drifted away to organize bands of their own, Johnson decided to explore a fresh medium—vaudeville. Here he found himself in competition with a popular feature of the four-a-day circuit in Professor Benjamin Harney, billed as the "Outstanding Exponent of Ragtime Piano." Johnson accepted the challenge and after a single season had overhauled Harney in popularity. He played the circuit for several years, finding time meanwhile to launch hit tunes of his own composition such as *Mama's and Papa's Blues* and the still durable *Stop It, Joe*.

Swinging back to New York City and the Palace just after Armistice, Johnson heard of a new field, one which was soon to feel the full force of his talents. Colored musical comedies, tailored for roadshow consumption, were usurping the place of minstrel companies. Johnson talked his way into the musical directorship of an elaborate production to be known as *Dudley's Smart Set*. After writing many of the lyrics and rehearsing the numbers, Johnson went on successful tour with the show, covering much of the South and West. The year 1920 found him back in New York again.

James Reese Europe had just returned from the Continent and was reorganizing the old Hell Fighter band for domestic exploitation. Europe asked Johnson to take over the piano. This offer, combined with his own urge to play live music once more, was too much for James P. to ignore. He accepted, and the Europe band went into the Clef Club for a long engagement. During this period James P. made his first player piano rolls for Ampico and Aeolian. In 1921 he was approached by the larger QRS company and signed to make rolls exclusively for them, as a "race" feature alongside the rococo but immensely popular efforts of Phil Ohman and Zez Confrey.

So far Johnson had never waxed a phonograph record. But this was soon to come, for the phonograph companies had tapped a field larger than that reached by the piano rolls. Once the Original Dixieland Jazz Band platters had tested public receptivity, Confrey and Johnson were won away from the QRS concern. Victor soon advertised solos by each in its ever-expanding catalog. Jimmy's first Victor pressing was *Bleeding Hearted Blues*. The popularity of this record, probably the first jazz piano solo on wax, is attested by other releases which followed in 1922 and succeeding years on Okeh, Columbia, Brunswick, Black Swan, and other competing labels.

Important as these items are to discographers, they were merely sidelines with James P. Now he can scarcely remember how many sides he made, or when; he is frequently confronted with something he knocked off one afternoon in a recording studio and has never heard since. When Alfred Lion and I talked to him at his home in Jamaica, Long Island, he had completely forgotten about *Harlem Strut,* for instance, and was still anxious to acquire copies of the far commoner Brunswicks.

At that time record dates were merely a useful source of side money, just like song royalties. In fact, James P. was better known as the composer of *Original Charleston, Ivy, Old-Fashioned Love,* etc., than as the virtuoso of Brunswick's *Jingles.* Most of these tunes were workaday products tailored to suit the needs of colored revues, for Johnson was still active chiefly in this field. He also did skits and lyrics for production shows at Connie's Inn, for Ziegfeld, Carroll, Schubert, and for the Cotton Club. One of his road shows, *Plantation Days,* did so well in America that it was booked for an extended tour of Europe, and Johnson was several months on the road in England and on the Continent.

Back in America once more, Johnson was attracted to Hollywood by a lucrative offer to do the musical score for the motion-picture short, *St. Louis Blues,* starring Bessie Smith. He had already done a great deal of work with Bessie, as tunesmith and accompanist both on the road and for record dates. After his scoring had been accepted, he remained in Hollywood long enough to play a supporting part in the picture.

It is quite impossible to keep up with James P. during the Roaring 'Twenties. In fact, as he says, he did well to keep up with himself. There was always something to absorb his interests and manifold talents. A new show to be rehearsed. Two more sides for Columbia. A short engagement as band pianist. A recording date with Ethel Waters or Roy Evans. A jam session at the Rhythm Club, where men like Duke Ellington, Claude Hopkins, Fats Waller, and Willie The Lion Smith spoke of "going to get their lessons" from the Grandfather. The Louisiana Sugar Babies date for Victor. Giving Fats, James P.'s boy, a brush-up lesson. Another show in production for the road. To Hollywood for a Warner Brothers short. Another celluloid role, this time for Pathé. Sitting in uptown with Bix Beiderbecke and Frank Trumbauer and Louis Armstrong. A four-week engagement as featured soloist at the Savoy. House rent parties and chitlin' struts.

Here was a man with vitality and personality, and besides that ability and perhaps not a little genius. A man who knew everyone, and worked hard and got his kicks and saved a little money. Looking back, we are interested mainly in the man's music—his records and the influence of his piano—but these things were just part of a larger pattern. We wonder how his records and his piano managed to escape the taint of commercialism, how he avoided becoming a bizarre medley of Confrey, Gershwin, and Irving Berlin, how the slender threads in the disorganized pattern came to acquire lasting form and color after the rest of the picture had blurred off. Jimmy wonders himself. If he has succeeded in salvaging something of value from the hectic, too successful career, he believes he owes it to his unflagging interest in after-hours music. At his busiest, he still found time to play at a house rent party or a jam session. A man with a tremendous vitality can relax at activities which exhaust another. So James P. went uptown to let his hair down and get his kicks; and the field of jazz music is permanently enriched by his efforts.

The fall of Wall Street marked the end of this fabulous decade. Out, with the G notes and the bootleggers and the It girls, went jazz music. Or rather, jazz went underground. And Johnson went home—to the two-story house he had purchased in the middle-class suburb of Jamaica. He was fortyish, growing a little fat, and a little bald. He took up pipe smoking and became quiet and philosophical. He slowed down, yes; but he had no notion he was through. During his career he had been a pianist, entertainer, performer, composer of popular tunes, director of musical comedies, amateur actor, dean of the eighty-eight among the jazz select. But one endeavor had eluded him, piqued his curiosity, challenged his ability. As a busy foreign correspondent might long for leisure in which to write a serious novel, Johnson had dreamed of trying his hand at serious composition.

The movie scoring had sharpened this growing interest and

the 'thirties finally found Johnson in a position to make a start. Gershwin's attempts to work jazz material into more serious form seemed imperfect to Johnson. Without conceit, he thought himself in a more advantageous position to succeed where Gershwin had failed—or rather, had managed to please only dilettantes. The great library of jazz music, or blues, rags, stomps, fox-trots, popular songs, had a vast wealth of material to offer, Johnson thought. He wanted a form of music which would give more lasting permanence to the material than the transient four-four, twelve and sixteen bar structures. So, in the quiet of his home, he sat down at the fine grand piano he had acquired and began his work. He had a big, tough job ahead. He is still at it, and expects to be as long as he lives.

The first serious effort was *Tone Poem*, begun in 1930. In 1932 he completed *Symphony Harlem* (four movements: *Subway Journey, Song of Harlem, Night Club, Baptist Mission*). *St. Louis Blues*, an elaborate improvisation on the Handy classic, followed in 1936. More recently he had been working on the most ambitious job yet, an opus tentatively entitled *Symphony in Brown*, which intended to trace out the rise of jazz music. The success of these challenging endeavors remains to be seen. Eugene von Gronna used *Symphony Harlem* for the Negro Ballet, produced at the Lafayette Theatre, New York, in 1937. There have been other performances since then. But this music finds itself poised between righteous jazz on the one hand and classical music on the other, subject to all manner of prejudice and suspicion. And it has never been easy for a new composer to interest important men in the classical field with his creations.

If Johnson's story ended here, many hard-shelled jazzophiles would be inclined to shake their heads and lament the passing of another onetime great. This judgment might be defensible had James P. remained in complete retirement. Fortunately, his selection as pianist on the important Hugues Panassié Bluebird dates of 1939 (Mezz Mezzrow Orchestra; Frankie Newton Orchestra) and, more specially, his subsequent recording work have furnished evidence to the contrary. James P.

plays a mellower piano these days, but it has lost nothing, in the opinion of this writer. The two opening choruses of his Decca *Stop It, Joe* (Rosetta Crawford) show that here is still the piano with more *pure swing* than any other in the business, not excepting Hines or Waller—and that with a minimum of effort, with greater economy than ever before. Here is no faded relic or dated exhibit, no tricky musical scholar or effete, meretricious Gershwin. Here literally, freshened by the latest acoustical advances, is the true Grandfather.

After all, a man who remained a top-flight musician while he was being all things to all people in the music business ought to be able to fluff off any softening influences of composing for full symphony. And maybe those more recent and most ambitious efforts will be the bridge, or the foundation for the bridge, between this incredibly rich native music of ours and the more timeless classic forms.

RECORD NOTE

Unfortunately, none of the recordings currently available, except for two tracks on Brunswick 54015 and three on Epic LN–3295, represents Johnson at his best.

These paragraphs are extracted, with permission, from the liner notes to Riverside LP-1048. It seems to me that in their clarity and succinctness they bring needed order to a subject which has been in a state of perpetual confusion, a fact which has significance as a revelation of the opposing claims which have been made for each jazz school.

ORRIN KEEPNEWS

Dixieland

The 1920's have come to be known as the "Jazz Age"—which is somewhat of a source of confusion to anyone concerned with jazz as *music*. For the term is usually intended much more as a description of the rip-roaring way of life of that far-off, apparently incredibly carefree span of years than as a reference to any specific musical style. . . .

There was, of course, an amazing quantity and variety of jazz afoot in the 'twenties. Big bands and small; a profusion of styles identifiable by one of the many geographical handles; an almost endless list of highly talented, memorable musicians. All this belonged to the 'twenties, and much of it made rather significant contributions to the sum total of jazz. . . . .

The music of Red Nichols and Miff Mole's Stompers and of the Memphis Five is also noteworthy as typifying one major force in shaping that prevalent form of small-band jazz which now goes loosely by the name of "Dixieland." Basically, Dixieland today is compounded of perhaps three main strains: white New Orleans style, as brought to New York by the Original

Dixieland Jazz Band and to Chicago by the New Orleans
Rhythm Kings; the Chicago style of Eddie Condon and his
cohorts; and the New York style of Nichols and Mole, with
which and with whom the Chicagoans merged when they
emigrated to New York later in the decade.

In his capacity as director of popular albums for Columbia Records,
George Avakian persuaded that company, beginning in the late 'forties,
to issue a series of collections of important recordings by Louis Armstrong,
Bessie Smith, and Bix Beiderbecke. Like the notes to the wartime
Brunswick reissues, the essays which he wrote for these Columbia LP's
opened the way for liner comment which could feature something besides
adjective-mongering spun through bits of "background" erudition—a
way not all have followed, alas.

Since this series was written, Benny Carter, Johnny Hodges, Harry
Carney, and others have attested to the influence of both Beiderbecke
and Trumbauer on their playing. More important, Lester Young affirmed
that his style was in part derived from Bix and Tram, which means that
indirectly they have affected all jazz since 1940.

This essay is a condensation of the notes to "The Bix Beiderbecke
Story," Columbia CL–844-6, and is used by permission of Columbia
Records and Mr. Avakian.

GEORGE AVAKIAN

Bix Beiderbecke

The Bix Beiderbecke story is the great romantic legend of
American jazz. It has everything: a sensitive young man who
just *had* to play that horn, after-hour sessions in smoky cellars,
gin, more gin, and enough crazy stories to fill several books.
And the setting was just right: a Scott Fitzgerald atmosphere
with John Held illustrations, complete to Stutz Bearcats and
raccoon coats.

Bix outlived those times, but not by much. Like the stock
market, he was riding high but shaky by 1929. He died on
August 7, 1931, his health shot, all but washed up professionally at the ripe age of 28. The standard story of his death,

which has been printed over and over again (as opposed to
the whispers involving gangsters), is that Bix, sick in bed with
a cold, got up to go to Princeton for a club date which would
have been called off if he didn't show. He drove down in an
open car, the story runs, developed pneumonia, and died.

Somehow, until now, no one (the present writer included)
ever questioned the anachronism of a Princeton dance in midsummer. One of Bix's Princeton fans, Frank Norris, who had
gone to Lake Forest Academy with him ten years earlier, recalls that Bix caught a beauty of a cold at the last of the week
ends that spring, and never did shake it off. "But die of a cold?
Bix didn't die of a cold," says Norris. "He died of *everything*."
Eddie Condon, who saw a great deal of Bix in 1931 when both
were proving that one transparent hamburger a day can keep
a man alive, confirms that Bix just gave out. "He was broke,
run down, and living in one stuffy room out in Jackson Heights.
He had this cold that you or I—well, you, anyway—could shake
off in a few days, but with Bix it was a case of having to stay
in bed. It was the end of July, and so hot that he rigged up a
couple of fans to blow on the bed. Two days of that and he
had pneumonia, but good." By the time Bix got to a hospital,
he couldn't have fought his way through a wet beer label.

So the legend got started faster than the biographers did. But
before we get into the life story, let's consider the big thing:
Bix's horn. It's something that will never quite fade away, as
long as there's a record around. Once heard, it's a sound you'll
never forget: the warm, mellow cornet tone, sometimes with
almost no vibrato at all; the attack that was sure, with every
note brought out as clearly as a padded mallet striking a chime;
the flow of ideas, sometimes bursting with spontaneous energy
and yet always sounding coolly calculated, as neatly arranged
as though a composer had carefully organized each phrase
and then plotted all the little inflections and dynamics.

Bix always played a cornet rather than a trumpet. This gave
him a rounder, warmer, more intimate tone, as opposed to the
more penetrating trumpet tone. There is always a reserved
quality to Bix's cornet sound; it's as though he never quite lets

himself go all-out emotionally, even on a barrelhouse Dixieland
performance like *At the Jazz Band Ball.* He was one of the most
exciting musicians who ever lived, but he did it by the individuality of his tone and the imaginativeness of his improvisations. Though his work was emotionally rich, it was always
tempered by a discipline which makes his work seem restrained
alongside the freedom of the great New Orleans Negro musicians, such as Louis Amstrong, Sidney Bechet, and Johnny
Dodds. To many, this quality enhances the spiritual excitement of Bix; it's like capping a geyser to get more of a kick
out of it when it lets go.

Bix had an inborn feeling for chords, and all his improvisations make use of the harmonic subtleties of whatever tune
he's playing. An untrained rebel at the start, he was quick to
sense the harmonic revolution of the early jazzmen. But as he
learned more and probed deeper into modern harmony his
dissatisfaction with jazz grew, and toward the end of his life
he was in the throes of a musical dilemma (to say nothing of
a physical struggle to overcome the effects of a youth strewn
with Prohibition-time jugs). Some musicians have felt that Bix,
in concentrating on kicking over the traces of conventional
music and studying the whys of his revolt, got bogged down in
more theory than he could handle.

Bix, who inherited the nickname from an older brother, was
born Leon Bismarck Beiderbecke at Davenport, Iowa, on
March 10, 1903. The Beiderbeckes were well-to-do and musical,
but Bix never studied music much, although jazz fascinated
him from an early age. His mother recalls young Bix playing
cornet to a record of *Tiger Rag,* which evidence shows pretty
clearly to have been the 1918 Original Dixieland Jazz Band
version. He certainly heard jazz bands on the riverboats that
came north as far as Davenport, although the story that he
heard Louis Armstrong is not confirmed by Louis, and is probably part of the legend.

In 1921, after two and a half undistinguished years at Davenport High School, Bix was sent to Lake Forest Military
Academy in the hopes that firmer discipline would keep him

harder at his books. But the school had a liberal week-end policy, and Bix constantly found himself getting down to Chicago's South Side, where New Orleans jazzmen had begun to find work. The New Orleans Rhythm Kings, a fine white band, hit town that year, too. It didn't help Bix's homework, but his cornet took on a new sound while he was at the academy.

Bix naturally gravitated into the student band that played for dances and during reel changes of movies in the gym. Social life was pleasant; a near-by girl's school, Ferry Hall, provided partners for the dances. The band played on a balcony which was reached by a trapdoor, and Frank Norris recalls the time that Bix was heating it up for the kids down on the gym floor and the headmaster, John Wayne Richards, poked his head through the trapdoor to call out, "Tone it down, Bix, tone it down!"

A year and a half of Lake Forest, and Bix had convinced the faculty that it was no use keeping him around any longer. Bix (who always was to have a reputation as a self-taught musician and a poor reader) continued to play cornet his own way. Not knowing that the first two valves of the horn are the principal ones, he used all three equally, and habitually played many notes "the hard way." This dependency on the third valve, however, probably helped more than not. Eventually he was able to play with ease passages that would have been tough going in orthodox fingering.

Bix's apprenticeship among the New Orleans migrants in Chicago paid off in late 1923, when with a group of other youngsters with whom he had been jobbing around he landed a steady job at the Stockton Club, a roadhouse in Hamilton, Ohio. This was the debut of the Wolverines. For a pioneer group, they played remarkably well, and Bix made the band swing almost as much as the New Orleans Rhythm Kings (which, oddly enough, included four musicians from southern Indiana and Illinois). Those who criticize the early-jazz sound of the Wolverines from the vantage point of more than a quarter-century would do well to consider that they gave Bix more of a jazz setting for his horn than any group of musicians he ever worked with. Bill Priestley adds: "I know of no other band that relied less for ideas on the other bands they were hearing."*

Squirrel Ashcraft, another Princetonian and a good pianist who frequently sat in with the Wolverines, points out that "the band pioneered ideas which meant so much to Bix that as long as he lived he repeated variations of things he played with them, or which other members of the band played." The tenor saxophonist George Johnson was especially an influence on Bix. He set the rhythm of the band, and it was from Johnson that Bix first picked up one of his most striking characteristics: a strong dependency on the whole-tone scale.

An Indiana University student named Hoagy Carmichael heard about the Wolverines that winter and brought them to the campus for a spring dance. There is a classic description, quoted by Eddie Nichols in his illuminating chapter on Bix in *Jazzmen,* of the Wolverines' arrival in an old phaeton, six musicians with beat-up instruments spilling over the sides. Even Hoagy, who hadn't heard them play, was worried, but they were a sensation and came back for ten week ends in a row. Hoagy became one of Bix's closest friends, and wrote a number for the Wolverines called *Free Wheeling,* which the boys went for in a big way because it gave them four breaks to blow in every chorus. Bix changed the name to *Riverboat Shuffle.* The Wolverines had no lack of jobs that year, although there was a lull during the summer of 1924, which Bix filled in with Mezz Mezzrow's band at the Martinique Inn at Indiana Harbor, a tough mill town near Gary.

Early 1925 saw the gradual breaking-up of the Wolverines. Bix joined Charlie Straight's band in Chicago, where he could once more hear the great Negro musicians who were pouring into town. He even heard Bessie Smith, who usually toured the South, and they say he was so moved that he gave her his week's pay to keep her singing.

In September of that year Bix joined Frank Trumbauer's

* The Wolverines' records are now collected on Riverside 12–123.—Ed.

band in St. Louis. When Tram broke up the band in 1926 to join Gene Goldkette in Detroit, Bix went along. Goldkette had an all-star crew that was pretty expensive to keep up, and when he had to let the boys go in the fall of 1927, most of them (including Bix and Tram) went with Paul Whiteman. The pace there got to be pretty tough on Bix, who always drank a lot and solved his problems by drinking more. It caught up with him, made him a semi-invalid, and when the chips were down he didn't have the strength to pull through.

The Bix and His Gang selections are the freest and least inhibited Bix ever made. They are in a loose, improvisational style which the public accepts as Dixieland. Good solos and solid ensemble work by other musicians are frequent, but Bix alone carries the stamp of greatness, and it is his playing that makes these records. He does the work of three or four men, often playing responsive phrases to his own melodic lines and blowing purely rhythmic explosions in his eagerness to kick the band along. With strictly jazz musicians on hand, Bix would not have had to work so hard, for the holes he plugs up himself would have been stopped up for him, but it is a special thrill to hear how he handles the shortcomings which he senses in his support as he plays. It wasn't just a fertile imagination and a lovely tone that made Bix a legend even before his romantically-timed demise.

The association of Bix Beiderbecke and Frank Trumbauer, begun in the fall of 1925 at the Arcadia Ballroom in St. Louis, is an unusual meeting of two musicians who were unlike in many ways, and yet collaborated successfully with mutual benefit to both. They were an odd combination even in appearance: Bix was husky, well-built, and blessed with a round, externally youthful, country-boy face, while Tram was the wiry type, a few inches shorter, with long, almost Mephistophelian, features.

Trumbauer generally played C-melody saxophone. The instrument has a whimsical tone, and Trumbauer played it that way. It suited the times, and it often suited Bix, who frequently served as Tram's foil. The many juxtapositions of Bix's cornet and Tram's sax blend well together, although oddly enough Bix always sounds dead serious and Tram always keeps the light touch.

Tram, a well-trained musician with a head on his shoulders, appreciated and encouraged Bix in every way he knew. He helped Bix with the technical side of music, but still more important he helped steer the impractical Bix (who often went for days without taking off his clothes, shoes and socks included) into the two best-paying and most famous bands of their time: Gene Goldkette's and Paul Whiteman's.

Second guessers have also claimed that this was the ruin of Bix. His death, brought on by alcoholism caused by musical and psychological frustration, bears them out in some degree. But the point is still highly debatable, and the opinion here is that Bix was doomed never to find his shadowy goal in life, and that the end might even have been hurried without the money that enabled Bix to pay half a buck extra for a better grade of the inevitable bootleg.

Bix still couldn't read worth a hang, although he'd managed to hold down a chair with Charlie Straight's eleven-piece band in Chicago for a while before joining Tram. But during the season in St. Louis he enlarged his musical development in two ways: in the loneliness of being in a strange city, Bix found time to indulge his interest in classical music and he used his ability to play piano by ear to delve more deeply into improvisation based on expansions of conventional harmony.

Contemporary European composers for orchestra fascinated him, particularly, Debussy, Ravel, Holst, and Stravinsky. In addition to going to concerts (usually with Bud Hassler of the Trumbauer band), Bix spent long hours at the piano in deserted bars, working out his own improvisations and teaching himself pieces by the Americans, Griffes, MacDowell, and Eastwood Lane. Bix always played with a consciousness for whole-tone scale (which also appears frequently in Debussy), and in this period he began exploring the non-jazz facets which were to influence more and more his improvisational thinking.

With Bix able to read a little better, Tram got him into Gene Goldkette's orchestra in the spring of 1926, along with some of the other Arcadia bandsmen. Goldkette, a rare combination of musician and businessman, owned the Greystone Ballroom in Detroit, where he would build up a band's reputation and then send it out to cash in elsewhere in the Middle West. He was primarily responsible for the success of McKinney's Cotton Pickers, the best Negro dance orchestra in the Midwest in the 'twenties, and later emulated Chicago's Husk O'Hare in booking two or three bands at once under his own name.

Goldkette's basic band was the finest white orchestra of its time, and consisted of musicians who could play both sweet and hot. It was the first white band to play jazz arrangements with real force, and it packed more of a wallop than most large Negro orchestras of that time. That summer Goldkette sent out a unit from the band to play a dime-a-dance joint called the Blue Lantern Inn at Hudson Lake, Indiana. The management frequently split the band so that the music could be continuous. Bix doubled in both platoons, playing cornet in one and piano in the other.

At Hudson Lake Bix shared a broken-down cottage with Pee Wee Russell, the colorful clarinetist from St. Louis, who was closer spiritually to Bix than the more business-like Trumbauer. Bix and Pee Wee didn't care about anything but playing and not letting their liquor supply get low.

A piano there helped Bix explore more and more the intricacies of harmony. He was beginning to split his musical personality—European form and discipline were beginning to encroach on the freedom of the New Orleans music which had been his first great influence. Soon after Bix was to record his piano solo, *In a Mist,* wherein the influence of Edward MacDowell wins out over jazz, though the latter is still there.

In a Mist, which grows in its importance in understanding Bix as one probes deeper and deeper into both the man and musician, could not have been more appropriately named. Bix never got out of the musical mist in his striving and searching for something that always eluded him, but what wonderful things he played as he strove. Further embattled as he was by the commercial music world, on which he was never able to turn his back, Bix's personal life became a mist in which he depended on alcohol to carry him through each disappointment.

The high points he found sometimes in his own playing, sometimes in the company of friends. Whenever Bix was in New York, he had a standing invitation to play at Princeton dances. Frank Norris and Squirrel Ashcraft, independently of one another and in almost the same words, made clear to the writer that when Bix was around the talk was seldom about music. "Bix had some unusual things in common with us," says Ashcraft. "We discovered that he could quote long passages from P. G. Wodehouse as well as we could, and we could spot the approximate page and the exact character who said any chosen line from his books—he had written 48."

The Goldkette days were the last in which Bix was to have any real degree of musical freedom, though even with this band there were plenty of times when he was playing under wraps half the night. The band traveled as far east as New York, where it played the Roseland Ballroom opposite Fletcher Henderson. Bix was the man the local boys pointed out on the bandstand; the word had already spread throughout the country among musicians. But it was the more practical Trumbauer who wangled a recording contract with Okeh (with the assistance of Red McKenzie and Tommy Rockwell). He used Bix and his friends on the dates, and later got Bix a contract, too.

But by the summer of 1927 it was apparent that Goldkette couldn't keep the band going at all-star prices. The break came in October, and Adrian Rollini, who had worked a couple of record dates with Bix and Tram, booked them (along with most of the other hot musicians) into a new club. In two weeks the joint folded, and it was with Paul Whiteman's orchestra that the nucleus of the Goldkette band finally landed, Bix and Tram among them.

The selections recorded under Frank Trumbauer's leadership were done during the period of the Goldkette band's east-

ern swings and the first year of Bix's association with Paul
Whiteman. They contain the most celebrated solos Bix ever
recorded. *I'm Comin' Virginia* and *Way Down Yonder in New
Orleans* are considered Nos. 2 and 3, with the top spot em-
phatically reserved for *Singin' the Blues.*

In fact, *Singin' the Blues* is usually considered one of the
three most celebrated solos in jazz history, a solo of intense,
brooding beauty, carefully built up to a typical tumbling break
in the middle, with a surprise explosion after it. There was
hardly a contemporary white musician of jazz pretensions who
didn't learn it by heart. Fletcher Henderson paid the ultimate
tribute by recording it twice in a version for his whole brass
section, and in the 'thirties Will Osborne and Adrian Rollini
both waxed similar arrangements for full orchestra. (The Trumbauer solo preceding Bix's was accorded the same honors, but
with the passing years it has taken a back seat to Bix's solo.)

Wriglin' and Twistin' and *For No Reason at All in C* find Bix
at the piano with Eddie Lang on guitar and Tram on sax. His
piano work on these numbers is not exceptional; the style is
typical of the period (Lennie Hayton's and Frank Signorelli's
solos are examples), but there is also an occasional flash of the
quality Bix shows in the famous *In a Mist*—particularly in the
fine intro he plays for *No Reason,* which is actually a variation
on *I'd Climb the Highest Mountain* as arranged by Bill Challis
for the Goldkette band. Each of these trio cuttings ends with
Bix picking up his horn to play the coda.

Ostrich Walk and *Clarinet Marmalade* are Dixieland favorites; the former contains an exceptional solo which twice uses the
descending phrase typical of Bix's concept of the blues. (He
bases his opening on *Way Down Yonder in New Orleans* on this
same phrase.) *Mississippi Mud* includes some minstrel-type
clowning by Bing Crosby and Frank Trumbauer, and *Crying
All Day* is obviously a follow-up on *Singin' the Blues,* a good
enough record on its own merits.

The Bix Beiderbecke who joined Paul Whiteman's band in
Indianapolis in early November 1927 was still pretty much in

a world all his own, although he had learned to make compromises such as clean shirts and nothing loud before midnight, please. He was good, and Whiteman liked him and paid him well, but Bix would have played for less if he had been allowed to play more.

Bill Challis, Goldkette's arranger, joined Whiteman just before Bix did. As before, he frequently wrote passages especially for Bix, either as lead horn or for ad lib solos with whatever sort of background Bix wanted. The other section men admired and respected Bix (with Goldkette, they were Ray Ludwig and Fuzzy Farrar; Whiteman usually had Charlie Margulies, Eddie Pinder, and Henry Busse, who was later replaced by Harry Goldfield), and they always made a point of helping Bix with the tough concert arrangements. But it was never enough to make up for the fact that Bix often had to sit there for an hour blowing section harmonies (or just plain sit through the Ferde Grofé productions), and when he finally got a chance to play something on his own it was over before he could really get started.

By 1929 the pace was really rough. Whiteman's radio show was packed with new tunes every week, and Bix had to work harder than ever at what he disliked most. Drinking didn't help much any more, because now drinking itself was pushing Bix around even more than the commercial music. It got to the point where Whiteman had to send him for a cure, and when Bix got out of the hospital in February 1929 he was scarcely able to return to the grind. He went home to Davenport for a while, and returned to New York, but it was obvious that he couldn't go back with Whiteman.

Challis tried to get Bix into the Casa Loma Orchestra, an ex-Goldkette unit that was just beginning to build a reputation which would make it the prom-trotter's favorite in the early 'thirties. Bix didn't have much confidence in his own ability to cut the tough Gene Gifford arrangements, though Challis had done several for the band which were based on arrangements that Bix had played often. After one false start that got no further than the Plaza entrance of Central Park, Challis and Corky

O'Keefe, the band's manager, drove Bix up to Connecticut to give it a try. Four nights of the constant repetition that the Casa Lomans needed to execute the precision arrangements were all Bix could stand, and he rolled back into town further off the wagon than ever.

For the first time in his life, Bix was broke. The considerable amount of money he had sent home to his sister through the years was lost in the crash; Bix had invested it all in bank stock, and the stockholder's double liability of those days wiped out all his savings. Club dates were few, but still he managed to stay on at the 44th Street Hotel. (Among his companions in those days was a fellow named George Herman Ruth, who had an afternoon job with a ball club up at East 161st Street. Bix, a well-built fellow with a physique that remained robust until his final illness, had always been a baseball fan and had even played for the Lake Forest Academy team, as an old yearbook picture attests.)

Bix turned more and more to classical music and playing the piano. He frequently spent the day at Bill Challis' apartment on Riverside Drive and 81st Street, where they gradually worked out a score of *In a Mist* and some other piano pieces Bix had developed through the years—*Candlelights, Flashes, In the Dark.* It was slow going; Bix never played anything the same way twice. He was very conscientious about the piano scores, though; he had a premonition that something might happen to him, and he wanted to be remembered mostly by them. The published version of *In a Mist* differs somewhat from the recording, partly because Bix wanted to make revisions and partly because the publisher wanted a slow section just before the return to the first theme. After Bix's death, Challis also edited Bix's *Davenport Blues* in the same style for piano.

Bix's last year was a downhill slide which his friends don't like to recall. There were a few commercial record dates, a short-lived attempt to take an all-star band to Europe, and finally the move to Queens, where the cold Bix had been curing for years caught up with him.

The recordings from the Paul Whiteman period are all cele-

brated Bix items, but for his solo work only. The right band for
Bix would have been Tesch, Condon, Joe Sullivan, Bud Freeman, and Gene Krupa, or maybe one or two of the other white
Chicagoans who worshipped him and who could play *with* him
as practically no one else ever did. But the music they made together was never heard beyond jam sessions, of which the
surviving musicians and others who heard them still speak with
reverence.

We asked musicians how it was that these perfectly mated
partners for Bix never got together in a studio with him. "Bix
actually traveled in a different crowd," said one. "He didn't
job with us, and in Chicago we got together only when he blew
in for a week or so between working elsewhere in the Middle
West. And our bunch got precious few record dates, remember
—small wonder Bix just wasn't around during them. In New York
Bix was established with that other gang. How many records
did we get to make at that time in New York? Six sides—and
three of them weren't released until more than ten years later!"

"As for Bix's record dates," said another, "he just recorded
whenever Trumbauer or somebody told him to come, and the
invitation didn't include guests. You know, Bix carried the
whole band on his back on all those dates—when he blows on
those records, he's blowing trombone, beating the drums, and
everything else. He had to—he was the only real guy on them."

Though this is essentially true of every session Bix ever made
in his life, it's especially so with these last recordings with the
Trumbauer studio band and the regular Whiteman orchestra.
The Trumbauer arrangements were getting to be more and more
commercial (as opposed to the freedom still present in such
earlier arrangements as *Riverboat Shuffle* and *Ostrich Walk)*
and almost all the tunes were current pops. Trumbauer sang
many of the vocals, with indifferent results. But Bix was used
to keeping his blinders on, and whenever he got up to play the
atmosphere changed immediately. His solos were like glistening
gems among the paste. Every facet of Bix's solo style is represented here, and his unflagging spirit is all the more remarkable
when one hears in full the barren music surrounding him.

The public liked Trumbauer's whimsical saxophone playing, and Bix, though far more serious in his playing, often worked hand-in-glove with Tram's musical ideas. On *Borneo*, for example, which contains not only a fine first chorus lead by Bix but a Scrappy Lambert vocal that lampoons the whole ridiculous idea of a Tin Pan Alley song about Borneo, Bix and Tram indulge in one of their favorite pastimes: a "chase" chorus. Bix plays two bars, Tram plays two. Bix answers him, and so on, for the whole chorus. They keep the melodic line going in one continuous improvisation, and when Bix mousetraps the last eight bars of the chorus with a pregnant little silence, Tram does it too when it's his turn.

They pull a variation on this trick on *Baby, Won't You Please Come Home*. Tram ends his chorus with an ascending phrase, and Bix comes in to start his chorus with a variation on the same phrase. Incidentally, this is a record which Bix scholars love to argue about. Andy Secrest also played the date, and until the last few bars only one cornet can be heard at a time. Who plays which? It's our guess that it's Secrest in the first chorus, Secrest again in the second, and still Secrest behind Tram's vocal, except for the first fill-in (second bar). After that, Bix plays the muted stuff, with Secrest returning to punch out the lead in the final chorus and Bix coming up over him in the last eight.

Bix and Bing Crosby steal the honors on the Whiteman recordings in this set. The Whiteman band was a truly top-heavy organization, and the arrangements were often the height of pretentiousness. The "concert" interpretation of *Sweet Sue* is a real period piece. (The celesta background behind Jack Fulton's piping vocal—which is also typical of the era—was once thought to be played by Bix, but it is by Lennie Hayton.) Fulton recalls that Bix was in bad shape that day, and wore everyone down by fluffing notes in the run-downs preceding the recording. "He had everybody about crazy before finally settling down into that cozy going, as if to say, 'Why didn't you guys say you wanted to get out of here?' " His solo, played with a derby over the bell of his cornet, is one of the finest muted choruses he ever recorded.

The Bix legend started fast and has never slowed down. The Princeton fans were the first collectors of his records. The word spread swiftly, and by 1936 reissues had been made of several Bix and His Gang sides and some of the better Trumbauers. Dorothy Baker wrote *Young Man with a Horn*; Rick Martin, as she pointed out, wasn't Bix, but there's no doubt Rick couldn't have been invented without Bix as the model.

Bix in his final year, living as best he could with almost no money, is something of a stranger to historians and to his fellow musicians as well. They grow uncomfortable in discussing Bix's last musical directions, and prefer to talk about the Bix they really knew, when he was one of the boys on and off the bandstand. The beauty of tone, commanding drive, and the fantastic, fascinating succession of ideas are what they remember, and they are what made him a legend that will live as long as jazz is known.

Like his notes to the Beiderbecke sets, Mr. Avakian's series on Bessie Smith was a result of new biographical research and a summary of previous biographical sources and critical comment.

The following condensation, made from the four essays for Columbia CL–855–8, appears with the permission of Columbia Records and Mr. Avakian.

GEORGE AVAKIAN

Bessie Smith

To the uninitiated, one blues sounds much like another, just as the compositions of Mozart may sound alike. But when a Bessie Smith is involved (or a Mozart), each new creation within the same basic framework is filled with freshness and vitality.

Bessie Smith could do more with a greater variety of blues than any other singer who ever lived. She left behind her 160 recordings. Each is a three-minute demonstration of why this great folk artist so richly deserved to be called The Empress of the Blues.

A mistress of vocal inflection and an artist of impeccable taste, Bessie was also blessed with a huge, sweeping voice which combined strength and even harshness with an irresistible natural beauty. She could cut loose when she wanted to, but was also capable of the tenderest nuances. Every note she sang had in its interpretation the history and heritage of her people, even in her last creative years when she was trying to "go commercial" and her texts strayed from the authenticity they once had. Her style and individuality always remained, no matter what the circumstances.

Bessie's control of her voice was without parallel; a subtle accent in one syllable could convey the entire meaning of a line. Her sense of pitch was as dramatic as it was accurate. She could hit a note on the nose if she wanted to, but she could also dip, glide, and "bend" a note to express her feelings. In short, she combined technique with the finest elements of folk art.

Bessie Smith was born in Chattanooga, Tennessee—when, even she never knew. As with many of the New Orleans jazzmen, Bessie was a victim of the casual attitude of southern officials toward Negro birth certificates. Jazz historians have placed the year as 1895 or 1896, but Frank Walker, who discovered her for Columbia Records and managed her affairs for a time, believes the right date is 1900.*

Bessie was a large, handsome woman; she was 5'9", and though she weighed 210 pounds in her prime, almost all of it was solid bone and muscle. Her appetites were as prodigious as the strength of her voice and body. She drank to excess in her youth, and increased her capacity as she rose to fame. Hers was a quick cycle. From the obscurity of cheap tent shows, carnivals, and honky-tonks that preceded her first recording in 1923, she shot right up to the big time, was riding high during 1924-7, but by 1930 was holding on and none too successfully. At fault was a combination of changing public taste, her own excesses, and gross errors of judgment after Bessie and her husband, a Philadelphia policeman named Jack Gee, began handling her affairs.

Her last New York appearance, presaging increasing appreciation by serious students of jazz and folk music, was in 1936 at a Sunday afternoon jam session sponsored by the United Hot Clubs of America at the original Famous Door on 52nd Street. Symbolically, she didn't even take off her cheap furs as she sang a few songs and returned immediately to the hit-and-miss gigs she was forced to play for a precarious living.

On September 26, 1937, on the eve of John Hammond's de-

---

* "Bessie had the rare good fortune of having a scrupulously honest man as her manager. . . . Frank Walker was practically the only man in the phonograph industry [of that time] who never exploited artists because of their color or ignorance, and he carefully put aside upwards of twenty thousand dollars in royalties for his protegée." (John Hammond, *Tempo*, Nov. 1937)

parture to Mississippi to bring her back to New York to record again with James P. Johnson, Bessie Smith was in an automobile crash just below Clarksdale, south of the Tennessee state line on the main road to Memphis. Her right arm nearly severed in the collision, Bessie died from loss of blood under circumstances that have never been clearly established.

Among Bessie Smith's early recordings is a group on which the chief accompanist is a young cornetist named Louis Armstrong, then a member of Fletcher Henderson's orchestra. Each is a rich blending of what are probably two of the greatest talents jazz has known. There is something of a dedicated air to the first session they made together (enhanced no end by the country-church sound of Fred Longshaw's harmonium on two of the five numbers), and Bessie is considerably more subdued and withdrawn than she is in the later collaborations.

For the newcomer, *St. Louis Blues* provides a wonderful initiation into the ways of blues singers and accompanists, for it is a "book" rendition of an orthodoxly constructed blues, which also happens to be the most popular blues of all time. Bessie's interpretation is slower and less spectacular than one might expect, but its projection of the song's meaning has never been equaled by any other version.

Each of Bessie's vocal phrases serves as a cue for Louis to pick up her last note and improvise in the same melodic line, or inject a contrasting instrumental commentary. Louis demonstrates both techniques in the first line of *St. Louis Blues*. Bessie sings *I hate to see,* and Louis plays a perfect bridge into Bessie's completion, *that evenin' sun go down,* at which point Louis injects a contrasting phrase that leads perfectly into Bessie's next words.

Throughout this group of nine collaborations, Louis and Bessie "send" each other, spiraling their improvisations to new heights as each blues is developed. Louis never abuses his role, even when he has a chorus to himself. He will usually begin quite simply, elaborate his part as the lyrics are developed, and if he has a solo, it invariably flows quite logically from what has gone before and flows equally into what follows.

Most of Bessie's early acoustical recordings are fine examples of her work, but lack the interesting accompaniments which characterize most of the electrical recordings. A notable exception (along with the first Armstrong session and Joe Smith's debut accompaniment) is *Ticket Agent, Ease Your Window Down*, in which one Robert Robbins uncorks an elastic, low-down "alley fiddle" which has to be heard to be believed. As with Irving Johns' fine piano accompaniment to *Jailhouse Blues*, the spirit is perhaps more of Chicago's South Side than the Deep South.

Down Hearted Blues is the very first record Bessie Smith ever made. It was released in the spring of 1923—the first "country" blues record ever issued. Frank Walker, spurred by the success of a few recordings by urban Negro singers* made in a peculiarly hybrid style resembling Sophie Tucker, felt that the time was at hand to record genuine blues sung in authentic style.

There was only one singer he would settle for to launch his revolutionary idea. He had heard Bessie Smith in an obscure honky-tonk in Selma, Alabama, and it had been one of the great musical experiences of his life. ("She was just a kid of 17, maybe 18. I had never heard anything like the torture and torment she put into the music of her people. It was the blues, and she meant it.")

Walker dispatched composer-pianist Clarence Williams, who had worked with Bessie from time to time, to find her and bring her back to New York. When Williams returned with his prize, Walker established her in Harlem for three or four months in order to acclimatize her. "She was so gosh-darn country—real Southern," he recalls.

On February 16, 1923, Bessie made a test of *Down Hearted Blues* with Williams at the piano. Next day she recorded a master and then cut *Gulf Coast Blues* for the other side. The

---

* Particularly Mamie Smith, whose *Crazy Blues* was a surprise best-seller for Okeh. (There were five Smiths who recorded blues in the early 'twenties—Mamie, Bessie, Laura, Trixie, and Clara. They were not related to one another, even in style.)

record was issued without fanfare, merely by announcing it to Southern distributors as a Negro blues record suitable for their territories. The Atlanta distributor refused to place more than a token order. But once the Negro public heard the record (up North as well as in the South), sales jumped until Bessie's first release outsold the leading record in the general popular series eight to one.

At the end of the first year she had sold over two million records and was the headliner in Milton Starr's top-ranking Negro vaudeville circuit. In the next few years Bessie was to become the highest-paid Negro entertainer in the country, booked solidly at $1,500 a week, and her records were to outsell those of any other Columbia artist before her time.

Bessie Smith, born in crushing poverty, got her first break when Ma Rainey's Rabbit Foot Minstrels passed through Chattanooga and Gertrude Malissa Nix Rainey herself heard young Bessie. Ma Rainey, unquestionably the finest of the pioneer blues singers (some rate her as tops, though she lacked the expressive range and fire of Bessie), took the young girl on the road with the show and taught Bessie how to use that magnificent voice.

Bessie served a long apprenticeship with such small-time traveling tent shows as Charles P. Bailey's company and Pete Werley's Florida Cotton Blossoms. It was not until after her first recording was a smash hit that she broke into the best Negro vaudeville circuits.* She covered the entire South and most of the major Northern cities in the middle 'twenties, always as the top attraction on the bill. She always closed the show, singing four or five of her current best-sellers and then asking for requests. All her tours were arranged so that she would have a week or two at regular intervals in New York, during which she'd learn her new numbers for recording.

* The best, at that, was often none too good. The Toby, or TOBA circuit, as the Theatre Owners Booking Association was called, was one of the most desirable at the time, but its initials were also said to stand for Tough On Black Artists.

For the first two or three years, Bessie recorded only what was assigned to her by Columbia. The material at first was real blues, either chosen for her or written by commission from Columbia's director of recording, Frank Walker. Many Bessie wrote herself, sometimes registering them under her husband's name. In later years, the type of material which Bessie recorded underwent drastic changes. This was a reflection of a change in Bessie's life, in which the underlying cause was her increasing addiction to alcohol as an emotional release.

To understand Bessie and the changes in her career, one must recognize that her personality was a strange mixture of contrasts. She was literally two people. One was gentle, tender, sentimental, and as full of pity and compassion as one would expect from the vastness and depth of the emotion with which she sang the songs of her people. The other was tough, aggressive, egocentric, with the violence that was suggested in her enormous and powerful frame.

Gin was usually the medium that brought out the rough side of Bessie, and by 1926 she took it—or any substitute, reasonable or not—a tumblerful at a time. She had begun drinking in her teens and drank more heavily with the passing years. Talking to various people who knew her well, one gathers that aside from the usual influences of her unfortunate environment she rebelled against the basic gentleness of her own sober personality. Bessie's inner self wanted to dominate situations and people, and only liquor could release the inhibitions she normally felt. The way she spent money was sheer exhibitionism (though Frank Walker put her on an allowance and made her buy a home in Philadelphia). If nothing else attracted attention, Bessie in her cups would shout down a whole saloonful of roisterers. Noise, fights, anything went as long as she was in the spotlight.

Yet the sentimental side of Bessie often ruled her, too. The Walker's son Johnny, two and a half years old, became seriously ill in the summer of 1926. Somehow Bessie heard about it, cancelled three weeks of bookings, and came by herself to their summer home in Long Beach, Long Island, and announced to

Mrs. Walker, "I'm Bessie Smith. You've got enough to do just taking care of your boy, so I thought I'd better come take care of everything else." Despite the Walkers' protests, she cooked, washed, cleaned house, and did the family shopping until Johnny got better—and then went back to her tour.

As alcohol got the upper hand in Bessie's life, the pattern of her career underwent marked alterations. Success made it possible for Bessie to throw her considerable weight around with more abandon than ever. But local managers got tired of her backstage didos—from time to time she would fail to show up at all. Eventually there were many places where she was not re-engaged despite sold-out houses; she was just too much of a headache.

Artistically, Bessie's high life carried her away from the folk roots whence sprang her great appeal. Like a plant torn from earth, Bessie withered as she substituted more sophisticated material for the country blues which had given her fame. Walker tried to keep her material along the old lines, but apparently Bessie felt the need for a change too strongly. By 1927, old-time blues began appearing less frequently on her releases, and within two years they stopped entirely.

Her record sales fell off, and on the road Bessie was no longer able to call her shots. She broke with Walker, handled her own money, and soon threw it away as thoroughly as the character of whom she sang so knowingly in *Nobody Knows You When You're Down and Out*. Spending more lavishly than ever, Bessie had to take any kind of work to make money, and soon she was accepting engagements for which she had to sing bawdy third-rate blues or do mammy routines in costume. She combined both in her one Broadway engagement—three days at Connie's Inn in 1928.

Bessie's recordings, from the viewpoint of performance, were still magnificent. To collectors, the variety of subject material and the better quality of most of the accompaniments make them more interesting than the majority of the 1923-4 hits. Bessie never lost the ability to put over a song with conviction and artistry; it was her increasing misbehavior on the road, fol-

lowed by her own insistence in deviating from the successful
formula of old-fashioned blues, which began to cut her earning
power.

Even so, it was only a matter of another year or two before
the Negro public was to turn its back on the country blues.
Walker, who still handled Bessie's recording sessions, tried as-
signing her a wide variety of pop-type tunes, jazz songs, and
blues with bizarre lyrics. But none of them sold the way the old
blues had. By 1931, Frank Walker reluctantly had to admit that
Bessie was washed up as a commercial recording artist, and her
last session (in 1933) was a sentimental gesture sparked by
John Hammond, who (like Walker) has never lost his enthusiasm for her.

A real vaudeville air pervades Bessie's last date; the tunes
were written by Wesley "Socks" Wilson, veteran of the Negro
stage, and the leader of the band was Buck Washington, pianist
of the famed team of Buck and Bubbles. The songs, all constructed in the style of 16-bar blues, abound in colorful slang.

Most exciting of these is *Gimme a Pigfoot,* a picture of Bessie
herself in the guise of Miss Hannah Brown. Her opening cry—
"Twenny-fi' cents! Huh? No, no! I wouldn' pay twenny-five cents
to go in *no*where!"—identifies a Harlem rent party which apparently follows the New Orleans custom of handing out pigs-
feet free to patrons on "pigankle night." (Despite Bessie's rowdy
air on this and many other records, one should not assume that
Bessie ever recorded while drunk or even mildly high. On the
infrequent occasions when Bessie showed up at the studio with
a load, large or small, the session would be called off rather
than run the risk of putting in a whole afternoon for nothing.)

Bessie showed her barrelhouse mood in the Clarence Williams
dance novelty, *New Orleans Hop Scop Blues,*° and the good-

° Bessie's majestic voice is more "shot" on this 1930 record than on any
other, including all four of her 1933 "comeback" session, leading many to
believe that she was straightening out her personal life and was able to
sing as well as ever, although the last session was the only one she made
during the last six years of her life. John Hammond confirms the last half
of this hypothesis.

natured hokum tune, *Jazzbo Brown from Memphis Town.*
Buster Bailey of the Henderson band (with Fletcher himself
at the piano) plays to bouncy perfection the role of Jazzbo, the
legendary clarinetist.

The Bailey-Henderson team also accompanies Bessie on her
intense *Gin House Blues,* certainly one of her finest records. This
tune, as well as *Me and My Gin,* is more than a bit autobiographical. But the most personally meaningful of all her recordings
is the unforgettable *Nobody Knows You When You're Down and
Out,* considered by many to be the greatest record Bessie ever
made. Her exposition and development of the text is a work
of classic beauty, and her accompaniment (particularly Ed
Allen's great cornet) is equally superb. Some recordings reflect
the variety of Bessie's "new blues" subjects. *Black Mountain
Blues* is a series of outlandish pictures of a tough community
("children spit in your face and all the birds sing bass"), filled
with the humorous exaggerations one finds in folk tales everywhere.

One of the great periods of Bessie Smith's recording career
lies between the two sessions, spaced twenty-two months apart,
made with Fletcher Henderson's Hot Six. Henderson himself
and two of his star sidemen, Joe Smith (trumpet) and Charlie
Green (trombone), were Bessie's most frequent accompanists
during this time.

Joe Smith, always a sensitive musician with a tone whose
delicacy hid a great inner strength, is considered by many to
have been the most effective accompanist Bessie ever had. He
was her favorite musician, and certainly Bessie made more
artistically fine records with Joe than with anyone else.

Bessie and Joe, who were not related, hit it off beautifully
from the time they made their first side together in 1924 *(Weep-
ing Willow Blues).* Joe could play with great warmth and tenderness, reflecting Bessie's moods on such poignant numbers as
Baby Doll and *Young Woman's Blues,* or go barrelhouse and
bat out a lead to a Dixieland ensemble, as he does on *Cake*

Walking Babies, Alexander's Ragtime Band, and *Hot Time in Old Town Tonight.*

The first Hot Six session was also the occasion of Bessie's first electrically recorded master. Previously all her sides had been cut by the acoustical method in which sound was picked up by large horns. Columbia was quite excited about the new Western Electric recording system, and was busily experimenting with Western engineers in order to steal a march on competition. (Some of the other systems left much to be desired. Ma Rainey was making records for a rival firm with "Electrically Recorded" on the labels, but a popular rumor had it that all the company did was turn on a light bulb in the studio).

One of the Western Electric engineers had a theory that the carbon microphone required confinement of the sound into as small a space as possible. For this session, he rigged a monk's cloth tent inside the studio, suspending it from the ceiling with wires. In those days everybody—musicians, supervising director, recording men, and even their equipment—was out in the studio with the artist. So Bessie, suffering from an occasional twinge of claustrophobia, was hemmed in with all seven (!) of Henderson's Hot Six, Frank Walker, and a bevy of extra engineers hovering over a mass of unfamiliar equipment. Two tunes were made before the whole business collapsed in the middle of a take, reducing everyone to a mass of bobbing bubbles under a sea of monk's cloth. That was the end of the session—and the tent theory of electrical recording.

But the sides recorded that day—*Cake Walking Babies* and *Yellow Dog Blues*—are fantastic in their integration and emotional impact. Bessie has seldom performed with such vitality, imagination, expressive power, and rhythmic swing. Almost every word contains subtle inflections.

The band, too, is in rare form, particularly in its interplay behind Bessie's voice. Few composers have ever written so tightly knit a chamber work as Bessie and the band improvise in *Yellow Dog Blues.*

Cake Walking Babies, except that the second half of the band's ensemble chorus lacks the wonderful unity of the first half (they are divided by a marvelous break played by Joe Smith), is equally perfect. It matters not at all that Bessie inserts an extra word toward the end of the record. (After the most sizzling rendition of the syllable "Aw" in the history of phonograph recording, Bessie sings of the champion dancers, "The only way is to win is to cheat 'em," but note how the extra word is absolutely essential in her perfectly conceived musical phrase.) This is typical of the poetic license of jazz and the blues, even when an extra syllable is not required. For example, earlier in this record Bessie twice sings, "They in a class of they own," which is much more effective in sound than the correct reading of the line. And—probably for no conscious or explicable reason—in her repeat chorus she interchanges the original positions of the words "demonstratin' " and "syncopatin'."

From a musical standpoint, it is a pity that Bessie did not record more of such rhythm tunes. But so different from other recordings was this one that Columbia did not dare release it at the time it was made, and *Cake Walking Babies* was not issued at all until the writer uncovered it in the Columbia factory archives in 1940. The fact that this great record would have been a lemon commercially in 1925 illustrates in an inverse way two points which can be demonstrated again and again: It was not for any ears beyond those of a particular time that Bessie's records were made; that they are art is incidental to the function they served in a particular segment of American society.

Yellow Dog Blues, one of the most popular blues of the period, is a mock-serious story of a search for a good-time girl's steady fellow. The saga of Susie Johnson and her runaway boy friend, Lee, is a great initiation into the Negro slang that began in slave days and continues today. Someone—memory is hazy here, but it might have been in one of the esoteric British jazz journals of the 'thirties—once provided a libretto for the final chorus. Certainly most listeners will require assistance, so it is not amiss to render here a translation of the last of a series of messages to the anxious Miss Johnson:

Dear Sue—Your easy rider (a character who subsists on the earnings of his mistress) struck this burg today(clear enough) on a southbound rattler, beside the Pullman car. (That's a beat-up box-car. The original text substitutes "side-door" for Bessie's "beside the." As in the example cited from *Cake Walking Babies,* the change fits perfectly Bessie's variation on the melody at this point.)

I seen him there and he was on the hog. (He showed up dead broke, lucky to be eating lesser cuts of pork.) Aw, you easy rider, got to stay away; he had to vamp it, but the hike ain't far. (Town was too hot for him; the only way he could leave was on foot, but he didn't have far to go.) He's gone where the Southern cross' the *Yellow Dog.* (Those cryptic words refer to a meadow just outside Morehead, Mississippi, where the tracks of the Southern Railway intersect those of the Yazoo Delta Line—Y.D., hence Yellow Dog. The Illinois Central now owns that segment of the Southern, and the latter line is now the Columbus and Greenville Railroad.)

The second and last Henderson Hot Six session employed less colorful material; four popular songs, in fact—a rare departure for Bessie. Irving Berlin's *Alexander's Ragtime Band* has never had the rousing, down-to-earth treatment that it gets here. (The clarinetist on this side, incidentally, is tenor saxophonist Coleman Hawkins.) Its companion piece, *There'll Be a Hot Time in Old Town Tonight,* is even better despite the fact that the usually dead-sure Joe Smith is thrown off-stride for a bar by the key change going into the band's ensemble chorus. Note that Bessie omits the article before "Old Town." That's not an accident—she's referring to Old Town, Louisiana, a sleepy hamlet which in the fall of 1896 was plastered with "teaser" posters heralding the coming of the famous McIntyre & Heath Minstrels. These posters promised "a hot time" for the residents of Old Town, and the phrase inspired Theodore Metz, conductor of the show's band, to write a special march for the forthcoming occasion. Minstrel Joe Hayden wrote words to the new composition, which was then set in ragtime.

After You've Gone, usually taken as a stomp, is interpreted as a blues in accordance with the meaning of its lyrics. Bessie's impassioned singing bears real conviction—her inflection of the word "gone" alone makes you know it. *Muddy Water* is a great record despite the puerility of its lyrics—it's a pop tune that, of all things, sentimentalizes the recurrent Mississippi floods! Compare the guff about "Dixie moonlight, Swanee shore" and the inevitable magnolias with the honest and compelling imagery of Bessie's personal reaction to the great Mississippi flood of the same year (1927), which she experienced while on tour—hear *Back Water Blues.*

Other numbers feature Joe Smith and Fletcher Henderson, sometimes with the addition of clarinetist Buster Bailey or trombonist Charlie Green. Of these, perhaps the finest is *Young Woman's Blues*, a sixteen-bar verse-and-chorus song which is a perfect vehicle for Bessie. The establishment of mood and theme is immediately made with a few drawn-from-life images, and gradually a picture emerges of a high-spirited outlaw who is more to be pitied than condemned. The development of the lyrics is of a high poetic order, and Bessie's interpretation is an artistic triumph of complete projection of every nuance to her audience.

Baby Doll, another tragic study of hope-without-hope, is offset by the light touch of *Money Blues.* As with *Cake Walking Babies, At the Christmas Ball* was so far removed from the successful type of Bessie Smith record that it was left unissued until the writer dug it out of the files. Joe Smith plays fine horn on this beautiful and sentimental tune which Bessie handles with a grace that the incongruous lyrics scarcely deserve.

Joe Smith's most remarkable accompaniment is perhaps the one on *Lost Your Head Blues.* While Bessie sings the reproachful lyrics with a touch of gentleness and resignation, Joe adopts a more uncompromising attitude and plays his accompanying part with a firmness and resolve which is a perfect psychological foil to Bessie's interpretation.

Fate linked Bessie and Joe together in more ways than one. Their careers reached a peak together; it was largely through personal shortcomings they began downward slides which were accelerated by factors beyond their control. Joe was only

26 when his fragile health broke in 1930, and he spent the last four years of his life in a Long Island hospital. He died on December 2, 1937, just 35 days after Bessie.

James P. Johnson and Charlie Green were close behind Joe Smith as Bessie's favorite accompanists. Pianist James Price Johnson first heard her in Atlanta in 1919, as a member of the Liberty Belles, a trio including two girls as enormous as herself. Jimmy, who was working a few doors up Decatur Street at a joint called Eighty-One, began an acquaintance with Bessie that was to result in a unique collaboration.

Jimmy was also a trained musician who could and did compose serious music, and his piano improvisations were far more sophisticated than anyone else's at the time. He and Bessie knew each other's styles perfectly, and their recordings are real duets instead of just Bessie-with-piano. Jimmy had a particular knack of underlining not only the lyrics but Bessie's varying inflections in a way that inspired Bessie to new heights.

Their first recording was *Preachin' the Blues,* which appropriately enough opens with a recounting of the atmosphere in which they first met "down in Atlanta, G. A." Jimmy injects a portion of his celebrated solo classic, *Snowy Morning Blues,* toward the end of the piece.

Its companion on the date, *Back Water Blues,* is one of the songs usually chosen among Bessie's very greatest records. A blues of the highest poetic quality, it contains unforgettable images of the Mississippi floods, interpreted in the most moving possible style without ever bordering on the maudlin. That was one of Bessie's greatest attributes: the ability to wring emotion out of any blues without being obvious.

The great variety of the Johnson-Smith duets is not only apparent within each record, but also in the type of song that was recorded. *He's Got Me Goin'* is one of the rockingest fast blues ever made, while *Blue Spirit Blues* is an eerie nightmare packed with wild pictures of Bessie's dream descent into hell. The fire-and-brimstone sermons of jackleg preachers are recalled in this literally gory blues.

Bessie actually indulges in a bit of backwoods preaching in *Moan, Mourners* (in which she and Jimmy are assisted by a male quartet, the Bessemer Singers), and they even inject some reality into the contrived 1930 pop, *On Revival Day*. Bessie imparts a life and beauty to this lightweight pseudo-spiritual which is no less than the charge she would give to a *Rock My Soul in the Bosom of Abraham*.

Outside the recording studio, Jimmy and Bessie enjoyed several joint ventures in show business. He helped Bessie no end with her 1929 show, "Midnight Steppers," and was the arranger and musical director of her Warner Brothers short, *St. Louis Blues*. Despite the quickie nature of the production and the fact that an adequate print of the film is no longer available, there are some fine shots of Bessie in this flimsy dramatization of the Handy blues. The sound track, unfortunately, has suffered.

Empty Bed Blues will always be notorious for the salacious interpretations which can be put on its colorful lyrics. A curious note is introduced toward the end: evidently the side was running overtime and some frantic signaling got Bessie, Charlie Green, and Porter Grainger to drop out the middle four bars in the final chorus in a scramble that might slip undetected past a first-time listener.

The wild atmosphere of *Shipwreck Blues* is highly appropriate for Bessie's rough-and tumble style. Old devil gin had worn her voice down, but Bessie was still Bessie and to many of her fans the roughness of her voice on this date makes it more exciting than ever. Her first two choruses are unusual in that Bessie, instead of singing the blues in the familiar a-a-b pattern, jumps the punch line each time to the second four-bar section and lets the band break it down alone in the last four bars. One cannot help but think it was because of fatigue, but the band's ensemble work is in itself a joy.

Long Old Road, prophetically enough for a third-from-last session in a long career, in many ways sums up Bessie's own life. Without, we can be sure, being aware of the General Longstreet quotation from which Ernest Hemingway was to draw the title for his *Across the River and into the Trees,*

Bessie sings the same thought in much the same words in the course of this touching blues.

It was even closer to the end of the long old road for Charlie Green. Equally a victim of himself, the depression, and changing public taste in entertainment, Trombone Cholly was found six months later under a light blanket of snow, frozen to death on the doorstep of a Harlem tenement.

Commercial success of any degree for a Bessie Smith would be next to impossible today. The musical tastes of the Negro public which once bought her records so avidly (in all, over six million were sold) have undergone radical change. Neither in material nor in style would Bessie now be a true representative of her people.

Another singer of Bessie's artistic stature in the jazz and blues field will not emerge, simply because it is socially and economically impossible for the necessary development to take place again. No part of the American public big enough to matter can produce one, or even wants one. Only among the best three or four contemporary Negro religious singers can one find voices comparable to Bessie's. She has passed to the jazz collectors, folklorists, and just plain people of sound artistic judgment (of whom there are always more but never enough).

Wrote John Hammond in 1937: "To my way of thinking, Bessie Smith was the greatest artist American jazz ever produced; in fact, I'm not sure that her art did not reach beyond the limits of the term 'jazz.' She was one of those rare beings, a completely integrated artist capable of projecting her whole personality into music. She was blessed not only with great emotion but with a tremendous voice that could penetrate the inner recesses of the listener."

The following is an expansion of a 1952 review of Riverside RLP-1007,
King Oliver Plays the Blues *with singers Sara Martin and Ida Cox (it
turns out not to have been Oliver accompanying Miss Cox) written for*
The Record Changer, *used here by permission. These remarks are a
result of my conviction about the poetry of the blues and the fact that I
was studying English in a certain graduate school at the time.*

MARTIN WILLIAMS

Recording Limits and Blues Form

Sara Martin's *Mean Tight Mama* is a blues about sex. In a
few brief verses, the singer is able to sketch a character and a
situation of pathos, honest earthiness, and an ironic and humorous acceptance of the facts of her life. *Kitchen Man,* on the
other hand, is a piece of cabaret smut, "clever" in its verses
and implicitly hypocritical in its outlook. Conditions and public taste and the fact that blues about sex somehow got the reputation of being "dirty" songs no doubt determined that the blues
artist must take on the role of buffoon: *Kitchen Man* is sympto-
matic. The dirty song, as opposed to the song about sex, may
have had its place, but once the folk singer commits herself
to it, there is clearly no way out for her but the one that leads
through the middle class "respectability" of Tin Pan Alley
tunes.

Ida Cox also had the gift to turn experience into poetry, and
in speaking of her I want to speak of the poetry of these records
in general.

At their own right tempo each of these singers could get in

about four blues stanzas on a ten-inch recording. Many singers have responded to the limitations of time on records by simply stringing together four stanzas on (more or less) the same subject; others have attempted some kind of narrative continuity. Both of these singers do more: they give each blues a specifically poetic development which takes subtle advantage of the four-stanza limitation and creates a kind of classic form within it. Ida Cox's *Fogyism* will serve as example. The first stanza states a subject, superstition:

> *Why do people believe in some old sign?*
> *Why do people believe in some old sign:*
> *You hear a hoot owl holler, someone is surely dyin'?*

There follow several examples, still in the realm of superstition:

> *Someone will break a mirror and cry: "Bad luck for seven years"*
> *Someone will break a mirror and cry: "Bad luck for seven years"*
> *And if a black cat crosses them, they'll break right down down in tears.*

The last line of stanza three makes a transition:

> *To dream of muddy water—trouble is knocking at your door,*
> *To dream of muddy water—trouble is knocking at your door,*
> *Your man is sure to leave you and never return no more.*

The vague *trouble* of the superstition, becomes a specific problem to prepare us for the last stanza:

> *When your man comes home evil, tells you you are getting old,*
> *When your man comes home evil, tells you you are getting old,*
> *That's a true sign he's got someone else baking his jelly roll.*

The rhetorical pattern she has set up in three stanzas remains the same but the subject has changed; she is no longer in the realm of superstition but of "realistic" deduction, and in that climax there has been an almost sonnet-like twist which throws all that has preceded it into an ironic, humorous relief. What had been a one-stanza verse form has become a four-stanza poem.

As always in good blues, in each of these the stock situation and attitude is so vividly dramatized and explored that even the expected phrases and images touch the reality behind the convention with the freshness of discovery.

Mr. Russell's reviews on Meade "Lux" Lewis and Clarence Lofton originally appeared in 1939 in the H.R.S [Hot Record Society] Rag, one of the earliest of the "little" jazz magazines. His comments on Jimmy Yancey were originally a booklet which accompanied an album of Yancey solos issued the following year by Victor records. The latter appears here by permission of RCA Victor, all three by permission of Mr. Russell.

WILLIAM RUSSELL

Three Boogie-Woogie Blues Pianists

I—CRIPPLE CLARENCE LOFTON

Solo Art's latest release offers solos by four outstanding boogie-woogie pianists—Pete Johnson, Albert Ammons, Meade "Lux" Lewis, and Cripple Clarence Lofton. In keeping with his fantastic and enigmatic career, Clarence again does the unbelievable and, even among this fast company, carries off honors as the month's most exciting soloist.

Cripple Clarence could well be regarded as the personification of crude, illiterate musicianship. And by the same token Clarence might be hailed as the ultimate in vitality, freshness, and originality.

It is a generally accepted fact that refinement and elaboration in any art are accompanied by a corresponding decline in vital ruggedness, spirited abandon, and in genuineness and intensity of expression. If one had any doubt of the validity of this observation in application to hot jazz, one need only consider the spontaneity, breadth, and forceful expressiveness of the early and cruder Hot Five recordings. Although Louis Armstrong had technique to spare, he played like a veritable wildman on his early records; and as for Ory and Dodds—they always sounded as though their instruments were in danger of being blown to bits.

Cripple Clarence would appear to be good evidence in support of the theory that the origin of boogie-woogie was due to lack of pianistic skill among those self-taught musicians who were compelled to keep their left hand in one position and constantly repeat a figure.

Clarence takes *Pinetop's Boogie Woogie* and virtually murders it. Some of the rough outlines are crudely sketched with broad strokes, and there is no difficulty during the first part in recognizing what Lofton is trying to play, but soon he rambles off, guided only by his own most individual and productive imagination. Clarence, who boasts that Pine Top was "his boy," and who attempts to show Yancey and Lux how to play, would not hesitate to cut Rachmaninoff, were he by mistake to get into Chicago's Orchestra Hall some evening.

In recent years there has appeared a lot of pretentious nonsense about the unconventional length of the "conventional 12-bar blues." Those who rave about this unusual "folk pattern" would have a tough time explaining Clarence's peculiar phrase and period lengths. In his version of *Pinetop's Boogie Woogie*, his first three choruses are respectively eleven, ten, and twelve measures in length. In the latter part of the piece Clarence favors a fourteen bar construction, with a final chorus of 14½ for good measure. Odd phrase lengths were likewise in his previous Solo Art recording of *Streamline Train* and *Had A Dream*, and in *I Don't Know*, in which pairs of 19 and 20 bar choruses are followed by one of 19½. Quite evidently Clarence did not set out either to make his music screwy, or mathematically complicated—he just played the notes to express what he felt, and couldn't be bothered to count out the number of beats. After all, Clarence does not even regard himself as a pianist, but simply as a singing entertainer who has made good money in his day: "Man, I've made as much as $3.00 a night," he has said.

The musician's union considers that Clarence is just an

amateur. Once upon a time Clarence was accustomed to rove around the vast desolate spaces of the dilapidated and dark South State Street section of Chicago, stopping in every joint that had a piano, "breaking it down" as soon as the regular pianist or orchestra got off the stand. But never having collected enough cash to join the union, he has been chased out of all the dives in which he was once welcome.

An amateur is not to be regarded with condescension, however. A perusal of the history of music and other arts shows that many important creative innovations have been due to the amateur. Usually in art a new style has its beginnings with the people, and not with cultivated performers. Although Clarence has his own kind of virtuosity, which could never be matched by any professional concert pianist, he has preserved much of the freshness, originality, and especially the enthusiasm of an amateur. He has the rare quality of being able to send himself, and is not dependent upon the inspiration of others, or certain favorable conditions, for a rousing performance.

Absolute steadiness in tempo is often considered one of the most essential skills of a good musician. An examination of Clarence's tempi discloses that not only is his closing tempo usually faster than the beginning, but that certain phrases within this gradual acceleration are frequently rushed or retarded. Unless one believes that metronomic rigidity is the rule of life, one must admit that Lofton's free and perhaps even lax procedure is more natural and normal. Certainly the effectiveness and excitement of many dances call for constantly accelerated tempi. It is rather an arbitrary and illogical standard which requires an immobile tempo to be maintained, as though the body of the dancer, once set in motion, must be considered a mechanical clock piece.

Just as Clarence plays in only two different keys, C and G, he tends to maintain his tempi, in all his pieces, around two general speed centers—fast (about 126) and slow (92).

I Don't Know is one of the most amazing piano solos ever waxed. After an amusing one-finger introduction (even then he hits a bum note), Clarence drives into his prize piece with great zest. This solo was originally a vocal number, and after five choruses, in place of a vocal, there occurs a most unusual interlude which sounds somewhat like the "vamp till ready" introductions of early ragtime days.

Especially in the left hand part, with its frequent open fifths in the manner of medieval organum, a distinct modal feeling is prevalent. Actually the bass line does lie within the Dorian mode. As Clarence develops the queer interlude motif and combines it with the original thematic material, some very weird and interesting clashing of harmonies occurs. Accidentally or otherwise, Clarence has stumbled across the most unusual harmony ever used in a blues or boogie-woogie composition. No one can complain of "monotonous tonic and dominant" harmonies in *I Don't Know*.

When Qualey hopped the bus and went to Chicago last year to record Clarence, he pulled a real prize out of the bag. Maybe Clarence never in his life got a vote in a favorite musicians poll, but there are more kicks and original ideas per inch on these sides than the big ten ever put on record.

II—JIMMY YANCEY

When Jimmy Yancey retired from vaudeville in 1915 and returned to his native Chicago, his really significant musical career had scarcely begun. It had been only natural for Jimmy to become a musician and entertainer. His father was a bass singer and played guitar in the shows with which he traveled. Jimmy was somewhat of a child prodigy, his talent being evidenced very early in singing and dancing. He soon became expert in the "buck and wing," which today would be known as tap dancing.

Jimmy first appeared on the stage in the early years of the century with "The Man From Bam" at the old Pekin Theatre. Until about 1914 the Pekin, on State and 27th Street, was the most famous Negro theater in Chicago, if not in the entire country. There, before the age of movies, all the best attractions played, from concert artists such as Black Patti to vaudeville acts.

At the age of ten Jimmy left the Pekin and toured with various acts headed by Bert Earl, Jeanette Adler, Cozy Smith, and others. He traveled from coast to coast but never went farther south than Louisville. Before World War I he toured abroad on the Orpheum circuit for two years. He visited many of the capitals of Europe, including Paris, Berlin, Budapest, Brussels, and London, where he sang and danced for the King in Buckingham Palace.

When Meade Lux Lewis of *Honky Tonk Train Blues* fame introduced his *Yancey Special* in 1936, no one knew the man who inspired the title. Many supposed it to be another train piece. Gradually, the mists were cleared, and today Yancey has a chance, through Victor records, to be heard by a world-wide audience.

Another misconception concerning Yancey is that he is an old man. Considering his early start and varied career, as well as his far-reaching influence on younger pianists, this notion is easily understandable; but actually he is still in his forties, and as these records show, still possesses all his youthful vitality.

Yancey's unusual piano style has become known popularly as the boogie woogie. The most noticeable feature of the boogie woogie is the rapid, driving rhythmic foundation of the left hand. Yancey does not remember any formative influence which definitely affected the evolution of his unique style. Naturally, he worked against the inescapable background of the blues and rags. Most American Negroes have heard the blues since birth. Although his father rarely sang any blues, Jimmy undoubtedly heard plenty of folk singers, and remembers hearing such professional blues artists as Stringbeans, Mamie Smith, and Lotta Grady. The boogie woogie is cast externally in blues form, uses in some instances similar melodic phrases, and bows to the conventional blues harmonic formula. But the blues style fails to explain many elements in Yancey's peculiar mode of piano playing. At its best Yancey's music contains certain features which, otherwise, appear most commonly in the thrilling dance music of Africa. In some manner there has survived among American Negroes certain characteristics and practices of African music. Some of these elements are found to a degree in all hot jazz, but they seem to be intensified in the case of Yancey, whose music is the closest approximation to African dance music which has been heard in North America for over half a century.

Admitting that all American Negro music is a hybrid art, at times with dominate European characteristics, and, especially in the case of spirituals, little evidence of African musical heritage, yet we must, nevertheless, concede that boogie woogie contains elements not found in any Western music. To attempt an analysis of the purely African elements in Yancey's style and to conjecture how they got there is beyond the scope of this article; however, a few general characteristics may be noted. The late E. M. Hornbostel, leading expert on extra-European music, pointed out that in general African music is not conceivable without dancing, nor African rhythm without drumming. The piano, an invention which enables one performer to produce more than one part of rhythm is in reality our most advanced percussion instrument. The very close resemblance of many passages in Yancey's solos, both in sonority and rhythm, to the highly developed music produced by a group of African drums of definite pitch is obvious.

Jimmy never played piano on the stage; in fact, he didn't start to learn it until he was fifteen. He had no teacher, but "just picked out his own stuff" by ear. By the time he returned to Chicago, still in his teens, he had developed his individual style. Several of the solos in the album, including *Yancey Stomp, Five O'Clock Blues*, and *Tell 'em About Me*, date from this early period. There exists a misconception that Yancey was never a professional pianist, since he was known chiefly as a singer and dancer. Actually, he played many jobs around Chicago, and worked for a while at the Cabaret Moonlight Inn, and in a saloon called The Trap. But most of all, Jimmy played at house parties and dances during the Prohibition era. His natural talent for comedy as well as music made him very popular on Chicago's South Side, and he was the life of many an all-night party. When Yancey wasn't hired to play at a party, he might have been found in almost any joint along 31st or State Street which had a "box" on which he could practice. Wherever Jimmy played, a group of young admirers and would-be pianists listened and later imitated. Among those who came under his influence were Cripple Clarence Lofton, Pine Top Smith, Albert Ammons, and Meade Lux Lewis.

For some inexplicable reason Yancey was passed by entirely in the mad rush to record hundreds of blues by "race" artists during the latter half of the Jazz Decade. In the swing revival of the late 'thirties some of his "pupils" became well known, while Yancey himself remained almost forgotten. Since 1925 he has worked as a ground-keeper at Comiskey Park, home of the Chicago White Sox baseball club.

Laura Bolton, outstanding authority on African music, throws more light on the relation of this native music and of boogie woogie when she suggests that some of the principal features of African music, such as rhythmic complexity, constant repetition of short phrases, and the tendency of melodies to progress downward, are present in the music of the New World Negro.

State Street Special, commemorating the street which a quarter of a century ago was Chicago's principal South Side thoroughfare, is a slower, more melodic dance. In the second chorus, a strange rhythmic development occurs. Out of the steady throbbing pulse Yancey evolves a common African rhythm which was used as the basis of the Charleston. All Western music is based on a system of rhythmic pulses or beats of even length, but in some African (as well as Oriental) music, some beats may be longer than others. The particular rhythm which is used in *State Street Special* is really one of three beats to the measure; the first two long, and the third short. This rhythm is best known to present-day Americans through its use in the Afro-Cuban Rumba. Yancey is able not only to sense the irregular beats, but to combine the halting rhythm with other more familiar patterns in the right hand, and produces one of the most varied and original piano solos ever composed. Some passages of *State Street Special* may suggest the influence of the player piano, but if anyone's player had ever behaved in such a fashion, an S.O.S. would have been promptly sent out to the repair man.

Yancey Stomp is a dance played at such rapid tempo that twelve choruses (variations) are contained on one ten-inch side. Comparable in its form to many African dances, this stomp, with its drumlike bass figure, constantly grows in rhythmic complexity as the feeling of excitement mounts to a climax. Although the 12-bar blues form is used, this piece has very little in common with vocal folk blues. Rather it suggests the convulsive dance, in which the participant is carried with frenzied passion to an exhilarant state in which all self-control is lost, and even consciousness may completely disappear. The convulsive dance, which is still found in parts of Africa and Asia in connection with hypnosis-controlled religions, was common in the Shouts of American Negroes a century ago, until secular music and the dance were suppressed by Baptist and Methodist missionaries. No real tune exists in *Yancey Stomp;* there are only short melodic figures whose repetition and development accelerate the rising tension. The unusual ending, with an abrupt modulation and final dissonance, need not surprise anyone who remembers that Negro improvised folk music has no fixed beginning nor definite end, and its formal length of no more consequence than the title. Such a dance as the *Yancey Stomp* could probably go on all night without decrease in effectiveness.

Five O'Clock Blues, in a more quiet vein, depicts the mood of a house party when it's about to run down, just before the "break o' day." In the *Five O'Clock Blues,* Yancey shows the direct relationship between the Charleston rhythm and another African rhythm popularized by Cuban and South American Negroes in the Habanera and Tango. The Habanera rhythm, which is used exclusively after the second chorus, has become commonly associated with melodies of Spanish flavor, but Yancey's wistful melody shows not the slightest Spanish influence. The *Five O'Clock Blues,* with its quaint charm, is much more reminiscent of a plaintive Haitian Meringue.

Tell 'em About Me is the most lyrical selection in the album. One of Yancey's very earliest, this Chicago classic has been used at times as vocal blues: "If you get to Chicago, Won't you tell 'em about me."

Though more tuneful than most of Yancey's solos, it nevertheless proceeds with his usual powerful drive. Yancey's ability to hold his composition together and keep it moving and rocking with such a sparseness of notes is astonishing. In the vigorous and rough, even crude, manner of *Tell 'em About Me,* can be observed the real beginnings of Yancey's solid and dynamic style.

Mellow Blues is rhythmically one of the most varied and intricate of Yancey's solos. The uneven Charleston rhythm is again used in part as the basis. Occasionally, in Yancey's improvisation there is a hint of something he has used before, but on repeated hearing no close resemblance is apparent. Rather, it is a distinctive personal touch which gives a unity to all that he plays. Yancey's extraordinary mastery of African rhythmic material and his use of the blues idiom combine to make the *Mellow Blues* an improvisation of unusual variety and melodic charm.

Slow and Easy Blues consists of forty repetitions, or rather developments, of one descending phrase. With his unerring taste and sense of form Yancey must have felt that the 12-bar blues, used in all the other solos in this collection, would involve too much repetition, and wisely adopted the eight measure form. His remarkable ingenuity in motive variation preserves throughout the freshness of the theme. Often it has been claimed that boogie-woogie and blues pianists are able to play in but one key. In dispelling this myth we have only to note that all except two of the pieces are in different keys.

Curiously, Yancey's conventionalized ending modulates in every case to the same key: E flat. Frequently, as if to em-

phasize the inconclusiveness of the ending, and the arbitrary
length of the composition, a final dissonance is used.

III—MEADE "LUX" LEWIS

The Blue Note Meade "Lux" Lewis piano solos again bring
to the limelight the talents of this highly imaginative artist.
His brilliant 12-inch recording of *Honky Tonk Train Blues* recalls to mind the greatness and vitality of a phenomenal composition which must be regarded as a masterpiece of modern
music.

That two seasons of countless repetition of the *Honky Tonk,*
in a necessarily stereotyped two-minute version, failed to curb
Lux's imagination or his enthusiasm is amply proven by his
latest recording session.

The *Honky Tonk* is taken at an amazing speed. Although
the piece is almost impossible for an ordinary pianist to attempt, even at a more moderate tempo, and misleads many
trained listeners into believing that it is for two pianists, the
music is so pianistic that the notes actually fall right under
the fingers. It is interesting to observe that although the composition is in the key of G, the left hand is so arranged as to
use only the white keys:

Of further interest is the unconventional use of "four-six"
chords throughout. The fact that the tonic chord does not
really appear until the final note of the piece may account
partly for the suspense as well as the feeling of momentum
which Meade Lux produces.

The characteristic rhythmic devices which Lux uses, such
as the cross rhythms of the second and third chorus, are perhaps even more exciting at the rapid tempo used on the Blue
Note recording:

Meade Lux Lewis has always been a marvel of inexhaustible inventiveness, and the new *Honky Tonk* contains eight effective and highly stimulative variations heretofore unrecorded in the shorter versions. The new *Honky Tonk* comes to a close with the familiar final variation:

which further illustrates the ability of Lux to create great swing and rhythmic effect from apparently so simple a polymetrical device.

Tell Your Story is a moderately fast boogie-woogie blues. The left hand plays a bass figure of even 8ths with insistent drumlike pounding. The bass, as well as certain melodic features, resemble the style often used by Pete Johnson. More remarkable than this evidence of Lux's long association with Pete at Café Society is his skill and discriminating taste in the selection of ideas and in formulating his distinctive and unmistakable style. Just as Lux once assimilated the best elements of the Jimmy Yancey blues style and the Cripple Clarence Lofton stomp style (*Tell Your Story*—9th and 10th choruses) he has now adapted ideas from Pete Johnson into his, the most personal of all boogie-woogie styles. Everything he plays bears his indisputable trademark. In his feeling for the subtleties of piano resonance, the sensitivity to tone color, the independence of hands in rhythmic complexities, as well as in the mastery of form by means of unity, compositional organization, and climactic development, Meade Lux has probably not been equaled by any known boogie-woogie pianist.

Another striking feature of Lewis' talent is his ability to make the piano seem a part of his being in expressing his feelings. Not only is the piano intrinsically a colder, less direct, and more mechanical means of individual expression than many instruments, but is also lacks the means of sounding the microtones (such as the lowered 3rd and 7th) and sliding tones peculiar to the scalar and harmonic structure which has long been regarded as essential to the blues style. Somehow Lux bridges the gap and makes the piano as intimately personal and expressive an instrument as a singer's vocal chords.

In producing a feeling of blues harmony and off-scale colors, he rarely resorts to the use of minor and diminished chords, but rather creates his impressions through the use of dissonance. Frequently his chords are built of clusters of superimposed seconds. Not that Lux makes an intellectual application of the theory of dissonant chord structure, but apparently he has the inherent faculty of "feeling out" the most poignant and appropriate tone colors for the blues.

As a master of rhythmic subtleties, Lux is also unsurpassed. The unaccompanied introduction of *Bass on Top* consists of a series of single notes, not one of which is played exactly on the metrical pulse, yet the tempo is instantly indicated and a rocking swing immediately set up as Lux's pudgy fingers pound out the staggering rhythm. Just as in the *Honky Tonk Train Blues*, Lux again proves that the most striking and effective music can be produced by the most natural and simple means.

Bass on Top is a remarkable composition in which a rhythmic and a melodic germ motive are developed over a "walking bass" figure:

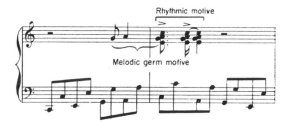

The rhythmic motive, consisting of two sharply accented chords, is augmented to form the *Charleston* rhythm (variations 2 to 4); is elaborated by extension (variations 6 and 7); is reversed in variation 8. This rhythm which might be considered as the retrograde form of the *Charleston* rhythm has always been a predominant rhythm in the boogie woogie. In variation 9, two forms of the rhythmic motive are combined.

A still more ingenious development is made of the three-note melodic motive. Lewis's music has occasionally been compared to that of Bach in its grandeur and sweep, and in its usage of improvisational and contrapuntal technique. However, in *Bass on Top* the motival development is more suggestive of Beethoven's painstaking elaboration. Naturally Lux did not consciously set out to develop his motives as systematically and laboriously as did Beethoven in his sketch books, but, nevertheless, a masterful use of his material is made. The germ motive itself is derived from the bass accompaniment figure. It is treated by extension (chorus 2), by diminution and inversion (choruses 4 and 6), twisted and turned about until its possibilities of elaboration are seemingly exhausted. Finally, in the eleventh chorus there begins a liquidation in which not only the melodic but the rhythmic motive and accompanying bass figure, as well, are reduced to their most essential features.

Six Wheel Chaser is another breathtaking piece of tremendous drive and elemental power. The bass resembles the figure used in *Honky Tonk Train Blues,* except that the chords are in root position. The music, often consisting only of repeated notes, chords, or short motives, has little melodic tunefulness. Pulsating percussive chords, such as Meade Lux uses in the sixth chorus, produce a powerful syncopated momentum. What Stravinsky did in parts of *Le Sacre du printemps,* Lux accomplishes with a minimum of tonal, technical, and instrumental resources.

Throughout the record there is an impelling logic to his rhythmic development. As his ideas unfold with incredible drive, and at times with frenetic outbursts of crushing force, the rhythm is not the only factor of interest. Fascinating and amazing sonorities occur during the surging of tone.

Boogie woogie, though cast in the structural and harmonic form of the blues, often (as in the case of *Six Wheel Chaser)* has little of blues *feeling,* but is more a jubilant stomp-like dance of rugged energy.

RECORD NOTE

The rights to Clarence Lofton's Solo Art recordings currently belong to Riverside Records, which has made one collection from them, RLP–1037. Pine Top Smith's *Pinetop's Boogie Woogie* is available on Brunswick 54014. Jimmy Yancey's Victor recordings were most recently available in the Label "X" collection LX–3000, but that set did not include all the recordings discussed here, nor were the specific "takes" on that issue the same versions originally issued. Meade Lux Lewis's *Honky Tonk Train Blues* is in the curiously uneven piano collection, Camden 328. Blue Note 7018 included Lewis's recording for that label.

I repeat the truism that the Europeans led the Americans in their recognition of jazz. Perhaps they still do. Yannick Bruynoghe of Belgium and Albert McCarthy and Paul Oliver of England could tell most of us about the blues.

This is the first of several essays in this volume which originally appeared in Albert J. McCarthy's Jazz Monthly (St. Austell, Cornwall, England), a magazine which in the past few years has found and published several of the very few critics that jazz has had. These essays are reprinted with permission of Jazz Monthly.

Maceo Merriweather is only one of many blues men about whom little is known. Not only are there few commentaries on such major blues artists as Peetie Wheatstraw, Leroy Carr, and "Bumble Bee Slim" but no records by them are currently available. The extent of our lack in this field begins to show itself.

The records to which Oliver refers are given with their original 78 r.p.m. release numbers.

PAUL OLIVER

Big Maceo

October 1929 brought to the United States the greatest economic disaster in her history when the stock market prices, ballooning through the results of a speculative orgy, collapsed with devastating effect. The Wall Street crash rendered a shock to the nation's system which rapidly paralyzed the arteries of trade and commerce and killed the vital organs of industry. Investments ceased, factories closed, and by 1932 between twelve and fifteen million workers were unemployed. Outside the shuttered entrances of the halls where they had so recently danced the Grizzly Bear and the Buzzard Lope to the music of the jazz bands, poverty-shocked men now stood in mute bread-lines with their backs turned to the driving sleet. Common to all, the nation's misery was mirrored in every facet of its multi-planed existence; was reflected in the minute aspect which is jazz as in any other. Except for a very few who were playing the Big Time, which could withstand even such a shock as the Depression without emptying its purse, the musicians and singers who had recently enjoyed a booming success at the clubs and cabarets, the dance-halls and roof-gardens, were now finding themselves "laid off." As the entertainment centers closed they went on fruitless tours in "the sticks" or, more wisely, sought work in whatever field to which they could adapt themselves where work was still to be found. As the effect of the economic crisis hit them the recording companies switched off their microphones, closed their filing cabinets, bolted their doors. Some were never to open again, the piles of unplayed wax passed into the hands of the official receivers.

So it was that the Classic period of jazz, the so-called "Golden Age," came to a close, and, at the same time, the more humble activities of the Northern city folk musicians, the boogie-woogie and blues pianists, were also called to a virtual halt. In some ways it is true their music may have meant more to them at this time than at any other, for above all the blues is a vehicle of self-expression, an outlet for emotions: to many a colored man his piano may have been his only solace in a time of the severest stress. This was the period when the familiar-unfamiliar names of Romeo Nelson and Dobby Bragg, of Charles Avery and Henry Brown, were to be seen on new issues for the last time. And it was to be many years before the names of Montana Taylor and Cow Cow Davenport, Jimmy Yancey and Cripple Clarence Lofton were to be seen—in some instances for the first time—on a record label. Some of those remote and singular musicians who recorded perhaps twice, or who recorded not at all, may never again have touched a piano. As personalities they have disappeared; as names they decorate the pages of this book or that with their strange evocativeness.

What appears to have been the first generation of recording boogie-woogie pianists had thus passed on. But the picture is

deceptive: it was the extreme youth of many of these musicians
—such as Eurreal Montgomery—when they made their first
recordings, or in the cases of such pianists as Pine Top Smith
or George Thomas's son Hersal, their equally youthful demise,
that causes them to appear to be members of an earlier generation. Were they alive or playing today, many of these seemingly
distant characters would be less aged than a number of the
piano personalities still admired for the youthfulness and virility
of their playing. It was natural of course that some pianists succeeded in bridging the recording gap and these, as one would
expect, were the most popular. Though he had started recording late (June 1928), Leroy Carr had been a resounding success. Before the effects of the Depression hit even as reliable a
financial certainty as this best-loved blues artist, he had made
some eighty recordings. It is no surprise to find that when the
first tentative issues were again put on the market that Leroy
Carr should be among the first artists to be recorded. Signifi-
cantly, his last title before a two-year gap was *The Depression
Blues,* and *Hurry Down Sunshine* was appropriately enough
among the first titles he made when he again faced the microphone. The sun was to shine on Carr for just one more year,
during which the style of singing and playing which had so
endeared him to the hearts of countless members of his race
underwent no change.

When, however, in the middle and late 'thirties the recording of "race" musicians recommenced in earnest there had been
a significant change in the nature of the music. The piano blues
and boogie woogie of the "first generation" pianists had for the
most part been a series of solo performances, augmented occasionally by perhaps a guitar. Boogie was a folk music, centered
in a Northern city and always closely related to urban surroundings, but it still retained a certain flavor of its Southern and
Mid-Western origins. For the most part such musicians lived
and worked apart from the development of band jazz. There
were of course the washboard and "hokum" bands which made
some tenuous link, but the strongest connection between the
current trends in band jazz and the music of the South Side

pianists was in the person of Jimmy Blythe, who succeeded in
having a foot in both camps. A prolific recorder with Dodds,
Dominique and Armstrong, he also played the blues of his
even less unsophisticated party pianist brethren. In his recordings with the Dixie Four, in spite of their vamping bass figures
which are often close to ragtime, he does give some indication
of the direction in which future trends in "race" music lay. While
the arc lamps shone with ever-increasing brightness on the great
but sensational Ammons-Lewis-Johnson team, and illuminated
the highway to Carnegie Hall, the emergence of the style which
may conveniently be called "Urban Blues" manifested itself. In
this subsequent development of Northern city folk music the emphasis was on driving rhythm sections with sometimes a single
melodic voice, playing in support of a blues vocalist. While the
structure of the bands varied inevitably, the groups led by
William "Jazz" Gillum, Yank Rachell, Sonny Boy Williamson,
Tampa Red, Joe Williams, Big Bill Broonzy, and Washboard
Sam—to name but a few—would have an instrumentation drawn
from drums, washboard, bass or imitation bass, guitar, piano,
harmonica, and alto sax. It would be difficult to say exactly
which musicians in these groups established a common thread
for all of them. Such a key instrumentalist might be found in
an unexpected quarter: in the ubiquitous Ransom Knowling,
for example, the bass player whose driving but unobtrusive work
is to be found at some time or another with most of these groups
and many more besides, not excluding the Harlem Hamfats.
Common to all are the guitarists, of whom Willie Lacey and
Big Bill Broonzy—the latter thoroughly urbanized at this time in
spite of his Mississippi origins and later recollections of his
early work—were more than usually prolific. In almost all these
bands those making the firmest contact with the music of the
pre-depression era were the pianists—Joshua Altheimer, Bob
Call, Black Bob, Simeon Hatch, Honey Hill, Memphis Slim,
Roosevelt Sykes, Eddie Boyd, Horace Malcomb, and Blind
John Davis—some, like Sykes and Call, having recorded in those
far-off days. Their boogie-woogie and slow piano styles, deeply
rooted in the tradition of the twelve-bar blues, laid the firm

foundations on which the new form of an old music was based.
And of these pianists none was the peer of Major Merriweather.

Major Merriweather—or Big Maceo, as his friends called him
—came to Chicago from Detroit in the late 1930s. Whether his
family was of Detroit origin or whether they came up from the
South during the 'twenties when the labor demands in the factories in Detroit attracted large numbers of Negroes to the city,
does not seem to be established. What importance can be attached to the verses of Big Maceo's *Texas Blues* (Bluebird
B-8827) is a matter of conjecture:

My home's in Texas, what am I doin' up here?
My home's in Texas—what am I doin' up here?
Yes, my good corn whisky, baby, and women brought me here.

It is more than probable that this blues has as much significance as the favorite stand-by of the blues singer: "Born in
Texas, raised in Tennessee . . ." Curiously enough, Maceo's
three "solo" recordings are named after Detroit, Chicago, and
Texas. If he did indeed come from that quarter it is unlikely,
though not impossible, that he should have learned the rudi-
ments of his music there. It is equally unlikely that he learned
his music by listening to pianists in Chicago; far more probable
that Detroit was the scene of his musical education, for when
he started to record he was already an accomplished artist. That
a school of boogie pianists existed in Detroit seems certain, but
how important it was is difficult to assess, for little investigation
has been made. The city's most famous son in the field of boogie
and blues was Charlie Spand, who recorded fairly extensively
in Chicago during the 'twenties. Spand was an unequal performer but his rendering of *Soon This Morning* is one of the most
powerful examples of the music on record. Spand may have returned to Detroit during the lean years, or he may be representative of a number of pianists of similar style. It would seem from
purely circumstantial evidence that the origins of Big Maceo's
formidable work may result from such an influence. Though he
did not employ the same lightness of touch, there are echoes in

his work of more than one recording by Leroy Carr, and if he did not learn from Carr personally he may well have learned much from his waxings.

That Maceo did benefit from the recordings that he heard is well demonstrated in his *Maceo's 32-20* (Victor 20-2028), in which he uses note for note Little Brother Montgomery's celebrated *Vicksburg Blues,* but crushes the notes and growls the bass figures to even greater effect. No slavish copyist, Maceo sings an entirely dissimilar blues with a tune of quite a different character. The verses of this blues are usually aggressive in nature for Maceo, who has named the blues after the 32-20 bore revolver which is peculiarly favored by Negroes, when, as Big Boy Crudup explains in his own *Give Me a 32-20,* it is "made on a .45 frame."

> I walked all night long, with my 32-20 in my hand [repeated]
> Lookin' for my woman, well I found her with another man,
> She started screamin' "Murder!" an' I had never raised my hand.
> Tampa, she knew that I had them covered, 'cause I had the pistol
>   right there in my hand.
> I ain't no bully, an' I don't go for the baddest man in town.
> I ain't no bully, an' I ain't the baddest man in town.
> When I catch a man with my woman, I usually tear his playhouse
>   down.

Even here where some positive action is implied there is more than a hint of the passivity that characterizes almost all the blues that Maceo recorded. From the blues that he sang and from the anecdotes told about him an impression is created of a man who canalized his emotions into words rather than actions. Though the theme of many of his blues may be fictitious and the women that he addresses in terms of rejection mere figments of the imagination, he still had a predilection for this type of material, a tendency which would present no problem to the psychologist. Anxiety, insecurity, the need for someone on whom to depend—these are the themes of his blues and, though it may be argued that they are the subjects of blues by innumerable singers, their constant recurrence to the exclusion

of most of the other major themes is indicative of an essentially
introvert nature. Maceo does not comment upon the world in
which he lives nor upon the people with whom he has to live and
work: he sings instead of himself and of his own feelings. Characteristically his very first recording under his own name was
Worried Life Blues (Bluebird B8827):

> *So many nights, since you been gone*
> *I been worryin' and grievin' my life along,*
> *But some day, baby, I ain't gonna worry my life any more.*

Notwithstanding this declaration, *I'm So Worried, My Own
Troubles, It's All Up to You, My Last Go Round*, and *It's All
Over Now* are among the blues which he subsequently recorded.
The despairing note of the latter title is echoed in *Won't Be a
Fool No More* (Victor 20-1870), in which he sings:

> *Everything I do, it looks like I do it wrong,*
> *Sometimes I hate the day that I ever was born—*
> *I'm so disgusted, I ain't got no place to go.*
> *But if I ever get lucky,*
> *I won't be a biggy fool no more.*
> *I don't have no money, ain't got no place to go—*
> *The Good Book says you gotta reap just what you sow.*
> *So I'm broke an' hungry, ramblin' from door to door,*
> *But if I ever get lucky,*
> *I won't be a biggy fool no more.*

Whereas too much importance should not be attached to the
surface values of his blues, following as many of them do the
popular conventions of subject matter—promiscuous living, de-
sertion, faithlessness, and so on—all of which are part of the
stock in trade of the blues singer, the underlying motives for
Maceo's thematic preferences can be readily deduced. He was
one of a family of six children, a family man with wife and
daughter, and when he sang, "Baby, I ain't goin' down that big
road all by myself, if I don't catch you baby I'll just have to
catch somebody else," he was underlining his need for the secur-

ity of home and family life rather than displaying a disregard
for one individual person. In his way of singing, no less than
his lyrics, Maceo gives evidence of his disposition: his voice is
sad, nostalgic, at times almost plaintive. He had a tweed-tex-
tured voice neither coarse nor smooth but with a certain roughness of quality, blurred at the edges, soft but with substance.
His voice had much of the same indistinct smokiness that is
common to such singers as Peetie Wheatstraw or Brownie Mc-
Ghee, but without the negligent ease of the former or the liveliness of the latter. In Merriweather's singing there is always
present a degree of strain, and, as one listens, one can visualize
the tightening of the throat muscles and the gathering frown at
his brow. Not a handsome man, Maceo had a kindly face with
small, sad eyes and well-molded lids. Heavy of jaw and with a
deep upper lip, he seldom permitted himself more than the faint-
est flicker of a smile in his photographs. Large features and
a receding forehead gave him a somewhat bovine appearance
which was sustained by his immense shoulders and powerful
physique. Weighing all of 250 pounds, he had thick forearms
and hands of considerable span. From such reserves of strength
he drew the ability to create his Herculean bass figures, but
his desire to do so stemmed from the proliferations of his own
personality. In a man of lesser artistic stature and identical
physical stature the need for action resulting from the circumstances which initiated his blues might have taken a violent
form, but with Maceo such emotional reactions were sublimated
in his playing and found expression in his dynamic blues improvisations.

Major Merriweather played the most puissant piano in jazz
and had no need for instrumental support, but in fact he seldom
played without at least a guitar for accompaniment. In Tampa
Red he found a guitarist whose style was sympathetic to his own
work, and a close friend in the man himself. Tampa Red was
actually born in Atlanta, Georgia, but before coming North in
the early 'twenties he spent some time in Tampa, Florida.
When he eventually reached Chicago his real name of Hudson
Whittaker was forgotten. In those early years he recorded pro-

lifically as an accompanist to Ma Rainey, with his own Hokum band, and with numerous other "race" artists. At that time he had a bird-like liveliness which in his maturity gave place to a quieter disposition. Together they made an ideal team, and Maceo played piano with the more experienced guitarist at numerous clubs and cabarets, and at many informal party dates. Though not perhaps as popular today as they were more than a quarter of a century ago, the parlor socials of Harlem and the "Bronzeville" of Chicago still form a colorful part of the local scene. Like the "first generation" boogie pianists who emulated Pine Top Smith and his recording of *Pinetop's Boogie Woogie*, Big Maceo has re-created on record the atmosphere of such a party and has recaptured its informality and the spontaneity of creation shared by the musicians. Against a rapid and unusual bass pattern Maceo plays a melodic riff on *Texas Stomp* which is fast and rippling but executed with strength as well as dexterity. It forms the basic melody line of the tune, and after a few bars Tampa Red joins in:

> "*Hey, Macey!*"
> "*Yeah, man?*"
> "*What kind of jive d'ya call that?*"
> "*Man I call this—is the 'Texas Stomp'.*"
> "*Texas Stomp?*"
> "*Tha's right!*"
> "*Say, you don' min' me an' 'T' comin' up here to help ya out do ya?*"
> "*No man, come up here with me now . . .*"

Tampa Red joins in with strongly designed counter-melodies against the right-hand work of the pianist while "Little T"— Tyrell Dixon—accents a different rhythm on the drums. The force of Big Maceo's rhythmic and melodic lines was so considerable that such interweaving of rhythmic and melodic patterns was always possible and added greatly to the textural variety of his recordings. As the record progresses Maceo follows a familiar routine calling:

"Hey, Tampa! . . . See that girl over there in the corner?
Man, she can dance! Come here girl—show Tampa how you can
*   jello!" . . .*
"She can cut it, can't she?"
"Yeah man. Come on Tampa, show me what you do in your home."
"This is the way we do it back in my home, Macey—listen here!"

and Tampa plays a singing chorus on his guitar against the driving piano background. On paper the words spoken are neither
impressive nor important; their significance lies in their placing
within the progress of the performance. The pauses, the excla-
mations, the emphasis on certain syllables are related intuitively
to the music played. It is as if only the bare chassis of a blues
was being driven with the music, with all superstructure, all
vocal upholstery, all but the mere minimum stripped away.
Before the record closes, Tyrell Dixon plays a succession of
drum rhythms against a stop chorus. Then Tampa plays two
whining notes, the bass rolls, and the piece swings on to the
finish.

   Detroit Jump, played to a forceful walking bass, is a continuation of the mood, with the informality of the session reaching
the point where Maceo and Tampa are discussing plans for
Maceo's return that October to Detroit. Without a doubt, however, Maceo's peak performance in fast boogie was his recording of *Chicago Breakdown* (Bluebird 34-0743), which must
rank among the greatest examples of the music ever recorded.
Tampa is again present and so is Chick Saunders on drums, but
their contribution is scarcely noticeable, for Big Maceo, playing
as one inspired, dominates the attention of the listener. A walking bass constitutes the fundamental rhythm, but there are in
fact some four bass figures employed, though the variations
are only played for a few sudden bars each before the pianist
returns unfalteringly to the basic left-hand pattern. Though
played at a furious pace and with arm-wrecking power, the
piece does not flag for an instant. Intricate treble variations
succeed those of monumental simplicity, and their inter-rela-
tionship with the changing bass is unerring. From the first

opening bars the "breakdown" rolls on inexorably to the end
with such tremendous mastery of the idiom that the existence
of this recording alone would establish Maceo's place in the
hierarchy of jazz and blues.

Unlike a great many boogie pianists Merriweather was a
master of the music in the slow and medium tempos as well as
the fast. Most of the recordings under his own name were in
the slower tempos, and all are notable for the rock-like solidity
of the basses. The treble passages were generally simple and
unadventurous behind the voice and had more decorative value
in the breaks between the lines. It was in the free solo choruses
which he usually introduced into his recordings that Maceo
displayed his pianistic inventiveness, but whether elaborate or
stark in their plainness, his improvisations had inherent blues
feeling, as such recordings as *Tuff Luck Blues* or *Why Should I
Hang Around* amply demonstrate.

As an accompanist to other singers Maceo excelled, and with
his attention undivided he created blues of majestic beauty on
recordings by several artists. Tampa Red recorded a great many
blues, and on a large number of these he had the support of his
friend. *Don't Deal with the Devil* is a characteristic blues song
composed by Tampa, which shows in its warning theme his
more extrovert temperament. Big Maceo plays the introduction
and settles down to a superbly blue accompaniment in 4/4
time, with a rolling foundation played by the left hand. To
Tampa's "Play that thing, boy," he responds with a change to
the boogie bass, and while Whittaker continues to call, "I got
that, Maceo. I hear you on that piano, boy! Git it now! Play
those blues, boy," he fabricates his variations with grim pur-
posefulness. The devices of *Don't Deal with the Devil* (Bluebird
B-8991) are used to even more devastating effect in Tampa
Red's *I Can't Get Along With You* (Bluebird 34-0748), in which
the guitarist half-sings, half-shouts his accusing angry verses.
From the start Maceo's ominous, thunderous piano sets the for-
bidding mood of the song, each verse of which is divided into
halves, the first punctuated by an arresting stop chorus, and
the second half played to a grumbling boogie. When Tampa

reaches for his kazoo and blows a fierce chorus, Maceo supports him in like manner and he can be heard shouting, "Lay it on me, Tampa!"—the phrase which seems to have a code-like significance to the two musicians so frequently do they use it.

The year 1945 was the peak in Maceo's recording activity, and besides the many couplings that he made with Tampa Red under their respective names, he recorded a number of sides with Big Bill Broonzy, whom he had met in 1941. Though a number of these are unissued, the fastish version of *Roll dem Bones* displays Maceo to advantage (Columbia 36879). Of the remainder several were recorded with Buster Bennett on alto. *Partnership Woman,* though dominated by Broonzy, has fine work by Maceo, but the record (Columbia 30143) is somewhat marred by the presence of the saxophonist. A good friend of Broonzy's, Maceo played with him on a number of club dates, but he does not appear as much in sympathy with him as with Tampa, just as Broonzy was happiest with Joshua Altheimer. Less applauded than the team of Leroy Carr and Scrapper Blackwell, such guitar-piano duos as these are of scarcely less importance. That Maceo's recordings with Sonny Boy Williamson are more successful is not surprising, therefore, since they have both Tampa Red and Chick Saunders, and it is of interest to note that they were made at the session that produced *Chicago Breakdown.* On *The Big Boat* (Victor 20-3218) or *Stop Breaking Down* (Victor 20-3047) Maceo gets no opportunity to solo, and Williamson's vocal or harmonica is to be heard throughout the sides. Nevertheless, Merriweather's contribution is considerable; an Atlas who could carry the whole rhythm, he lays a firm foundation the worth of which becoming readily apparent when these recordings are compared with those in which the far from negligible John Davis or Eddie Boyd play.

In the subsequent two years Maceo appeared with Tampa Red at the Flame Club in Chicago—the nightspot where Sonny Boy Williamson played on the night of his murder. But now his health was beginning to break up. Some evidence of this is to be found on his recordings with Jazz Gillum made in 1946, for although he still plays with much of his past strength his ideas on such sides as *Keep on Sailing* (Bluebird 34-0747) seem on the wane. For his friends, and particularly for Tampa Red, who had known him so intimately, the break-up of his health must have been almost as distressing as it was for his family. Late that year he suffered a stroke which left him partially paralyzed. Recovering to a degree, he made the sad sides in which Eddie Boyd played the piano while Maceo sang, and during the next couple of years he played when he could and sang intermittently, even making one more vocal session for Speciality early in 1949. Then came the final paralytic stroke from which he never recovered, and on February 26th, 1953, at the early age of forty-eight, he died. A major figure in a minor art, Big Maceo had arrived at the day when he would not have to "worry his life any more."

The inclusion of two essays on Ellington, this and Vic Bellerby's which follows, as the only representation of "big band" jazz points to the deplorable fact that evaluations of the achievements of Don Redman and Fletcher Henderson, of Bennie Moten and Count Basie, of Jimmie Lunceford, of the 1946–47 efforts of Dizzy Gillespie at big band bop simply do not exist. Thus, the two essays have to stand for the whole area of big-band jazz.

That Ellington is a major figure, one of perhaps less than a dozen that jazz has had, has long been acknowledged, yet before the 'fifties little written on Ellington attempted to deal with him as if he were that. Then essays by Bellerby and Burnett James began to appear in Jazz Monthly. Mr. Fox's essay was written for Peter Gammond's anthology, Duke Ellington, His Life and Music, in 1958.

Mr. Fox's account of the long-neglected subject of Ellington's musical development and specific achievements is included by kind permission of editor Gammond and of the publishers, Phoenix House, London.

CHARLES FOX

Duke Ellington in the Nineteen-thirties

"The most ambitious effort we have heard in this country since *Washboard Blues*," wrote Spike Hughes in 1931, "*Creole Rhapsody* is the latest development of a form which Ellington has made his own. . . . It is, in fact, the first classic of modern dance music. The individual player is, for the first time, completely subservient to the personality of the composer."

One of the most percipient British jazz critics, Spike Hughes cared little about who played on a record or exactly when it was made. The qualities that made him a good critic were his ability to detach the genuine from the spurious and his flair for relating jazz to a wider musical context. Within a few years his opinions on Duke Ellington's music and musicians were to harden, a note of petulance even to creep in, but writing in 1931, listening to *Creole Rhapsody,* Hughes realized that here was a composition which took jazz an important step forward. If his immediate reaction was to compare it with a Red Nichols recording, that was only because the jazz records issued in Britain during the late 1920s had given critics a limited, rather lopsided view of the music.

The important thing about *Creole Rhapsody* was not the fact that it occupied both sides of a ten-inch disc, unusual as that was for jazz in those days. Red Nichols had made a double-sided *On Revival Day* only three months earlier, while in 1929 Ellington himself had recorded *Tiger Rag* on two sides of a Brunswick record; in both those instances the extra playing time had been used to crowd in more solos. *Creole Rhapsody* differed from these recordings in being a genuinely extended composition.

It is always misleading to select a particular moment in musical history and to assert that there, exactly at that point, a specific style of playing or composition ended and another began. It would be truer, perhaps, to suggest that by a particular date certain conventions had become established. That is really what happened with Duke Ellington. Throughout the latter part of the 1920s his orchestra contained plenty of brilliant soloists, men whose playing was integrated by their leader's compositions. But with a few exceptions *(Black and Tan Fantasy, The Mooche,* and *Creole Love Call,* for instance) these compositions went no further than the provision of sympathetic backgrounds for the soloists; they were comparable, in fact, to the work of Jelly Roll Morton. Slowly, however, Ellington's compositions began to impose a pattern upon his soloists. By the time *Creole Rhapsody* was recorded—January 20, 1931, to be exact—the process had been completed.

Collective improvisation can be vigorous, sometimes it even achieves a transitory profundity; but if an artistic creation is to possess either breadth or depth it must be the work of one man, the concept of an imagination that can hold its several parts together. The greatest jazz performances have never been communal exercises; always they have been dominated by a strong personality—either a soloist like Louis Armstrong or Charlie Parker, or else a composer like Duke Ellington.

By 1931 Duke Ellington's orchestra was already a highly subtle instrument. Sketching out a composition, Ellington could always anticipate the manner in which his soloists would interpret the theme. He commanded a variety of trumpet styles: the plaintive accents of Arthur Whetsol; Freddy Jenkins' brash exuberance; the choked growl—not quite so tigerish as Bubber Miley's—of Cootie Williams, as well as his vibrant open playing. Trombonist Joe Nanton added a forceful almost raw quality, while Juan Tizol's valve trombone—rarely heard in jazz solos—gave many tunes a faintly exotic tinge. Barney Bigard retained the mobility of a New Orleans clarinetist, soaring against brass and reeds as well as taking extravagantly phrased solos. The other members of the reed section were Johnny Hodges, creator of many exquisitely lyrical alto solos, and Harry Carney, his baritone saxophone a sedate, good-humored voice.

"Duke sure loves his brass!" said Fred Guy once, a little grudgingly. Certainly it was the brasses that dominated Ellington's music in the 1930s, endowing it with a character both elusive and unmistakable. By comparison, the reeds—as a section— seemed subservient, echoing the trumpets and trombones, occasionally deployed against them, yet rarely taking the initiative, seldom being entrusted with the statement of a melody or the creation of a mood. Ellington's contemporaries—men like Fletcher Henderson and Benny Carter—balanced reeds and brass against each other in a symmetrical musical pattern. Ellington preferred to blend the sections together, his conception basically orchestral. Yet he has always retained what Sidney Finkelstein calls in *Jazz: A People's Music,* "the two-voiced character of the blues." His use of antiphony, however, relies as much upon the contrasting of a solo instrument against a section or the full orchestra—a challenge between textures—as upon the linear call-and-response of brass and reeds.

Most artistic problems resolve themselves into problems of form, the artist's continual search for a contemporary mode of expression. Sidney Finkelstein has analyzed very intelligently the way Duke Ellington solved the problem of form and content for the large band. He did it "by re-creating all the elements of New Orleans music in new instrumental and harmonic terms," writes Finkelstein. "What emerged was a music that could be traced back to the old roots and yet sounded fresh and new."

Having accomplished this, it was hardly surprising that Ellington's ambitions moved beyond the limits of a three-minute recording. *Creole Rhapsody* stands out today not only as one of Ellington's finest and most completely integrated works, but also as a landmark in his musical development. All the longer compositions he has written in recent years stem from this simple beginning. There was even a gentle attempt to evade the convention that jazz must split up into four-bar phrases. As Gunther Schuller, the American horn-player, has pointed out: "In *Creole Rhapsody* he experimented with a 16-bar phrase made up of a pattern of 5 plus 5 plus 4 plus 2:" The passage Schuller refers to is the chorus played by trombones just over halfway through the work. Yet although *Creole Rhapsody* was conceived in terms as rigidly formal as those used by any European composer, spontaneity and an element of improvisation still crept in. Comparison between the original 78 r.p.m. disc and the LP re-issue reveals the use of alternative masters for the second half of the work. The piano passage with which Ellington ushers in this section turns out to be completely different in each case. Five months after making the Brunswick recording, Ellington cut a twelve-inch version for American Victor. Padded with out-of-tempo rhapsodizing, the logic of the original abruptly disappeared. Previously a strict, relentless tempo had defined the form of this work; now the slackening of tension destroyed its unity.

Apart from this, Duke Ellington recorded only four more sides during 1931. Three of these—*Echoes of the Jungle, It's a Glory,* and *The Mystery Song*—rang among the orchestra's finest performances. Belonging to days when patrons at the Cotton Club liked to imagine themselves listening to music which went straight back to Africa, *Echoes of the Jungle* was, paradoxically,

extremely sophisticated in character. Finkelstein has described
it as mixing blues with sweet mountain folk song. From its pro-
cessional beginning, the brass choir floating languidly; Cootie
Williams, first open, then growling ominously above rustling
banjo chords—the mood of this work is beautifully sustained.
It's a Glory, a magnificently exuberant stomp, belongs to Ellington's earliest style, the scoring mainly a setting for the string
of superb solos. Like *Rockin' in Rhythm, The Mystery Song* was
used as background for dance routines; hushed brass state the
theme, then sustain chords behind warm-voiced reeds playing
a delightfully casual variation.

The changes that occurred in Duke Ellington's orchestra during 1932 had a considerable effect upon its music. Otto Hardwicke, one of the band's original members, returned, bringing
the reed section up to a quartet. Even more significant was the
addition of Lawrence Brown, a studious twenty-six-year-old
trombonist whom Ellington heard working with Louis Armstrong in California. Not only did this give Ellington a three-
piece trombone section, opening up new possibilities for tonal
blending, it also introduced a powerful solo voice into the Ellington ensemble.

Lawrence Brown was a virtuoso, a trombonist of immense
technical resources, his tone rich and strong, his phrasing often
suggestive of Louis Armstrong's trumpet playing. His appearance within the Ellington orchestra provoked an outcry among
European jazz critics and *aficionados,* an outcry to be repeated
—if less vociferously—every time Ellington introduced a new
soloist or experimented at all ambitiously. The sensual tone,
the suave, almost slippery phrasing—these were aspects of
Brown's playing that attackers picked on. "His solo work is altogether too 'smart' or 'sophisticated,' " wrote Spike Hughes, "to
be anything but out of place in Duke's essentially direct and
simple music. Brown is as much use to that band as Kreisler
would be playing first fiddle in the New York Philharmonic. It
is not that his individuality is too strong; just misplaced." But
whether European critics liked it or not, Brown was to stay
with Ellington for the next nineteen years.

Ivie Anderson, who also joined the Ellington orchestra at this time, has suffered from indifference on the part of the critics. Probably this attitude had its origins in the fact that she was often featured on the more commercial Ellington performances, recordings of tunes from shows or films the band appeared in. For many people, therefore, she became associated with the second-rate in Ellington's music, a grossly unfair judgment. Easily the finest singer Ellington has ever used, Ivie Anderson had a cool, curiously restrained style that now sounds unusually modern, while her influence upon other singers has probably been underrated.

It was in February 1932 that Ivie Anderson made her first record with Duke Ellington, a beautifully relaxed performance of *It Don't Mean a Thing If It Ain't Got That Swing*. The same session also produced *Lazy Rhapsody (Swanee River Rhapsody)*, one of Ellington's most fragile themes, backed on the original Brunswick issue by *Blue Tune*, a composition making impressive use of the trombone section. In contrast to these two works, both complex in texture although simple melodically, *Baby When You Ain't There*, a twelve-bar blues from the same period, is notable for some exceptionally imaginative solo playing.

An interesting aspect of Duke Ellington's work has always been his adaptations of other men's tunes. Sometimes they survive for us only in the thin, functional arrangements he often scored quickly for use at the Cotton Club; sometimes he would entirely transform a melody, virtually making it his own property. That happened with *Bugle Call Rag*, where Ellington completely shifted the rhythmic accents of the original; at one point the treble voicing implies a 6/8 tempo, at another the tune becomes a boisterous stomp. *Rose Room*, scored with masterly reticence, its melody discreetly hinted at, was used as a vehicle for Barney Bigard's clarinet playing. *The Sheik of Araby* opens with one of the only two solos that Lawrence Brown ever planned from beginning to end (the other occurs in *Rose of the Rio Grande*, recorded six years later), while Johnny Hodges's solo on the soprano saxophone is a reminder of the fact that he once studied that instrument under Sidney Bechet.

On the whole, 1932 was a good year for Duke Ellington's music. As well as the records already cited, there were outstanding performances of *Blue Harlem, Blue Ramble,* and *Ducky Wucky.* Even more interesting, perhaps, *Lightnin'* represented Ellington's earliest attempt at describing a railway engine in music, a forerunner of *Daybreak Express* and *Happy-go-lucky Local.*

Duke Ellington not only came to Europe in 1933, he also created a controversy with his recording of *Sophisticated Lady.* Spike Hughes, who visited the United States that spring, came back annoyed at the way Americans had turned "sophisticated" into a vogue word, misusing it in every conceivable situation. Ellington's maudlin recording of *Sophisticated Lady,* with glutinous trombone playing by Lawrence Brown and Otto Hardwicke's oily alto-saxophone solo, reflected fashionable New York values too nakedly for Hughes's taste, even before a lyric writer began rhyming "nonchalant" with "restaurant." Much more satisfying were the hard-swinging *Merry-go-round,* a melancholy *Eerie Moan,* and *Slippery Horn,* a slow version of *Tiger Rag* featuring the trio of trombones. *Dragon's Blues* (later titled *Bundle of Blues*), more elementary in pattern, presented fluent blues playing with the minimum of orchestral work. Most charming of all Ellington recordings from this period, however, was the disarmingly simple *Drop Me Off at Harlem.*

On Friday, June 9, 1933, Duke Ellington and his musicians landed at Southampton from aboard the S.S. *Olympic.* The following Monday evening jazz fans packed the first house at the London Palladium. Already annoyed because the programs spelled Otto Hardwicke's Christian name as "Ottox," they waited impatiently from six-thirty—when the performance began—until eight o'clock. Thirteenth on a bill that included the comedian Max Miller, Duke Ellington's orchestra could be heard playing *Ring Dem Bells* as the curtains swept back to reveal fourteen musicians, all dressed in pearl gray suits.

It is interesting to recall exactly what the band played on that occasion, its first appearance in England. *Ring Dem Bells* was followed by *Three Little Words;* then Ivie Anderson sang *Stormy Weather,* with *Give Me a Man Like That* for her encore. After *Bugle Call Rag,* Bessie Dudley ("the original Snake-Hips girl") danced to *Rockin' in Rhythm.* The show officially ended with *The Whispering Tiger* and *Black and Tan Fantasy,* but applause forced two encores—*Some of These Days* and *Mood Indigo.*

During the past two years, ever since the Musicians' Union began allowing American jazz artists to play in Britain again (1956), the visits of Louis Armstrong and Lionel Hampton have incited criticism from people who found their perform-ances unnecessarily commercial and exhibitionist. Looking through twenty-year-old copies of the *Melody Maker,* it is fas-cinating to discover that exactly the same objections were hurled at visiting American musicians in those days. Not even the Duke Ellington orchestra escaped, particularly for the con-cert it gave at the Trocadero Cinema on Sunday, July 16, 1933.

This concert, sponsored by the *Melody Maker,* was arranged in order that Ellington could perform a program of his own mu-sic without any commercial restrictions. It began well enough with *Echoes of the Jungle, The Duke Steps Out, Blue Tune, Jive Stomp, Creole Rhapsody, Lightnin', Ducky Wucky, Bugle Call Rag,* and *Black and Tan Fantasy.* Some of the audience laughed whenever Cootie Williams or Joe Nanton took a growl solo, and Ellington, sensing that the slower numbers were not being ap-preciated, decided that his vaudeville routine would go down better. During the second half, therefore, Lawrence Brown played his solo version of *Trees,* Freddy Jenkins performed *Some of These Days,* and the band played *Minnie the Moocher, Sophisticated Lady,* and *Tiger Rag.*

Outrage spread among the readers of the *Melody Maker.* One whose anger burst into print was Laurie Lee, well known today as a leading English poet. "I had always considered Ellington the prophet of a new art," he wrote, "but on Sunday I found a prophet who continually debased himself." A second concert, three weeks later, went off more happily. Meanwhile the Elling-ton orchestra visited the Decca studios in Chelsea to record four sides: *Harlem Speaks, Hyde Park* (originally *Ev'ry Tub*), and head arrangements of *Ain't Misbehavin'* and *Chicago.*

One effect upon Duke Ellington of his visit to Britain, France, and Holland was to show him how seriously jazz was being treated by many cultured Europeans. The late Constant Lambert, in his columns in the *New Statesman and Nation* and the *Sunday Referee,* regularly praised Ellington's music. Even in the United States, during the course of a lecture at New York University, the Australian-American composer Percy Grainger had compared Ellington's music to that of Bach and Delius.

Soon after the band returned to America, Ellington recorded a simple, swinging arrangement of *In the Shade of the Old Apple Tree,* containing masterly alto playing by Johnny Hodges, as well as another version of the ebullient *Harlem Speaks.* Much more significant, however, was a recording Ellington made that September—*Rude Interlude.* For the first time comparisons with Delius and Ravel took on genuine substance. Reputed to derive its title from a habit Mrs. Constant Lambert had of referring to Ellington's best-known composition as "Rude Indigo," *Rude Interlude*—heavy in texture, reflective in mood—possessed no tangible melody, only a somber harmonic sequence. Linear development was supplied by the snarling trumpet of Cootie Williams and the mournful, wordless lyric sung by Louis Bacon (Ivie Anderson's husband). Only during the final chorus, exquisitely scored for brass and reeds, did the contours of a theme emerge. *Dallas Doings,* recorded at the same time, moved much more lightly, the reeds stating a sprightly tune against brasses playing wa-wa phrases. In both compositions, however, Ellington showed a new concern for harmonic richness, a desire to create more sensuous textures. The year ended with recordings of *Daybreak Express,* more strictly programmatic than *Lightnin',* and a delicately scored *Dear Old Southland,* notable for Joe Nanton's gruff trombone playing and a lyrical solo from Johnny Hodges.

Delta Serenade, Stompy Jones, Blue Feeling, Solitude—these were the first titles Ellington recorded in 1934, all of them made within the space of two January days. *Delta Serenade* was remarkable for its subtle tone coloring, *Stompy Jones* for warm-hearted vigor, while *Blue Feeling*—velvet warm in texture—started with a superb open trumpet chorus by Cootie Williams. Yet the side that proved most successful—more successful than any tune Ellington had written before, in fact—was *Solitude*, rather a commonplace melody, wistful but lacking the four A.M. grisliness of *Mood Indigo*.

Duke Ellington's orchestra recorded only ten more titles—eight of them songs by Arthur Johnston—during the remaining eleven months of 1934, partly because the band moved out to Hollywood for a time, playing at Sebastian's Cotton Club and making two films for Paramount. In the first of these, *Murder at the Vanities*, they played *Ebony Rhapsody*, a free adaptation of Liszt's *Second Hungarian Rhapsody*. But it was a song from *Belle of the Nineties*, their second film, which gave Ivie Anderson an opportunity to sing with unusual sensitivity and emotional power. Few vocal jazz records are more moving than her interpretation of *Troubled Waters*, with Cootie Williams fashioning a restless obligato behind her voice. *Saddest Tale*, a melancholy blues, and the perky *Sump'n 'bout Rhythm* were the only other recordings of major interest that Ellington made in 1934. But if it was a dull period for admirers of Ellington the composer, important changes took place within the orchestra. Wellman Braud, the bassist, was replaced by Billy Taylor and Hayes Alvis (for a time both of them played in the band), while Christmas week found Rex Stewart taking Freddy Jenkins's place in the trumpet section.

Rex Stewart is a performer of unusual versatility. He can growl as ferociously as Cootie Williams or else roll notes lazily from an open horn, his tone and phrasing uncannily like Bix Beiderbecke's (his solo in *Kissin' My Baby Goodnight* is a remarkable example of this). At other times he exploits his unique half-valve technique, or tightly muted, traces an audacious melodic pattern. His talent is explosive, mercurial, capable of both lyrical flights and empty virtuosity.

Although Ben Webster did not become a regular member of the Ellington orchestra until 1939, he played with the band on occasional dates and recording sessions from 1935 onwards. A tenor saxophonist whose style, like that of most of his contemporaries, took shape from the playing of Coleman Hawkins, Webster managed to sound entirely individual within that idiom. No tenor player has used his tone quite so skillfully, suggesting contrasts of light and shade, while his phrasing—whether he was playing a fast tempo or in slow rhapsodic mood—always remained muscular and tightly controlled.

Easily the most disappointing years in Ellington's career as a recording artist were 1935 and 1936. Not only did he make fewer records than at any time since 1925, but no more than a tiny proportion of those he made could be ranked alongside his best work. In 1935, for instance, only fifteen sides were issued, four of them making up *Reminiscing in Tempo*. And apart from this longer work, *Showboat Shuffle* was the only recording of more than ephemeral interest. *Showboat Shuffle*, however, is one of Ellington's most successful creations, a brilliant musical picture of a Mississippi stern-wheeler. Staccato brass simulate the churning of the paddle wheel, while Johnny Hodges's bubbling alto saxophone and the throttled cornet of Rex Stewart are heard in gay solos.

Reminiscing in Tempo, although it lasted twelve minutes, was in its way a less ambitious work than *Creole Rhapsody*, not so dynamic in form, the mood much more passive and subdued. A quiet, melancholy tone poem, it makes few emotional or intellectual demands upon the listener. In a technical sense, of course, the work went beyond *Creole Rhapsody*, Ellington experimenting with more advanced harmonies and coupling fourteen- and ten-bar phrases together.

After recording *Reminiscing in Tempo*, Ellington's first reaction was to wonder what England would think of it. "I wrote it just for them," he declared. "That's partly the idea of the title." Spike Hughes minced no words: "A long, rambling monstrosity that is as dull as it is pretentious and meaningless." Over in America, John Hammond, his article headed "The Tragedy of Duke Ellington," suggested that Ellington kept his eyes averted from "the troubles of his people and mankind in general. . . . His new stuff bears superficial resemblance to Debussy and Delius without any of the peculiar vitality that used to pervade his work." Only Leonard Hibbs, at that time editor of *Swing Music,* really got down to analyzing the work and discovering how its themes were stated, re-stated, and finally resolved.

By 1936 the "swing era" had begun in America. As a result of the phenomenal success of Benny Goodman's orchestra, a much wider public was beginning to listen to jazz. Duke Ellington, however, occupied rather an isolated position. Young swing fans preferred the large white bands—Benny Goodman's, Tommy Dorsey's, Artie Shaw's; to them, Ellington's music sounded less exciting, its forms too complex, its moods too subtle. And unhappily 1936 was a bad year for Ellington recordings: out of fifteen titles made by the full orchestra, six were popular songs. On some—particularly *Isn't Love the Strangest Thing, Kissin' My Baby Goodnight,* and *It Was a Sad Night in Harlem,* as well as Ellington's own *Oh Baby, Maybe Someday*—Ivie Anderson showed just how mature and expressive her singing had become. Most of the orchestral performances around this time, however, were rather commonplace. About the only creative development in Ellington's music during the year was his use of concerto form; these compositions, however, were not concertos in the classical sense of that word, but settings which gave scope for the virtuosity of certain of the band's soloists. The sentimental *Yearning for Love (Lawrence's Concerto)* and the vulgar *Trumpet in Spades (Rex's Concerto)* were failures, but *Clarinet Lament (Barney's Concerto)* with its sweeping clarinet glissandi and *Echoes of Harlem (Cootie's Concerto)* both proved triumphs for the soloists and the composer. At the same time, as if responding to the fact that jazz was turning into swing, the Ellington orchestra began to achieve remarkable rhythmic integration, swinging as a whole band rather than brass and reeds above a rhythm section. *In a Jam*—the most uninhibited of all Ellington recordings—is a fine example of the drive and fervor which could possess these musicians; it contains, incidentally, a superb chase chorus between Johnny Hodges and

Cootie Williams, their phrasing contrasted yet interlocking perfectly.

Between 1937 and 1939 Ellington's music passed through a transitional stage, moving away from the heavier, somewhat static orchestrations of the early 1930s toward the more dynamic, swinging patterns of the 1940 band. Arthur Whetsol, the trumpet player whose pale tone and gentle cadences had given so many Ellington themes their wistful character, left the band in 1937 and died shortly afterwards; his place was taken by Wallace Jones. Otherwise the orchestra's personnel remained the same throughout the whole of this period.

At the end of 1936 Ellington had begun recording for the Master and Variety labels, both owned by Irving Mills, his manager and booking agent. Unhappily these records were not made available to the British market. Even when American Brunswick and Vocalion took over the catalogue, Mills still controlled the overseas issue and continued to deny them to Britain. For that reason, British collectors—apart from those who imported the records direct from the United States—heard nothing of Ellington's contemporary work until 1940, when HMV began issuing records by the new band. Without a knowledge of the intervening period, the changes in Ellington's style at first seemed overwhelming.

As well as recording the full orchestra, Mills put out discs by small contingents of its musicians. While keeping an Ellingtonian texture and pattern in their ensemble playing, these groups had a light, intimate quality of their own. Perhaps the best music came from those led by the two trumpet players—Rex Stewart's Fifty-second Street Stompers and Cootie Williams' Rug-Cutters. These two groups usually produced virile, unpretentious music, nearly always featuring outstanding solos by their leaders. Barney Bigard's Jazzopators, on the other hand, attempted to be both more fragile and more sprightly, although records like their *Clouds in my Heart* and *Frolic Sam* equal anything in this genre. The only thoroughly disappointing records came among those made by Johnny Hodges's orchestra;

some were of commercial songs, while quite a few featured Hodges playing in the lachrymose, rhapsodic style he started using around this time. Yet, in common with the other small Ellington groups, Hodges's orchestra created a large number of charming and exciting performances.

Too many excellent recordings were made during those years for any listing to be other than personal or cursory. It should be pointed out, however, that it was at this time that Ellington began making new versions of some of his older tunes, beginning with *Birmingham Breakdown* and *East St. Louis Toodle-oo.* A year later he recorded both the brilliant *Prologue to the Black and Tan Fantasy* and the *Fantasy* itself, two sides which record companies still persist in putting on separate discs. *Harmony in Harlem* dates from 1937, also *Caravan,* Ellington's best-selling—though far from his best—record that year. But the most exciting and ambitious work was the double-sided *Diminuendo* and *Crescendo in Blue,* an exercise in dynamics as well as an extended exploration of the traditional twelve-bar blues.

The lazy reflective *Lost in Meditation,* the truculent *Braggin' in Brass,* the lyrical *Gal from Joe's*—all these were made in 1938, a prolific and distinguished year for Ellington. His only major commercial success, however, was *I Let a Song Go Out of My Heart,* one of his most delightful melodies. Other outstanding performances during this year were of *I'm Slappin' Seventh Avenue with the Sole of My Shoe* (dedicated to the dancer Peg Leg Bates), *Blue Light, Old King Dooji,* and *Boy Meets Horn,* the last-named virtually another—and better—concerto for Rex Stewart.

The spring of 1939 found the Ellington orchestra returning to Europe. They gave concerts in France and the Scandinavian countries, but had to miss playing in Britain because of the Musicians' Union ban on American instrumentalists. That year also saw Billy Strayhorn join Ellington as an arranger and second pianist. Strayhorn made his first appearance on an Ellington record in *Something To Live For,* an item Ellington picks as one of his favorite recordings by his own orchestra. Ellington's other choices, incidentally, are *Birmingham Breakdown*

(1927), *Old Man Blues* (1930), *Creole Rhapsody* (1931), *Reminiscing in Tempo* (1935), *Showboat Shuffle* (1935), *Harmony in Harlem* (1937), *I Let a Song Go Out of My Heart* (1938), *Country Gal* (1939), *Flamingo* (1940), and *The Brownskin Gal* (1941).

Ellington celebrated his visit to Sweden with *Smorgasbord and Schnapps*, recorded just before the band left America. *Pussy Willow, Subtle Lament,* and *Portrait of The Lion* (a musical sketch of the pianist Willie The Lion Smith) were other outstanding titles made during the spring of 1939. Later in the year came *The Sergeant Was Shy, Grievin',* and *Tootin' Through the Roof.* By this time bassist Jimmy Blanton had joined the orchestra and Ben Webster was about to enter its reed section. These two musicians, together with Billy Strayhorn, were to exert a catalytic effect upon Ellington's music. Blanton completely changed the band's rhythmic structure, creating an amazingly light, swinging beat that set all the musicians moving forward spontaneously; Ben Webster's tenor playing, relatively pugnacious compared with Johnny Hodges's urbanity or the calmness of Harry Carney, gave Ellington a new and powerful voice to exploit in his orchestrations.

Jazz history rarely splits up quite so neatly as critics would like it to. Yet each phase of Duke Ellington's musical career coincides almost exactly with one or other of the last three decades. In the 1920s he led a band of brilliant individual musicians, their solos occasionally given unity by his compositions; during the 1930s he took on stature as a composer, becoming increasingly concerned with problems of harmony and form, yet never losing the essential impetus of jazz; the 1940s and 1950s saw his music move into new—sometimes simpler—patterns. Yet throughout his entire career Ellington has preserved a strong central identity.

As well as being the most imaginative of jazz artists, Duke Ellington is also one of the most practical. He has always been aware of the restrictions that surround his music, of the commercial limitations, of the concessions that must be made. Yet these, like any artistic discipline, have only served to liberate his imagination more effectively, canalizing it within a narrow form. Ellington once defined a successful performance as "Being at the right place, doing the right thing, before the right people, at the right time." The nature and the extent of Duke Ellington's achievement seem to be summed up exactly in those words.

Most of the commentary on jazz that has reached print has modeled itself on the impressionistic literary and art criticism of the late nineteenth century. Unfortunately, it has far too often substituted a kind of vague and primitive enthusiasm for the perception and for the elucidation of quality and content which good impressionistic criticism can contribute.

Mr. Bellerby's essay is critical impressionism, and its approach has the further intrinsic advantage that it presents Ellington himself as an impressionistic artist. This version of it is a condensation of a series of articles in Jazz Monthly; *it is used by permission of the author and editor Albert J. McCarthy.*

VIC BELLERBY

Duke Ellington

To spend an hour browsing over an Ellington discography can be a fascinating experience. The titles themselves are often possessed of charm, poetry, and wit; their literary and musical association spin the imagination into a whirligig of American Negro life: the irrepressible gaiety, superstitious fears, profound thought, bubbling humor, childishness, and spiritual sadness. Many voices speak to us through the titles—Tricky Sam Nanton, the complete orator; Johnny Hodges, the prince of architects; Tyree Glenn, persuasive and elegant; Ray Nance, the romantic reader—but it is always Ellington who is the supreme background commentator, leading his players, and ourselves, to blues of such rich and varying experience as the ebullient *Stompy Jones,* the macabre, fear-stricken *Mooche,* the awful quietness of *Saddest Tale,* and the mystical structures of Billy Strayhorn's *Blue Serge.*

In an uproarious interview with Leonard Feather (*Melody Maker*, January 1955), Ellington expressed his disgust with jazz critics, not simply for adverse criticism but for so consistently misunderstanding what he was *trying* to achieve in so many of his compositions. Jazz being such a small art form, so restricted in its rhythmic and harmonic development, one might logically expect its critical world to be one of catholicity and tolerance; on the contrary, it has so often been cursed by critical writing unique in its prejudice and narrowness. Ellington, the elusive, has suffered more than anyone from indifferent criticism, because he cannot be "typed." Creole music influenced his early style, the crisp rhythms of the swing era effected the voicing of his orchestra, the jerky accentuation of bop is shown in his later-day brass techniques, but above and around these things we have the creative person of Ellington, always experimenting and changing—like the boy in Whitman's poem:

> *Cautiously peering, absorbing, translating.*

Spike Hughes of the *Melody Maker* was so shocked by the *Reminiscing in Tempo* of 1935 that he refused to review any more Ellington records—and never did. This delicate, dreamy introspective, conservative jazz work was condemned as a clever, phony experiment. Over the years this work seems to have the very essence of warmth and feeling when compared with the flashy effusions of Stan Kenton. John Hammond, then on a Basie-Goodman kick, wrote, "All is not well in the Ellington menage," when he reviewed *Cootie's Concerto* and *Barney's Concerto* in 1936. We are indeed grateful that Ellington has never recovered from the sickness which produced two such wonderful blues.

The rediscovery of New Orleans by a penetrating minority of jazz critics in the late 'thirties and early 'forties gave jazz criticism a desperately needed basis. In England the Jones-Mc-Carthy music magazine had tremendous influence out of all proportion to its immediate sales. The greatness and importance of such artists as Oliver and Morton began to be understood, and hundreds of us were made to realize the previous inadequacy of our jazz listening.

The excesses of the New Orleans revival could never have been anticipated by its originators; realizing far too late their own omissions and neglect, many critics jumped the New Orleans bandwagon and nearly overturned it in a frenzy of conversion, a conversion whose emptiness was emphasized by its fanaticism. Old men were literally and physically revived and asked to play the music of their youth—woe to any critic who might nervously point out that at times they played out of tune or even without inspiration, for this was AUTHENTIC. Jazz played in anything but New Orleans style and instrumentation was listened to only with a superior condescension.

Formalism went berserk. No one has ever seriously propounded or developed a thesis that the style of the Brandenburg Concertos of Bach is a touchstone of style and instrumentation from which later composers should never have departed; yet a remarkably similar proposition has been propounded by a number of critics who have misunderstood the significance of early New Orleans jazz. It would seem almost naïve to state that an artist should be judged from his ability to achieve truth and beauty in his chosen medium. It is very difficult in fact impossible, to state objectively who is the greatest musician—Dodds, Hawkins, or Parker—and easy to dismiss the styles of two of them because they do not play the period music of the other. Formalist critics of both the revivalist and modern school often attempt such astonishing judgments.

One reason why the Ellington band has existed for over thirty years is not that Ellington's inspiration is unceasing, but that it is ever changing and developing. Many large bands have risen to fame and aroused our admiration by their individual styles and their unique ensemble voicing; after a few years their original ideas have soon become clichés, the basic inspiration so obviously in need of refreshment. As the bands of Luis Russell, Andy Kirk, Don Redman, Bob Crosby, and the early Count Basie all reflected the mood of their own period in jazz, their demise was inevitable. It is so infuriating to hear people saying, often with an air of great profundity, "The Ellington band does not play as it used to," as if this in itself is a heinous fault. Being the first and perhaps the only great creative composer of jazz, Ellington has to change, develop, or die and, consequently, has often had to suffer from an attitude of unthinking reaction by critics, many of whom laud themselves as being progressive in matters social and political.

Duke has always kept one foot on the path of the blues; he has never deserted his keyboard nor his orchestra for the lure of abstract concert symphonic compositions or the phony glamour of film music and popular tunes. Indeed, Ellington's blues are not a revival but a continual refreshment, a remarkable fusion of detached, creative thought and the vitality of the improvising musician. Rarely does Ellington resort to a monotonous riff style in his blues; sections and soloists are linked together by a collective understanding, rich in counterpart and color.

Even in such a simple blues as *In a Jam* we at once become aware of the understanding between Bigard and Tricky Sam in the first chorus and Cootie and Hodges in the second. Discerning critics have commented on this character of Ellington's genius:

"The difference between Bigard's clarinet, soaring like a falcon against cliffs of brass in *Jack the Bear,* and that in a raging New Orleans collective, is in spirit so slight as to be meaningless. In each case the cumulative effect of sound is strong and natural, and delightful to the ear." (Stanley Dance)

"Ellington has the ability to restore in terms of the new conditions he had to face, something of the social character in New Orleans music." (Sidney Finkelstein)

Jazz has been described as vocalized music, the heavy vibrato of African speech expressing itself in the overtones of great Negro players, the essentially singing qualities of soloists such as Armstrong and Dodds being directly related to the lines of the voice. Ellington's most distinct contribution to orchestral blues has been his continual exploitation and developing of a style of brass playing which has a close affinity to that of the great blues shouters. He has elevated the semi-comic preacher trumpet style to solo and ensemble blues techniques of a unique character. The bewildering variety of Ellington's brass effects are often referred to as the "growl" or "jungle" style.

The growl is but one facet of a bewildering selection of mute, plunger, and bowler effects. The use of the term "jungle" style is the more annoying since it is often found typifying one of the most subtle and essentially sophisticated of Ellington's blues forms and expression. The classical critic who enjoys slumming in what is fondly imagined to be Duke's "jungle" music would be horrified if such a phrase was applied to Stravinsky's *Le Sacre du printemps*, yet in its simulation of barbaric tribal rhythms the Stravinsky masterpiece is far nearer to the pulse of the African rhythm than *Echoes of the Jungle,* which is essentially the richly colored, detached impressionism of a sophisticated Negro city dweller.

Much of the exaggeration about Ellington arose from the strange neo-African cult which grew in the late 'twenties—a near-fanatical movement finding its literary expressions in such novels as Carl Van Vechten's *Nigger Heaven* and political expression in Marcus Garvey's "Back to Africa" campaign. If in some respects a healthy reaction against the color bar, the movement hardly served to enchance the status of the Negro by its pointed elevation of the colored man as a purveyor of barbaric culture.

Many of Ellington's compositions were hailed as uninhibited jungle music, and Irving Mills was shrewd enough to exploit the style at the Cotton Club, where rich white patrons and their womenfolk would revel in "authentic" barbaric sounds. Actually, the primitive African Negro would have listened as uncomprehendingly to the Cotton Club Orchestra as to a Bach Prelude.

The first of Ellington's growlers was Charlie Irvis, who joined the Washingtonians in 1923 at the Kentucky Club. By the trombone chair he placed a bottle cap and bucket, weird accessories to the standard mute. His left hand worked unceasingly inside the instrument's flare, cajoling forth cries of derision, cynicism, and raffish delight. If the customers were at first bewildered by the pungent aside of the trombone, they soon learned to accept and welcome the novelty—just as a well-known public figure will take delight in a cartoon of himself, however derisive.

We can hear Irvis on *L'il Farina,* where he plays a short, effective growl solo, but if it is hard to evaluate his work on such slender recorded evidence, his influence on the subsequent development of Ellington's blues is unmistakable. At a time when he was little more than a moderate ragtime pianist revealing a most limited faculty for composition, Ellington instinctively sensed the importance of Irvis's grotesque style.

In 1924 when Arthur Whetsol packed his sweet trumpet and returned to Washington, he was replaced by the great Bubber Miley. In 1925 Tricky Sam Nanton joined, his protests that he was in no way capable of taking over Irvis's chair being overridden by Ellington in a most determined mood. Thus in 1927, when the true Ellington character was to emerge from the rambling style of the Washingtonians, Tricky and Bubber were to add the most distinctive contribution of the orchestral pattern —the bizarre, menacing mute-and-plunger blues style. Were it not for Ellington's quick perception of the unique character of such a technique, it would seem certain that the power and might of Miley and Nanton would never have been appreciated.

In the middle and late 'twenties, the great Armstrong was to emerge as the most influential jazz personality, his throbbing vibrato being echoed by clarinet and even piano players. At the same time Bubber Miley was to perfect a trumpet style which, with few exceptions, was to influence only his successors in the Ellington band. He is the finest of bizarre trumpet players because we instinctively feel it to be his natural, logical expression: his famous rubber plunger was as logical a corollary to his trumpet as the bow to a violin.

At the heart of all Bubber's playing there is a sadness which echoes life's protests in savage derision and a frenzy of excitement. His playing has wonderful poise; his use of the plunger is of incomparable subtlety. If a phrase or even a note was repeated, he could transform and alter its whole meaning by a

slight movement of the plunger and lips. Bizarre playing demands above all a magnificent open tone and a distinctive feeling for the blues. Miley had these qualities—indeed, the melodic
construction of his phrases and the changing hues of his note
sequences conjure the image of a blues singer bereft of the expression of words.

Although freely discussed as Ellington's first growl trumpeter,
Miley rarely growled at all in the strict, physical sense, rather
hinting at the throaty sound by quick variations of the mute
and plunger. Cootie Williams was the first of the band's trumpeters to transfer the basic sensation to the throat itself. It is
probably his powerful tone and deep blues feeling which led
Ellington to pick Cootie as Miley's successor in 1929. For months
he sat by Tricky Sam mastering the complex bizarre techniques
originated by Miley and increasingly demanded by Ellington's
developing inspiration. His playing was never to have the
naturalness of Bubber, and he was not to achieve the master's
sense of frenzied excitement and intimate poignancy. At quicker
tempos his playing occasionally revealed a slight self-conscious-
ness when compared with the suppleness of Miley's creations;
but this is criticism by the most exacting standards, and only
the most blind of purists could fail to recognize his tremendous
contribution to the Ellington band during its most formative
years. He brought to the band a sweeping majesty of the growl
phrase, and injected shivers of intensity to the most powerful
of ensembles. His departure in 1940 tore a great hole in the
brass section.

Since he joined the band in 1940, the trumpet of Ray Nance
has been consistently underrated. Though he does not possess
the power of Cootie, his warm tone and romantic phrasing have
restored much of the Miley sensitivity to Ellington's muted
trumpet solos. He has recorded many fine growl solos, one of
the finest being the *East St. Louis Toodle-oo* of 1956—fine playing, rich in tradition, vivid in imagination.

Cat Anderson is another trumpeter with a highly personal
muted style. His playing has not the depth of Cootie but reveals
a litheness excelled only by Miley. He is essentially the most

extrovert, flamboyant, and technically proficient of all the growlers and adds ornamentation peculiarly his own—sudden bursts of perfectly tongued staccato phrase and shivering tremors of sound. His *Cat Walk* is a remarkable creation, a blues of elemental ferocity, a hymn to the atom age.

The trombone playing of Tricky Sam Nanton is so essentially personal that one cannot discuss it with the same detachment as one can the contribution of, say, Dicky Wells, J. C. Higginbotham, or Charlie Green. Indeed, one does not know whether to class him as a great blues singer or a wonderful trombonist.

Tricky Sam seemed to be a warm-hearted raconteur between the band and its audience, voicing thoughts which were in turn humorous, satirical, and sad. Barry Ulanov called him "a grown, throated human, talking, laughing or crying." His style of the late 'twenties was never to alter. Quite indifferent to the experiments and changes around him, he simply took us aside and uttered his own personal comments—the smooth elegant composure of *Just a Sittin' and a Rockin'* (1941) is quickly shattered by his typical imprecations. On one number he will strut through the band with the impishness of a mischievous child, and on the very next, the bell of his trombone seems to echo the sadness and torture of humanity. Sometimes the mute was forced so tightly inside the trombone bell that the sound could hardly escape; he would often explode a phrase in whinnying cascades. His variety of effects with the mute, plunger, and bowler were seemingly inexhaustible, all dependent on a prodigious trombone technique.

His loyalty to Ellington was sincere and intense, even to the point of refusing to record outside the band. For twenty years his trombone mouthed across Ellington's white piano, its grotesque expressions always reminding Ellington of the uncompromising truth of the blues.

Tyree Glenn's simple open phrasing sometimes recalled Benny Carter in its elegant construction. His achievement in adapting his phrasing to Tricky's trombone style was very remarkable. At times, as in the extended *Mood Indigo*, the smoothness of his phrase gave his mute effects a ludicrous rather than

satirical effect, but he was often to drive with tremendous power
and achieve a delicate, individual shake effect. In the *Liberian
Suite* he inspires the fierce tension of the closing passages with
his controlled playing. His subtle style was a contrast to the
more throaty growls of Quentin Jackson, who follows Tricky's
example with more authority and understanding than Glenn
could manage.

Ellington's brassmen's most significant contribution has been
to a particular style of Ellington expression which can be described as a sounding of the sinister and the occult. While
Henderson and Redman entered this realm in their respective
Queer Notions and *Chant of the Weed,* no other jazz composer
has so thoroughly achieved and mastered such an atmosphere
as has Ellington.

Black and Tan Fantasy is one of the great jazz creations,
and one feels that on the Victor version of October 1927
the atmosphere is exactly right, with the soloists being re-
lentlessly propelled by Freddy Guy's fierce banjo. The work
is essentially a fantasy in its knitting together of elements so
utterly opposed. The sweet, sentimental alto passage of Otto
Hardwicke, Ellington's dreamy blues piano, and the Chopin
Funeral March have little in common with the opening hymn-
like chant and the weird solo creations of Bubber and Tricky;
yet everything is so fused together that one would not add or
subtract a note from this record. This challenging masterpiece
has the weird imagery of a Blake poem and the macabre sense
of a Fritz Lang film of the late 'twenties. Miley's uncompromising protests sound like hoarse shouts forced from the subcon-
scious to the lips of a colored man as he dreams of the indigni-
ties of the life about him.

Ellington's deep love of the *Fantasy* led him to re-record it
many times. The earlier Brunswick version is excellent, but
Bubber and Tricky do not achieve the mature expression of the
Victor disc. An Okeh version of November 1927 is much slower
and comparatively sentimental; where Bubber indicts, Jabbo
Smith pleads, revealing none of the firmness of texture required
by the important trumpet part.

The *Prologue* and *New Black and Tan Fantasy* of 1938 on Columbia is magnificent Ellington, having a lovely duet between piano and clarinet and Carney's blues solo against rich brass chords, but it has none of the vital unity of the early records and is rhapsody rather than fantasy. The only serious challenge to the early Bubber version is the big orchestral one of 1945 on Victor again, taken at a slow, earnest tempo. The solo brass work falls entirely on Tricky, who plays with tremendous vehemence against powerful brass flares. The 1955 version on Capitol is a romantic conception, with Ellington's shimmering celeste creating an atmosphere seductive rather than defiant. Russell Procope, Nance, and Jackson play good solos in a fine, dreamy blues record.

The Mooche differs from the *Black and Tan Fantasy* in that its solo passages can be freely varied without any weakening of structure. Of the early versions the Miley-Baby Cox is the most successful in sounding the weird atmosphere of this fierce blues. The first downward swirl of the clarinet set against Miley's swaying trumpet and Greer's temple blocks at once sense the macabre; the wordless chant of Baby Cox adds a strange hue to the bizarre coloring, Johnny Hodges's saxophone seizing this atmosphere with occult tension. This conception is in no way weakened by the expansion and colorful scoring of the 1951 *(Ellington Uptown)*. If lacking the aggressive qualities of the early record, the orchestral flashes illuminate the picture brilliantly, without any revolting excess of color. With superb solo work by Procope, Harry Carney, Willie Smith, Quentin Jackson, and Nance, this is the finest *Mooche* in its sense of fantasy. Nance's climb to the shattering climax is in the great tradition of Ellington brass.

Ellington's increasing love for orchestral color and the rapid technical improvements within the orchestra inevitably found influence in the bizarre conceptions of the early 'thirties. *Echoes of the Jungle* (1932) is of tremendous importance, great music in itself and a significant piece. Here the solo work is just as inspired as in the early Ellington's, but it is inextricably welded to the orchestral passages; the section work anticipates the structure of the *Blue Ramble* (1933) in its ever-growing assurance. In *Echoes* we have an uncanny intermingling of solo and ensemble passages. From the first growls of the brass to the last wails of the clarinet choir, an imaginative mood of fear is seized and wonderfully explored. As every soloist steps forward, he is provided with a backing exactly designed to illuminate his style.

So much nonsense is still talked about great jazz being "essentially improvised," but so many of the greatest jazz records owe their apparent spontaneity to detached preparation by a mind of strong, singular purpose. Ellington, like Jelly Roll Morton, so influenced his soloists that their improvisations are a logical function of a greater unity. The natural flow of *Echoes of the Jungle* is due less to hours of rehearsal than to years of patient experimentations and the careful development of collective understanding.

We find a continuation of such powerful orchestral techniques in *Black-Out* (1935) and the *Ko-Ko* (1940). *Black-Out* is a blues of desperate terror and sadness, the finale conveying tremendous feeling, as soprano-led reeds protest violently; behind them we have the relentless drive of the brass and the two string basses. Cootie's growl solo echoes the fierce despair of the whole orchestra. In the furious *Ko-Ko* the string bass of Blanton takes a logical part in the development of the orchestral tenseness. His two short solos are as vital to the work as Tricky's opening four choruses. *Ko-Ko* is a miracle of urgent compression.

In *Rude Interlude* (1933) and *Echoes of Harlem* (1936) we change to a mood of brooding fear. In both records Ellington enhances the dramatic feeling by roving syncopated piano figures of unusual accentuation. In *Rude Interlude* there is no escape from the somber atmosphere of the opening chorus; rarely has the organ-like tone of the brass been used to greater effect. This wonderful conception depends highly on Ellington's subtle, harmonic sense, as there is no obvious theme or melody. In *Echoes of Harlem* Cootie is given a concerto of spectral shapes and visions; the power and sadness of his playing is forcefully revealed against the chanting, ghostly patterns.

After *Ko-Ko* we can find no pieces solely developed to a similar bizarre blues creation; this feature of Ellington was used more to create atmosphere in other compositions, as in *The Strange Feeling* from the *Perfume Suite* or in many of the touches in *A Tone Parallel to Harlem.*

To play *Black and Tan Fantasy* and *Delta Serenade* one after another makes one aware at once of the astonishing extremes in Ellington's mind. The *Fantasy* is uncompromising in its fierce protests, the *Serenade* a delicately tinted pastoral evocation serene in mood. Never has any jazz composer been able to sound such completely different moods as Ellington. If at one moment the band is shrieking cries of protest, the next we find it swaying gently in a trance of wistful meditation.

In the scoring of many of his impressionistic blues Ellington has often been accused of copying the Englishman Frederick Delius. It is true that there is a definite link between the impressionistic style of the two composers. Both have a deep love of color for its own sake and will often deliberately eschew melody and rhythm for subtle harmonic developments, thus making the music seem to be hung on the merest shred of thematic phrase. It is interesting to play over a remarkable passage toward the end of *Dusk* scored for trumpets, trombones, and baritone saxophone and then Delius's *Intermezzo* from *Hassan.* In both selections the composers reveal an instinctive capacity for *suspending a chord in space,* creating a dreamy effect by seductive use of rich color and the subtlest of harmonic changes. It is interesting to note that Ellington had never heard of Delius until 1933, after he had already explored this style of composition, and it is even more significant that the most formative years of Delius's life were the five he spent in South Carolina, where he was greatly influenced by the nostalgic harmonies of Negro spirituals and work songs.

While Ellington drew instinctively on the harmonic progression of the blues and spirituals, Delius consciously absorbed these elements into his musical sensibility. It is important to realize that had Delius never lived among the Negroes of South Carolina he could hardly have produced his first masterpiece—*Appalachia—Variations on a Negro Slave Song*. One feels that *Dusk* and *Under a Turquoise Cloud* would still have been written had Ellington never acquired an interest in the Englishman's music.

Ellington's dreamy impressionism is most exacting in its demands on the technical proficiency and tonal blending of his musicians. In quick and medium tempi, a lapse into faulty intonation can quickly pass unnoticed; with the emphasis on color and subtle harmonic change, the slightest coarseness in execution is intolerable. It is, therefore, hardly surprising that this mood was to show little maturity in expression until the early 'thirties. In the late 'twenties Arthur Whetsol was the only musician who instinctively captured Ellington's wistful mood. Just as Bubber tremendously influenced Ellington's bizarre style, so Whetsol was to play a tremendous part in the development of the dream-like creations. Whereas Bubber chanted the blues, Whetsol was to sing the nostalgic line of the spiritual. In no sense a solo improvising player, Whetsol brought to the blues fragile poignancy rather than defiant feeling. His wistful tone gave the orchestral sound an unmistakable timbre and under his leadership the Ellington brass section of the early 'thirties brought a unique tonal splendor to jazz.

In the late 'twenties Whetsol was often to state perfectly the mood of many Ellington compositions when the rest of the front line often had little understanding of Duke's intentions. In the early *Misty Mornin'* (1928) he is the only player to achieve the true atmosphere of the piece; the jerky phrasing of the reeds and the brass are so hopelessly out of sympathy with the mood Ellington was trying to realize, and even Lonnie Johnson's superb guitar playing had little in common with the atmosphere of the composition.

One feels that the orchestra of the 1930's was best able to sense the delicate atmosphere of Ellington's conceptions. *Swanee River Rhapsody* (*Lazy Rhapsody*) epitomizes the way the trumpets and trombones were welded into an instrument of enormous flexibility and tonal range. From the first touch of the trombone the brass play with the great delicacy and ravishing beauty of tone.

This delightful intimacy, greatly aided by Wellman Braud's bass, sounding like the gentle flow of the river has a pastoral sense of innocence unparalleled in the jazz world. The coloring is wonderfully subtle, with the alternation of Carney's baritone, Hodges's alto, and Bigard's clarinet. One can but marvel at the fact that of the fourteen members of the orchestra who recorded the *Swanee River Rhapsody* twelve played in the *Misty Mornin'* of 1928. In five years this ragged ensemble had been molded into an instrument of unique understanding.

The period 1935-38 was one of great creative activity for Ellington. The flow of dreamy blues continued with the delicately tinted *Azure* (1937) and *Blue Light* (1938) and the *Subtle Lament* (1939). Many of the small band records such as *Blue Reverie* (1937) and *Wanderlust* (1938) have a rich, romantic strain.

With the turn of the 'forties the band's character was to change. Webster's tenor imparted thicker voicing to the reeds, and the astonishing agility of Blanton's bass revolutionized the rhythm section and inspired Duke to more powerful ensemble voicings. The band acquired tremendous power but lost much of its wistful charm. Indeed, between the *Subtle Lament* of 1939 and the *Transbluency* of 1946 we can think of only two orchestral contributions of similar style—*Dusk* and *Blue Goose* in 1940. *Delta Serenade* of 1933 and *Dusk* of 1940 show the difference between the orchestral style of the two periods. The *Serenade* is a watercolor of plaintive, misty shading; *Dusk* is painted in oils by a firm brush.

In 1946 the acquisition of Kay Davis was to inspire a series of Ellington compositions which recaptured the intimacy of the early 'thirties. In no sense a hot singer, Davis's straight phrasing was to re-create the mood of Whetsol and to continue the delightful form of the 1927 *Creole Love Call*, where Duke used Adelaide Hall's wordless chant above the clarinet choir.

Blending so perfectly with trombones and bass clarinet, Davis was to inspire the Duke to write the lovely *Transblucency* and *Under a Turquoise Cloud*. Perhaps her finest achievement is in *Minnehaha*, where she is given an exquisite wordless ballad which blends with the colors of Lawrence Brown's trombone and Jimmy Hamilton's clarinet. From approximately the same period we had the stately grace of the *Lady of the Lavender Mist* of 1947 and *New York City Blues* of 1948, the last-named being a set of wistful variations shared between Hal Baker, Hodges, and Duke. Rarely have the singing, penetrating tone, and rich harmonic subtleties of Ellington's piano style been so faithfully captured on record. In this portrait we feel the awful loneliness which can be felt in the heart of a great city, a remarkable parallel to the mood and bare outline of Aaron Copland's *Quiet City*.

Bigard's swirls from high to low register clarinet and the remarkable flexibility of his romantic creole phrasing were to add different flashes to the Ellington dreamy blues. *Rose Room*, with its perfect setting for Barney's clarinet, has almost come to be regarded as an Ellington composition. In contrast, at first Jimmy Hamilton's tone was thin and legitimate, hopelessly out of sympathy with the great library of Bigard's creole lyricism. However, his tone was to mellow and his feeling broaden so that at times he was able to re-create the Bigard mood with some success, but Ellington was often to prefer the liquid flow of Russell Procope's clarinet in such re-creations as *Creole Love Call* and *Black and Tan Fantasy*.

When discussing Ellington's dreamy impressionism we are dealing with the re-creations of the blues in terms of color and delicate feeling rather than the sadness or protest. The slightest touch of false sentimentality can throw sickly lines across the whole picture. It is, indeed, difficult to understand why in the 1940's Ellington encouraged the great Hodges frequently to indulge in a welter of self-pity; the more so since Hardwicke was always at hand to achieve the same style much better. The Hodges on *Come Sunday* and *Sultry Sunset* would seem to be a victim of Lawrence Brown's smear campaign, a strange de-

fect in an excellent soloist. In a few similar compositions Ellington has allowed his love of color to degenerate into sickly
painting and his fine feeling for the blues to descend to the
saccharine.

The question of Lawrence Brown's trombone will rightly
cause controversy wherever Ellington's blues are discussed. No
one can doubt his contribution to the brass; his magnificent
technique and firm tone were to impart a tremendous mobility
and sonority to the trombone section. Sometimes his playing
was so perfectly tuned to Ellington's mood that one would
not wish one note to be altered; the middle eight bars of his
solo in *Delta Serenade* hang perfectly across the music; his
twelve bars in *Blue Feeling* are beautifully constructed, but
much too often his excess of sentimentality and exaggerated
glissandi destroy the blues mood of the blues on Ellington
records. He is the most unpredictable of Ellington soloists, at
his finest a good link, at his worst a dangerously weak one.

Four of Ellington's finest impressionistic studies have been
devoted to mechanical transport—three inevitably to the steam
train, for the iron road has been the cradle for the majority
of Ellington's compositions. Few living people can have spent
more time in trains than Ellington; the railway carriage has
become to him almost a mosque, a refuge from the ballyhoo of
the outside world. Ellington himself has said, "When I board
a train, peace descends on me, the train's metallic rhythm
soothes me. The fireman plays blues on the engine whistle—big,
smeary things like a goddam woman singing in the night."

The thoughts of Ellington composing in a train has been
brilliantly drawn in a profile which appeared in *The New
Yorker* in the 1940's. On reading it, one's first impressions are
to think that Ellington would write much better if he could
retire to some lavish study and work uninterrupted; later one
realizes that the ever-present rhythm of the wheels, the screams
of the engine, and the immediate contact with noisy humanity
have inevitably contributed so much to the warm, personal
character of Ellington's blues.

In the early 'thirties Duke gave us two fine train pieces.

Daybreak Express was a vivid picture of a locomotive hurtling into the dawn. In *Lightnin'* we relaxed in the luxury of a pullman car.

Happy-go-lucky Local is the finest of Ellington's train compositions. This wheezy antique was most appropriately exhibited in the *Ellington '55* LP, where microgroove recording enables us to hear every note of its aging machinery. There are many touches of sheer delight: the magic of the opening with the Emmet-like train swaying precariously round a curve, bassist Wendell Marshall doing a hula below Duke's clanking piano; Paul Gonsalves's tenor blowing itself up with the impudent pride of the pompous antique, only to be deflated by the obscene pop of the safety valve; the hilarious passage where, gathering speed down a gradient, the train and its occupants burst into an exultant chant, Cat Anderson screaming delight above the uproar. The triple counterpoint of the ending is a stroke of sheer genius: Anderson jerking at the rusty brakes, clouds of steam rising from Ballard's cymbal, and Marshall's bass jerking the wheels to a standstill. Anderson's trumpet recreates the feeling of the great humorists, Bubber and Tricky. The whole band revels in the warmth of its blues classic, breathing a human personality into this dumpy locomotive.

In 1935 Duke gave us *Showboat Shuffle*. Made at a time when Duke cut down on rehearsals because of Arthur Whetsol's illness, it shows the band in a strangely ragged state: the reeds sometimes out of tune, the brass rough in tone (faults not quite so serious in the turbulent *Showboat Shuffle* but very obvious in *In a Sentimental Mood* from the same session). Duke's portrait symbolizes the movement of the showboat and recalls the days of Fate Marable and of New Orleans by means of Rex Stewart's fine trumpet, a blues solo of broad, sweeping invention, full of nervous intensity. Rex's solo is followed by a remarkable piece of orchestration, as deep trombones and two-part reeds imitate the threshing of a giant paddle wheel, with Bigard's clarinet whirling amidst clouds of spray. For once we can excuse the fade-out as the boat disappears up-river, the staccato brass sounding the pulse of the engine.

The fast and lightly swinging blues has always inspired Ellington and his musicians and has produced a wide variety of treatment. In the late 'twenties Ellington was often content to give his soloists a merest hint of an arrangement, as in the exuberant *Hot and Bothered* with Bubber, Baby Cox, Bigard, and Hodges at their most fierce. The orchestral sense of Ellington was to assume greater command in the lightly swinging *Jolly Wog* of 1929, which shows the merging of soloists into an orchestral pattern. A year later, with the great *Creole Rhapsody,* we can feel a sense of exaltation in Ellington's piano, and we sense the power of the band at its full maturity, as the brass drives into the opening twelve bars, with Bigard twisting above them. *Merry-Go-Round* is highly organized blues, solos and section passages intermingling with amazing coherence. *Stompy Jones* is a creation of delirious excitement, a virtual battle between the brass men, Bigard, and Tricky Sam.

Throughout the 'thirties the Ellington band was to compose many swinging pieces, scoring ensemble passages with a minimum of solo interjections. The *Gal from Joe's* and *Riding on a Blue Note* are typical examples, exquisite relaxation being achieved by the gentle pulse of the two string basses and the wonderful understanding between the sections.

The raging *Jack the Bear* of 1940 at once reveals the tremendous impact of Blanton's bass on the Ellington ensemble, dominating not only the rhythm but taking its logical place as a lithe solo instrument. If the middle 'forties were to see more changes than any other period in Ellington history, the shifting of personnel was only excessive by Ellington's standards, and always of less frequency than in the bands around him. Great soloists were never absent, and in the *Hy'a Sue* of 1946 the band roared into one of its best blues. Glenn's trombone conjures the image of a great blues singer; indeed, one can almost visualize Big Bill Broonzy throwing back his head as Glenn leads into each of his choruses. Hodges is at his very best, both in his obliggato to Glenn and in his solo passages, which sound the naked truth of the blues. The *V.I.P.'s Boogie* of 1951 is full of rich humor. Modernist techniques are subtly trans-

formed by delightful touches, particularly in the gaily swinging
unison reed chorus in which Ellington seems to be balancing a
straw hat between Charlie Parker's *Cool Blues* and his own early
Jolly Wog.

Ellington's blues are conceived and developed from within
the band. When playing his records one realizes that in no
other orchestra can the individual soloist attain such dignity,
for by some mysterious process the individual solo becomes a
contribution to a greater conception. Listening to Bigard in
Barney's Concerto one becomes convinced that he is an important blues clarinetist. However, after he left Ellington in the
mid-'forties and was given the "freedom" to improvise with
Louis Armstrong's small group, his playing became dull, spine-
less, and wearying. The difference is a measure of Ellington's
genius; indeed, Morton is the only musician to have ever challenged Ellington's uncanny sense of making musicians play
above their natural ability.

Count Basie's band has been designated the band of the
blues, but we must quickly narrow our perception if we are
to accept this dictum. Great indeed is the drive of this band
but, it never reveals the mystery of exploration or the surprise
of creation which we find in Ellington. Ellington's blues can
soothe, frighten, and excite.

Duke's blues can also touch the profound sadness of jazz.
From the time Ellington waxed the bitter *Blues with a Feeling*
in 1928, he has often sounded moments of sad truth in his blues
conceptions. From the first solitary wail of Bigard's clarinet
to Ellington's last spoken aside, the *Saddest Tale* of 1934 brings
us into the presence of music as deeply moving as Bessie
Smith's *Gin House Blues*. In 1952 there slipped almost unnoticed from the barrage of commercial drivel Duke recorded
for Capitol the mystical *Ultra-DeLuxe*, a remarkable creation
slowly expanding from Gonsalves's opening tenor phrase. In
the great surges of harmony and color rising from the orchestra
we sense the thoughts of the most profound of jazz musicians;
the original form of the blues is distorted, its rich spirit re-
created in shades of orange and deep red.

With the possible exception of Charles Ives, it is doubtful if America has produced a musician of such originality as Duke Ellington. For over thirty years he has succeeded in translating the changing patterns of society around him into hundreds of compositions, which show a mixture and a range of moods not seen before in American music.

RECORD NOTE

Riverside 12–129 has several sides by the Washingtonians, among them *L'il Farina*. Ellington's Cotton Club period of the late 'twenties and early 'thirties is currently represented by two LP's: the valuable Brunswick 54007 (from Vocalion masters), which includes *Black and Tan Fantasy, Birmingham Breakdown, Mood Indigo, Rockin' in Rhythm, Tiger Rag*, and the best version of *Creole Rhapsody;* and Camden 459 (from Victor masters), which includes *Ring Dem Bells* and an unfortunately padded version of *Creole Rhapsody*.

Columbia CL–558 contains the original versions of the following recordings from the 'thirties: *Sophisticated Lady, In a Sentimental Mood, Caravan, Solitude,* and *I Let a Song Go out of My Heart*. In addition there is an early recording of *The Mooche*, 1938 versions of *East St. Louis Toodle-oo* and *Black and Tan Fantasy*, and a 1949 *Creole Love Call*. *Reminiscing in Tempo* and *Blue Light* appear on Columbia CL–663. Epic LG–3108 features the small Ellington groups of the 'thirties and includes *Clouds in My Heart* and *Echoes of Harlem*. The 1939–42 band is represented by Victor LPM–1364, which contains *Just A-Settin' and A-Rockin'* and *Blue Serge,* and by Victor LPM–1715, which has *Jack the Bear, Concerto for Cootie, Ko-Ko,* a 1944 version of *Black, Brown, and Beige,* plus the 1927 *Creole Love Call* and *Transbluency*.

There are several Ellington recordings from the postwar period available. Columbia CL–848 has the two extended compositions, *Liberian Suite* and *A Tone Parallel to Harlem*. There are extended treatments of familiar Ellington pieces on Columbia CL–830, "Ellington Uptown," which includes *The Mooche,* and on Columbia CL–825, which has versions of *Mood Indigo, Solitude,* and *Sophisticated Lady*. *Happy-go-lucky Local* is available on Capitol T–521; an earlier version has appeared on the cut-price Allegro-Elite and Rondo labels, as has *Minnehaha*. *Diminuendo and Crescendo in Blue* appears in an inflated, frantic version on the 1956 Newport Jazz Festival recording, Columbia CL–934.

The demise of the ten-inch LP has deprived the catalogue of much valuable Ellington, including a Victor collection on Label "X" LAV–3037, with recordings of *Creole Love Call* and *East St. Louis Toodle-oo*. Victor, Columbia, and Decca own the rights to the bulk of the Ellington output from 1928 to 1942, but they have not provided adequate representation for what is in their vaults. The British and French companies which have rights in their areas to the same material have done far better for Ellington recordings of all periods.

Billie Holiday had been a major jazz singer (perhaps the major jazz singer, certainly one of two) for almost twenty years before any comprehensive essay on her had appeared. In 1956, came Edward Fowler's (Jazz Monthly, March 1956) and Glenn Coulter's in the short-lived magazine called i.e.: The Cambridge Review. Coulter's point of departure was the publication of Miss Holiday's biography "as told to William Dufty." The following, slightly condensed, was his review, and is used here with his permission.

GLENN COULTER

Billie Holiday

Up to the present, jazz has been primarily an instrumental music. Yet in its origin it was a sung music, and, though there has been less development and more perversion of this branch of jazz, the voice may still be accounted its primary instrument. Apart from the blues tradition, the great role in vocal jazz has been played and continues to be played by Billie Holiday. Virtually all the method, all the style, which we hear from other jazz singers and from most of the juke-box idols spring from Billie; yet her singing is in intention and effect quite different from any other, and indeed runs counter to most jazz.

In the first place her method seeks its inspiration from the leaders of instrumental jazz. These in turn must have been influenced by the very early blues singers (as classical instrumental techniques strive to correspond with the music of the human voice); in reversing this process, Billie set jazz on a new course. The great blues singers worked with a scale that is not identical to that known in legitimate music. This is the origin of the "blue notes," a remnant perhaps or an approximation of the notes in

African music. The result is a vaguely modal quality which re-inforces the sense of a true folk music and may mislead us into seeing a stronger link between it and the ancient, rural music of other cultures than perhaps exists. How much early jazz tended to conscious exploitation of these unclassical pitches I dare not say. Judging from old recordings, one finds that much of it must have been at first spontaneous and inadvertent. In any event, when instrumentalists attempted to parallel the new vocal scale, they were deliberately introducing a new expressive technique.

When Billie sings, we notice that nobody relies more em-phatically on these modal changes. But the voice is more limited in melodic variation than any instrument. Billie, therefore, de-pends on other weapons, particularly on a tight control of what resources she has, and so we have a whole spectrum of blue notes: A note may begin slightly under pitch, absolutely with-out vibrato, and gradually be forced up to dead center from where the vibrato shakes free, or it may trail off mournfully; or, at final cadences, the note is a whole step above the written one and must be pressed slowly down to where it belongs. To de-scribe these things is only to describe what we cannot avoid hearing from any popular singer of the day; Billie's use of devices is not only more skillful but different in intention.

Her distortions of pitch are wedded, welded rather, to her manipulations of the beat. It is impossible here to go into a fair discussion of this most important musical element, the element of time. Words are not adequate to deal with the heart of music, with what music does uniquely. We know how greatly the expressive quality of musical performance depends on the most minute hastenings or slowings of the expected beat. We all know of particular jazz musicians who pay more attention to the underlying beat in order better to fly free of it in solo phrases.

Billie's incessant modifications of the pulse are the most ex-pressive devices in her art. It is a pity we can't illustrate with recordings such daring and such taste. The skill in question obviously defies written analysis and eludes musical notation.

Billie's remarkable control of metrical organization was part of her equipment from the start. The freedom of Louis Armstrong must have been her primary influence. It is misleading to suggest, as many writers on jazz have done, that such an influence resulted in resemblance. Rather, a most important and quite original twist was given to the history of jazz.

Altered pulsations, produced instrumentally, convey a sweeping lyrical *élan*; when they are not played, when they are sung, they emerge as dark distortions, interferences. Even in jazz, vocal music strove for regularity; a certain smoothness is the ideal in vocal performances as well as an act of fidelity to the regular beats in simple poetry. By setting this aside, Billie had discovered a way of singing that could be put to use with profound effect. Obviously, any irregularity of the pulse in singing will bring the voice to a closer accord with the patterns of current speech, and every song may take on a dramatic value not guessed at before. Dramatic value is a term almost meaningless in this place and time, for traditional dramatic art has maintained a separation between artist and audience. Most of the personality kids who win the awards nowadays—I refer to singers as well as actors—use their skill to establish a spurious intimacy with their admirers. Surely the true communion is arrived at inadvertently, and it is this relationship which Billie can establish.

If her style has this declamatory quality, it follows that she is able to impart great interest to the texts she sings. What may be simple doggerel on paper will sound like honest prose, or perhaps arbitrary irregularities of accent will convert this doggerel to a subtler poetry than the lyricist had in mind. Billie's taste in musical invention corresponds naturally to these features of her style. She is driven, apparently, to strip all melodic excess from her songs. When the harmony does not alter, she is not compelled to follow the curve of the tune, but will reduce it to a couple of notes that lie in a narrow compass. She avoids stepwise progressions, singing the notes of the chord instead. On many occasions, her procedure is different; dull lines are transformed, but in the utmost simplicity, or a more astringent harmony is suggested than that actually written—but, whatever the procedure, the result almost invariably is the substitution of an austere, spiky line for what would have been an indecisive, undulant melodic curve.

All these elements in the Holiday style can be traced back to other artists, and they can all be found here and there among numbers of musicians whose careers started later than hers. Yet her style, taken as a whole, is quite unique; vocal jazz without Billie would have developed in quite another way. Jazz by and large is rightly considered a lyrical music whose darkest tone is pathos, whose gait normally is exuberant, delighting to conceal its intricacies beneath a broad freedom of approach. I do not think it far-fetched to see resemblance between Billie Holiday's relation to this art and John Donne's relation to the characteristic note of Elizabethan poetry. There are the same intricate surface, complicated rhythmic patterns, the same tendency to favor the prosaic to the poetic, and the same anti-romantic attitude.

All this is so much background for a closer look at Billie's singing. In any art, method and system follow after the fact. This is particularly true when the instrument used is the human voice, that gift so lonely and so frail. Those words are as well suited as any to the impossible task of describing the voice of Billie Holiday; clavichord-small and intense, it is of a monotonous color that only the passage of time can vary. Many a singer has tried without success to copy its color, clear and cold, so bitingly cold that like dry ice it can suggest great heat. Time-capsules have passed out of fashion in this hydrogen age, but surely even a posterity inconceivably remote could use any Holiday record as a source in sound for the American twentieth century.

When Billie's singing career began, her voice conveyed a curiously expressionless quality, and her first records are to a careless ear almost crudely straightforward. These early records were not designed to spotlight Billie. The musicians with her were some of the best men jazz has known; simply to list

their names gives a jazz fan pleasure—Buck Clayton, Roy Eldridge, Teddy Wilson, Lester Young. . . . There never was such
jazz as this for lyrical ardor and informal elegance, natural as
breathing and yet as perfectly balanced as the most sophisticated art. Billie's choruses are utterly different in method and
intention from their instrumental setting, a perfect counter-
balance to the work of Teddy Wilson, for example, whose
beautiful transformations of melodies force the listener into a
seemingly permanent attitude of wonder and delight.

Billie's deadpan actually conceals a good deal of intricate
treatment. She is not afraid to sound awkward if that is the best
way for her to nail a song home: *Nice Work If You Can Get It,*
is a good instance of this rigidity. *Fooling Myself* is one of the
best early examples of her dramatic approach; she gives the
words of the release a spondaic vehemence which almost turns
them into nonsense and in the process conjures up a weight of
bitterly humiliated desire. True simplicity rarely appears in
these records, and naturally it is all the more impressive when
it does appear, as in the directness and intimacy of *Easy Living*;
Teddy Wilson's solo work and his accompaniment of the other
musicians are enough by themselves to put this on any ten-best
list, and Billie never surpassed this vocal with its repose and
warmth.

Such warmth and repose disappear from Billie's singing as
her career advances. When she struck out on her own as a
night-club singer, her style became more elaborated, and the
surface simplicity of her first records (highly misleading as this
was) gave way to that curious paradox of expression which is
as elliptical and ambiguous as it is exposed. The records of this
period, those released by Commodore, offer performances at
incredibly slow tempos which in themselves draw attention to
irregularities in the musical line and to the startling, almost
surrealist manipulations of the words. It is easy to understand
why many listeners have found Billie's singing at this time to be
affected and pretentious. It tends to frustrate the intention of
every song and does so with an air of detachment which is not

to the taste of those who value sincerity above all other qualities in art. At least one of these records, however, draws its power from this remoteness; I refer to *Strange Fruit,* that uncanny expression of horror which transcends its willful lyric when Billie sings it, and becomes a frozen lament, a paralysis of feeling truer to psychology than any conventional emotionalism could be.

In a reversal of the usual story, Billie's popularity increased during the same time that her style became more complex. This was also the period when her own life seemed tangled in difficulty. Her voice grew darker and more worn by time, and the audacity of her musical approach was intensified. At the same time the elusive, remote character of her emotional communication began to harden. All this resulted in some of the most painful performances ever engraved and put on public sale. A touch of self-pity might have made them less painful, but Billie Holiday does not show mercy, least of all to herself. I have mentioned before her reliance on dramatic qualities rather than lyrical ones, and we must now remind ourselves that if drama intensifies it may do so by means of irony. To this weapon Billie now turned, and as she sang a love song it became a cry of hatred and contempt. Some of her recordings at this time, the time of the Second World War, carry a load of insulting ambiguity that music is seldom asked to bear. (One can only marvel that such bitter honesty could become the delight of café society, although it seems clear enough from her biography that Billie never expected anything less than the big time, that curious condition of success of which nightclub acceptance is often the prelude.) This unpleasant quality is conveyed through the tricky Holiday way with words and her cruelly intricate rhythms. She did not sing with freely progressing movement, but in a series of spasmodic outcries which did not so much attain a point of repose as collapse in discouragement. The very progress of the music represents mimetically a desperate inner situation: the struggle to escape from a disgusting constraint made more galling by the knowledge that escape is not only impossible but unwished for. Melodramatic words, of course, but they attempt to evoke a state of being which we are all acquainted with; in giving voice to it, Billie's art forever lost that quality of remoteness prevalent earlier.

Not all Billie's records were marked by tortured irony. *Porgy* is another of those rare and unusually moving expressions of tenderness: a wistful and confiding piece of art that can be listened to a dozen times without diminution of its pathetic effect. More characteristic of her singing at this time is a whole series of dull performances. These are depressing to listen to in any quantity, nor could anyone enjoy writing about them. It is valuable nevertheless to consider what causes them to be dull, and thereby realize that even when Billie is wrong her weaknesses involve her skill. It is evident, for one thing, that she is unusually sensitive to the quality of her accompaniment. Most of these bad performances take place in an over-arranged, be-violined setting, and the gait never seems to be an honest jazz tempo, or indeed any tempo that allows music to breathe naturally. Here was recognized the interfering hand of some businessman intent on converting Billie into a super-personality cranking out million-copy sellers. It is a shock to realize that Billie saw no incongruity in this attempt; we even learn with dismay that the throbbing violins are there at her express wish; it is only her demon that kept her from abandoning her art for the big money.

Most of the songs Billie used at this time seem to me bad ones, also, but Billie's way of capitulating to this state of mediocrity was also her own. She errs with too much restraint, as it were. The best jazzman has his off days of trying to please the crowd by any vulgar means, stunning his listeners with sheer volume or with displays of blank virtuosity. Billie, on an off day—and she has had more than her share of these—simply ceases to communicate. These listless performances are especially sad because she will not allow herself to fall below a certain standard of musicianly skill, and what results is a bored display of stylistic tricks which conveys little more than a vague impression of cynicism.

This cloudy period, lit occasionally by flashes of venom or disgust, dragged on for many years. It gave rise eventually to the common criticism that any Holiday performance is simply a parade of mannerisms; just so, critics who came immediately after the poets of Donne's school could see only frigid eccentricity.

Most recently, Billie has been singing in a way to surprise not only her detractors but her most fanatic admirers. It is clear her private misfortunes have not abated; they came close to swamping her career. The passage of time could not be expected to leave her voice unscathed. The temptation to exploit stylistic tricks is known to grow in strength with the years. True enough, when you listen to her latest records, you are distressed to hear a voice so frayed. But soon you begin to respect the perfect control of these resources, and you end by wondering how your admiration of her singing of years ago could possibly have increased so much. The voice has been getting smaller and darker with the years, but there is at last a compensating warmth. The melodic alterations which vocal convenience made necessary now have a miraculous simplicity. Best of all, Billie has at last recaptured delight in her own singing, and her sense of suffering is no longer cruel but compassionate. In place of the angry outcries so noticeable before, we now hear a sad acceptance, not only of pain but of the truth that pain is not an individual thing. An excellent foretaste of this further range may be found in the second record of *Travelin' Light,* the record of a public performance, and one of the few things in jazz that can stand the word sublime. It is noteworthy also as one of the rare occasions when Billie has risen triumphantly above an inept accompaniment.

There is more balanced work on a body of records wherein Billie is backed by Benny Carter, among others. Carter's invention is strongly horizontal, a matter of extending a solo by means of brief repeated motifs that evolve continuously from themselves (as the web of a spider from its own entrails); the results are not only in themselves lovely but stimulate Billie to a more flowing style than she ever before interested herself in. All these records are beautiful and can put to shame most recent jazz. I must single out three: *It Had To Be You* is a good sample of this late warmth in tone, and is a lesson in how to transform a banal little tune; *I Get a Kick out of You* has a chorus by Carter that is a classic, and is one of the most hair-raising instances of Billie's way of accenting the melody and the lyrics in a new and more convincing way. Billie's pleasure in her own work (an extra dimension that is always responsible for the glow of true art) is very noticeable on the last chorus. *Isn't It a Lovely Day?* is the latest of those rare performances that strive for an intimate warmth and simplicity, and with its melting tenderness it is the best of them all. A fusion of the warring elements in jazz—the lyrical strain with the ironic-dramatic strain for which Billie is chiefly responsible—would seem an impossibility, but is foreshadowed here.

To turn from an art so admirable and severe to a book about the artist which shows almost nothing of these qualities is an amazingly difficult task. Evidently someone has made an effort to fit this book into a category where it does not belong. Of late the national craze for entertainers, actors, generals, and the like has resulted in a steady flow of quasi-biographical writing about these magical beings. It is a sort of hagiography previously confined to the fan magazines but now extended to every medium of mass entertainment. Movies and television plays are devoted to these saints of our century; books abound. If such work were carried out properly, it could be of profound service, but the way the work has been done it has scarcely any value at all. Whether real talent is forced into the maw of pressure advertising because truth would be too unpalatable for the general public, I cannot say. At all events, this popular biography inevitably turns aside from the honesty that should be its first aim.

A more sophisticated subdivision of this species of biography has come to popularity the last few years. This genre details the triumphs over adversity—over vice or simple poverty—resolved by the hero when he finally hits the big time. One advantage of this type is that the books usually appear high on best-seller lists.

Lady Sings the Blues is a mistaken attempt to succeed in this way. It would be idle to blame Billie for this—the book is no doubt exactly what she wanted—and I do not think the whole trouble rests with William Dufty, who assisted her with it. Rather there must have been some editorial interference, the obvious clues to which are the gagged-up chapter headings, the tremolo ending, and indeed the title itself.

The biggest mistake, of course, was in deciding to cast the book in a racy, side-of-the-mouth idiom. Perhaps Billie in conversation does refer to herself as a "hip kitty." But the illusion of actual conversation is not wanted here; a book is supposed to be written, after all, and unfledged writers are more inclined to formality and elegant variation than to cant. There is also a preservation of tone so blatantly professional that it could not be Billie's own.

The most annoying device of the book is the vast amount of insignificant name-dropping that takes place, together with a refusal to tell us any of the things that might give point to this habit. A number of musicians are spoken of, but so sketchily that those who do not know the names already will not be able to guess what they stand for, while those to whom the names (Count Basie, Lester Young, and the like) mean a great deal are disappointed not to have anything said of Billie's feelings toward their art. Billie is one of the most sensitive musicians alive; there are anecdotes to prove it, to say nothing of her performances. Surely whatever she might say about her peers must be of great value. But we are not given any of this, perhaps for fear lest the untutored reader be bored.

Where the book does succeed in illuminating Billie's life and art is in areas that can hardly be discussed tactfully. There is, after all, no delicate way of pointing out that her life has been one of harshness and suffering. Those who wish to guess at the sources which have nourished Billie's galling art do not have to read far before coming on scenes of horror, of unpleasant sexual experiences at an early age, of a frightening death, of beatings, misunderstandings. There have not been wanting reviewers to chide Billie for appearing rude and ungenerous. Yet who could look for kindliness from one who until lately never knew what it was?

Strangely, it is this painful personal story which is given most attention, while very little is said of her career. (Here I want to say a word in praise of the very thorough and enticing list of Billie's records. It was compiled by Bill Galletly, and in itself is a good reason for buying the book.) One might perhaps hold that it is the pressure of the career which has made the life so hard. Billie's book may finally do some good if it forces us to examine our narcotics laws more realistically; and the cruel light cast on the difficulties of the life of a Negro may cause us all to search our hearts and bring from them the right response at last.

From this mass of personal detail an effect ensues which may be unintentional. It is the opposite of what one expects. That is, the book fails to bear any certain imprint of its chief figure. There is no lack of unflattering narrative, and yet the actor still eludes us. Billie can conjure up with some power impressions of terrible places like Welfare Island and the reformatory at Alderson; yet while we gaze at these wretched backgrounds the figure in the foreground fades out.

It is not fanciful to see in this reticence those qualities which bear up Billie Holiday's art and will cause it to endure. Rather, they are not qualities but virtues, and their names are bravery, and honesty, and dignity. Listen to her records, and read her book, and learn at what a price these have been retained.

RECORD NOTE

Fooling Myself and *Easy Living* are on Columbia CL–637, which is devoted to the early Billie with Teddy Wilson and Lester Young. Commodore 30006 includes *Strange Fruit* and other recordings of the early 'forties. *Porgy* now appears in Decca 8702. The concert version of *Travelin' Light* was issued on Clef MGC–169. Verve 8026 contains *It Had To Be You, I Get a Kick out of You,* and *Isn't This a Lovely Day?*

M. Hodeir's essay on the late Art Tatum is the only partly negative analysis in this collection. Written in 1955, it is a review of the first group of a subsequently continued series of LP releases collectively entitled The Genius of Art Tatum *(Clef and Verve). When it was first published by* Down Beat *something of a controversy ensued, but the burden of most of the protests was that not to have heard Tatum playing "after hours" for just the right audience was not to have heard Tatum. Hardly anyone attempted to deal with M. Hodeir's real point, nor did anyone attempt to question whether Hodeir had applied his distinctions correctly and fairly to Tatum's recordings.*

M. Hodeir's essential point is a crucial one for all jazz and one that must be dealt with: There is a comparative value among decorating and embellishing a melody, playing a melodic (or melodic-harmonic) variation-on-theme, and improvising new "harmonic" variations on chord structures.

The review is reproduced here through the courtesy of Down Beat *magazine and M. Hodeir.*

ANDRE HODEIR

The Genius of Art Tatum

What is genius? The ability to create, fertility of ideas, taste, feeling, and technique—are these qualities, when combined in a high degree, indeed when unequaled by any other jazz artist, enough, ipso facto, to justify calling the man who possesses them a genius?

In his notice on Art Tatum's albums, Norman Granz does appear to think so. He goes even further—he entitles these albums *The Genius of Art Tatum,* having first observed that "in the past, the word genius has been flagrantly abused."

And so Granz is running risks—risks, however, which his choice of subject diminishes. Perhaps no other jazz artist has been so highly and so unanimously praised by his fellow artists.

Even among the avant-garde modernists it would be hard to find a jazz pianist for whom Tatum is not the greatest of them all.

This extraordinarily gifted artist seems to have cast a spell over the younger generation of pianists. What else but admire a man able to conceive and then execute things which others, sometimes able to conceive, simply cannot execute?

So then let us grant that Tatum stands out above every other jazz pianist. And even grant, too, that the sum total of his creative power, his ideas, his taste, his feeling and technique, is greater in Tatum than in any other jazzman.

I am by no means sure I agree, but let us grant it for the sake of argument. Taken altogether, Tatum's abilities average out as something amazing; but should we assign an absolute value to an average, in a field where, obviously, some elements are infinitely more important than others? Certainly not. Add up a man's abilities, find the average, and it may be remarkably high; but even so, added-up averages never result in and never express genius.

The release of five twelve-inch LP records entirely devoted to Tatum is an event whose importance has struck everyone in the world of jazz. True, Tatum has recorded a great deal in the past. But now for the first time this phenomenal musician has been given plenty of room, and about three and a half hours to do what he pleases; until now the clock (in the case of his 78-r.p.m. recordings), presence of an audience, and the playing of fellow musicians always hampered his freedom of expression. Here we have Tatum on his own, free.

For Tatum, no doubt more of a *pianiste d'orchestre* than any other great jazz pianist, to be by himself at the piano, to be allowed to do just what he wants, are factors that definitely go into making up his success. It is not often that a jazzman has had such an opportunity to show his real self and whatever he can do. The intention here, Granz writes, is to record Tatum for posterity.

Granz has done his duty as producer; mine, as critic, is to make an impartial examination of the results. Apart from their

remarkable technical quality, they belong in a class by themselves. The European critic, handicapped when he has been
unable to hear a particular jazzman in person, in this case can
come very close to getting the same effect an American listener
would have when listening to Tatum playing in person. We
can consider these albums as a panoramic picture which the
celebrated pianist, at the high point of a long and brilliant
career, has drawn of his own work.

Has the freedom Tatum was given in these recordings had
any effect on his repertoire? Have any nonmusical considerations influenced his choice of music?

Nothing indicates that the choice of *Body and Soul, Humoresque, The Man I Love,* and *Begin the Beguine*—all old favorites
of Tatum—was imposed upon the pianist. This is where I wish
to make my first objection—this choice is a little too facile.

Would it not have been possible to arrange a program
amounting to a sort of anthology of the finest jazz numbers?
For example, one could have included *Black and Blue, Boplicity,
Lover Man, Minor Encamp,* and *Squeeze Me.* But as things
stand, these albums deliberately sacrifice beautiful melody for
sentimental ballads and authentic jazz pieces for popular hits.
Too much space has even been given to some particularly
doubtful "characteristic" pieces.

But it is not repertoire alone which determines the success
or failure of an album of jazz records. Everything depends on
the jazzman's attitude toward the material. Louis Armstrong
has transformed many a silly tune into a majestic one by simply
shifting a few accents or altering a few values; Fats Waller
managed to give an unaffected, bantering, and even poetic feeling to the most stupidly sentimental songs; Charlie Parker knew
how to play the magician by making appear and then disappear
scraps of a melody that should have been rendered in full,
hiding them up his sleeve; and Lester Young sometimes from
the very first bars of an exposition, has brought out an entirely
new melody and made it look like the negative image of the
basic theme, but purified, touched up, and disconcertingly improved. Every one of these approaches is valid. What is Tatum's?

Unfortunately, the one Tatum chooses is the most conventional. Every jazz pianist, even a fourth-rate saloon pianist, ornaments a theme as he plays it; in other words, he does his best to revise it, to re-animate it either by introducing "personal" harmonies or by fitting arabesques, runs, or arpeggios between the principal motifs so as to bring out the value, by contrast, of the simpler passages which surround them. This also gives the player a chance to display his virtuosity. This is the method Tatum uses.

He shows no evident desire to depart from the main theme. It is all played according to the rules. One need hardly say that Tatum does this better than anyone else. Equipped with greater technical means and a better imagination than one finds in any other pianist, he has an easy time doing superbly what I would have preferred not to have seen him bother with at all.

Actually, this lack of ambition comes out in a series of ad lib theme renditions which, it seems to me, occupy too important a place in these records. Why are these ad lib renditions here at all? One could understand that a pianist of limited resources might wish to avoid monotony at any price; considered in this light, as something modest, the ad lib rendering has some justification; and it would be surprising, indeed, if the ordinary pianist were not to make use of it. But Tatum is no ordinary pianist.

And so the element of variety thus introduced seems to carry little weight when one considers the major disadvantage that results from it, the however momentary dropping of the tempo and the consequent loss of swing. As soon as the swing's magic subsides, or is lost, the listener is forced to take this music for just what it is, and then he has to judge it on its musical substance alone. One must be willing to make plenty of allowances in order to find some superior qualities in a formless flow of music containing little by way of original ideas.

As usual, Tatum displays virtuosity and an extraordinary sense of harmony and even tries now and then to bring an unexpected element into the recurring monotony of these theme renditions. He draws upon—and in vain—his extensive imagination, trying to revive themes whose intrinsic weakness could only be saved by radical reconsideration—which is something Tatum has not dared to do.

These theme renditions are generally too long. That is their main defect. The rendition of *There'll Never Be Another You* lasts almost three minutes, and the coda (also ad lib) is of nearly the same length!

Fortunately, when Tatum starts off on a jazz tempo, the light switches and, more often than not, we are faced with Tatum at his best. This back-and-forth shifting is sometimes scarcely perceptible, sometimes abrupt. In *Louise,* for example, the tempo gradually glides into the musical discourse and, as phrase follows phrase, little by little brings out a pulsation that has been absent up until now. On the other hand, in *Humoresque,* it appears suddenly, striking a violent contrast which leaves the listener gasping. One should also mention the "false departures" in quick tempo in *The Man I Love.* All this is excellent.

The album's high points come in the improvised passages. It is when Tatum seems frankly to abandon the theme that he illustrates it best. The more he frees himself from his material, the more his powers to enrich it increase.

One cannot possibly list all the interesting things, indeed the treasures, to be found on these ten sides. Nor is this the occasion to enter into an analysis of Tatum's style. It is enough if we can point out that, while some of his brilliant passages soon show up as formulas—one thinks particularly of a type of "improved arpeggio" which he is apt to use a great deal—others stem from authentic musical ingenuity.

Tatum likes to take advantage of a break in the beat to slip in one of those long, confusing runs of his—a favorite trick he has borrowed from Earl Hines but which he is able to use more decisively and more richly, thanks to his incomparably superior technique.

There are frequent passages where Tatum, elsewhere adeptly faithful to the Waller "stride" or the bass tenths à la Teddy Wilson, stops beating out the rhythm—and yet the tempo keeps

right on. A "suggested beat" is what results. It is likely to dis-
concert a good many listeners, and the intervals, void of the
pulse of bass or drum, will perplex those for whom the mystery
of swing depends entirely on a well-defined afterbeat. It is here,
in precisely this suggesting of an unexpressed beat, that, in my
opinion, one will find the most captivating part of Tatum's playing. These breaks in the beat frequently give the freed left
hand an opportunity to weave subtle rhythmic patterns with
the right hand. It is then that Tatum best succeeds in giving
the impression of an orchestral style, with its multiple possibilities; it is then also that he comes nearest to modern jazz. This
rhythmic ingenuity reflects the very best in his personality,
more than do his brilliant playing, which is perhaps, too uniform,
or his harmonic language, which may appear too constantly
rich in altered or polytonal chords.

A close analysis of Tatum's work may bring a number of
paradoxes to light; the most difficult of all to explain has to do
with what I might call confidence. It has been remarked, and
rightly, that Tatum is not a pianist who "inspires confidence"
(in the sense that Fats Waller or Teddy Wilson give an element
of support to their sidemen, a certain security, enabling them
to play with an entirely free mind). Even Tatum's solo playing, from a rhythmical standpoint generally perfect in slow
or medium tempo, often becomes jerky, choppy, and sometimes
feverish in fast tempo.

Despite the manifest ease and sheer mastery with which he
overcomes instrumental problems, one has nevertheless, from
time to time, the fleeting impression that his sense of time is
loosening. This fugitive impression, which we receive when
listening to certain passages of *Yesterdays, Elegy,* or *Taboo,* is
something Bud Powell, King Cole, or Billy Kyle never give us.
In fact, oddly enough, this "unreassuring" pianist is one of those
whose taste—or need—for intellectual security has blocked off
certain avenues.

In Tatum's playing, the harmonic embellishments, the rhythmic patterns, and the fluent runs form a mosaic which is purely
decorative. This idea of decoration and ornament also would

appear to be Tatum's basic preoccupation in *This Can't Be Love,* *Memories of You,* and *Begin the Beguine.* But over all, too many decorative effects only stand in the way of the continuity and even of the unity of a musical discourse; and Tatum is surely too fine a musician not to realize it.

Is it that Tatum, knowing just what he is doing, deliberately chooses to impose these limits upon his own creations? Or, on the contrary, has the great pianist shied from objectives more difficult to attain and contented himself with a complacent and comforting security?

There are no ready answers to such questions. But the mere fact that they can be asked bodes ill for future interest in Tatum's work. The future sets little store by the complacencies of the present.

A few words remain to be said about the characteristic numbers. Jazz has a small place in them, but Tatum has found it necessary to keep them in his repertoire. At this point we stop believing in the "taste" of which Granz makes so much in his notice.

Tatum does by all means produce some great things in his jazz variation of Dvorak's *Humoresque*—which he maltreats uselessly in the rendition of the theme—but what can one find to say in favor of *Elegie?* Our entire musical education and culture founded on the necessity for masterpieces revolts against that. Furthermore, is there in the entire European repertory of wishy-washy music anything more derisory than Massenet's *Elegie?*

Let there be no claim that Tatum is able to renovate everything. For here, Tatum renovates nothing. He is content to play a kind of little arrangement, in form and content similar to the encore pieces that Horowitz tosses off in defiance of the snobs, pieces whose extreme musical poverty makes their inclusion in the program justifiable only because they emphasize the virtuoso's technical dexterity.

Far from audacious in other respects, Tatum throws caution to the winds when he creates the possibility for making such a comparison: since there is virtually no music here, unless it is of the worst, and hardly any jazz, there is nothing but the virtuoso left to judge. How then, when matched against Horowitz's perfection, can inaccuracies, unevennesses of touch, and a broad range of minute imperfections help but appear? And how can these faults help but rid these exercises of their last *raison d'etre?*

Such errors invite the severest criticism. It would be unjust to exaggerate them, but, everything taken into consideration, these disagreeable interludes are of little importance when one compares them with an outstanding success like *Tenderly*. All the same, they are elements in a portrait the artist has painted of himself, and painted with sincerity, in these five records. They strengthen the impression of extreme unevenness one gets from listening to them.

To be sure, unevenness is not always irreconcilable with genius. But if the artist of genius runs this risk, he does so almost always through an excess of boldness, and very rarely through complacency or caution. One discerns numerous flaws in Tatum's playing; they all stem from the same source. A greater share of discipline, toughness, and audacity would undoubtedly have given richer outlets to his brilliant gifts.

If finally, after having paid homage to Tatum's outstanding qualities, I refused to recognize in him a jazz musician of genius, it is because it seems obvious that his very conception of jazz bars his entrance into the world of real artistic creations. In concluding, one could echo that toughness, ruthlessness, indeed cruelty, are the secrets of genius. These secrets seem in no wise to have been confided to Tatum.

RECORD NOTE

The original five volumes "The Genius of Art Tatum" appeared collectively as Clef Album ♯1 and individually as Clef 612/8. The series was continued through twelve individual LP's in all. These twelve records of Tatum alone have been supplemented by several trio and quartet recitals, possibly the best of which is Verve 8118.

In the mid-'fifties, Columbia issued an LP collection of Benny Goodman Sextet recordings (CL–652) which included some "warm-up" playing in the studio and portions of alternate versions of some previously issued numbers. These notes on Charlie Christian's style and importance accompanied the recording. We should add that Ralph Ellison in his excellent essay on Christian's boyhood and the milieu *in which he learned to play, in* The Saturday Review, *explained, "In their excellent notes to the album, Al Avakian and Bob Prince are mistaken when they assume that Christian was innocent of contact with musical forms more sophisticated than the blues." Both at home and in school Christian was exposed to many influences.*

The essay is included by permission of Messrs. Avakian and Prince, and Columbia Records.

AL AVAKIAN AND BOB PRINCE

Charlie Christian

Oklahoma is essentially blues territory and the guitar is essentially a blues instrument down home. Charlie Christian's Texas birthplace and Oklahoma home were areas relatively untouched by more sophisticated forms and expressions than the blues. Charlie's father played guitar and so did Charlie.

In 1934, at the age of fifteen, Charlie began playing guitar professionally in Oklahoma City. He played with his brother's band, with Alphonso Trent's band (in which he played bass), and then with Anna Mae Winburn throughout the Southwest. Tired of touring in 1937, at the age of eighteen and at the time when he was already playing electric guitar, he organized his own little jump band in Oklahoma City.

The next year, he rejoined Al Trent's sextet and played for a while in Bismarck, North Dakota. Here, a young guitarist, Mary Osborne, went to hear him play. She recalls that on entering the club she heard a sound much like a tenor sax strangely distorted by an amplification system. On seeing Charlie, she realized that what she was hearing was an electric guitar playing single line solos, and voiced like a horn in ensemble with the tenor sax and trumpet. She says, "I remember some of the figures Charlie played in his solos. They were exactly the same things that Benny recorded later on as *Flying Home, Gone with "What" Wind, Seven Come Eleven,* and all the others."

At that time, Christian's prominence was established locally to the extent that a Bismarck music store displayed the latest electric guitar model "as featured by Charlie Christian." Musicians traveling through the Midwest and Southwest took notice of his talent and spread the word.

In 1939, the word got to Benny Goodman through John Hammond, who, on his way from New York to a Los Angeles opening of the Benny Goodman Band, stopped at Oklahoma City to hear Christian. Charlie was booked for Goodman's Camel Caravan show and was consequently installed in the new Benny Goodman Sextet. Although his two-year stay with the band resulted in a profound influence on the group and produced the main body of his recorded work, Charlie was dissatisfied with the limitations of his role in this large organization.

This lack of fulfillment led him to play after hours, principally at Minton's Playhouse in Harlem, the cradle of bebop in 1941. He was able to improvise ad infinitum. Unknown, but searching young musicians (curiously, of Charlie's age or older) were exposed to the clear logic of his conceptual originality. Among these were Charlie Parker, Dizzy Gillespie, Kenny Clarke, Thelonious Monk.

During most of his life, Christian suffered from tuberculosis. In the summer of 1941, he suffered a relapse and remained hospitalized until his death in February 1942. When he died at the age of twenty-four, he was considered by his fellow musicians to be the most advanced jazz influence of his time.

The Benny Goodman Sextet was a cohesive group of excellent musicians. The original numbers included in this album were constructed at rehearsals and were conceived by departing from a riff or a basic chord progression such as the blues.

Count Basie's Band was the first modern blues force to profoundly influence the Benny Goodman Band. Charlie Christian, whose blues riff approach sparked the Sextet, was the second.

Charlie was self-sufficient as a soloist in that he formed his own rhythmic impetus (riffs) and created melodically from these figures in paraphrase of blues tradition. The numbers in this album, which included only blues and riff originals, demonstrate this self-sufficiency of Charlie's. And the form of these originals would seem to demonstrate the principle of his improvisation, which was feeding riffs as a basis of melodic invention. The band would state a riff and the soloist would develop his melodic line, in a pattern of tension (riffs), relaxation of tension (melodic line), tension (reaffirmed riffs). This riff-melodic line-riff sequence was also the way Charlie constructed his improvised solos. Indeed, it was Charlie's construction which gave graphic form to the Sextet and stamped him as a basic innovator in swing.

Before Benny arrived at the session that produced *Air Mail Special* and *A Smo-o-o-oth One,* the musicians were jamming for their own pleasure. The engineers were testing equipment. Fortunately, the disc on which the jamming was recorded was preserved. In *Waiting for Benny,* Charlie, in the process of warming up, builds simple riffs, one leading into another, until he comes to a logical conclusion: the riff statement of *A Smo-o-o-oth One.* Then he rhythmically feeds Cootie Williams chords à la Basie, then riffs behind the trumpet, and Cootie proceeds with the only free, jamming, swing-era trumpet he has ever recorded. Before the end of his improvisation, Charlie is briefly heard reaffirming his simple riffs.

The comparatively sophisticated and formalized version of the same number as played by the full Sextet follows. This is succeeded by a more elaborate application of the riff principle, Christian's tune *Seven Come Eleven,* in which three basic riffs set the tension.

It is in this number that we find the clearest illustration of Charlie's construction of a solo. The Sextet, as always, follows this pattern, opening with a riff by the ensemble against a bass figure. Then Charlie launches his solo with a repetitive single-note riff, develops a series of riffs through the first sixteen bars (tension); then, in the eight-bar release, he contrasts this by playing melodic lines characteristically made up mainly of even eighth notes (relaxation), then returns to eight bars of riffs (tension), giving his solo contour and movement.

As an instrumentalist, Charlie Christian gave a full range of expression to the guitar, utilizing all its basic rhythmic, melodic, and sound potential. He was the first to master the electric guitar, and in his footsteps Barney Kessel, Billy Bauer, Jimmy Raney, Johnny Smith, and others followed.

But even more important is Christian's innovation and influence as a musician. His improvisations sound simple and effortless, but, when analyzed, prove complex and daring in their exploration of musical principles. These complexities were not contrived, but were the result of Christian's natural inventiveness and drive, bringing forth a new, mobile, swinging jazz that resulted in a basic influence on modern musicians.

Charlie's greatest asset was his command of rhythm. He had a natural drive to swing at all costs, and this, coupled with his spontaneous exploration of rhythmic principles, led him to a flexibility of the beat that was unique. This flexibility became a prerequisite in all forms of jazz to follow.

Charlie's basic beat was the modern even four-four, but his solos are full of metric denials. They are remarkable illustrations of mobile swing. His uses of off-beat accents and syncopation are engaging in their humor and impressive in their clear conception and execution.

This album opens with *Blues in B* (an unusual key at that, and an indication of the challenge that Charlie and the members of the Sextet posed themselves in rehearsal). At the end of the second chorus there are four bars of clean off-beat accents, and at the beginning of chorus three we find a neat example of syncopation. We also have here an unparalleled

example of Charlie playing basic, down-home blues. Many
examples of a more complex rhythmic technique (subdivid-
ing measures) can be found in his solos. Probably the most apparent of these is in the first three bars of the bridge in his
first chorus on *Air Mail Special,* in which he breaks the basic
four beats to the bar into units of three. This is done in clear
definition. He also establishes a rhythmic pattern and then
creates a contrast by restating the figure on an off beat, as in
the eighth-note triplets in the second eight bars of his second
chorus on *Air Mail Special.* This chorus was spliced from an
unissued take.

There are many more examples of these and other rhythmic
elements in his solos in this album, always unpredictable in
their juxtaposition, yet familiar in their basic blues allusion.
Christian had complete and easy control over rhythm, and on
the basis of this rhythmic freedom he constructed his phrasing.

A singular aspect of his phrasing is the unusual length of
his melodic lines, consisting of even and cleanly executed
eighth notes. His meter was delineated by the subtle accent
of certain of these eighth notes. There are several varied
examples of this technique on *Breakfast Feud,* which was
spliced together from three previously unissued takes. These
solos are individual and original, the phrasing and accents
within each one being unpredictable. In the initial three-bar
phrase in the first of these solos, Christian shifts the metric
accent from the normally strong first beat to the secondary
third beat, thereby creating the illusion that he is starting his
phrase on a pick-up from the previous chorus, when in reality
he is starting on the first beat of the chorus. He molded the
contour of this phrase so that the melodic peaks also occur on
the accented third beats. This type of practice, unusual to
jazz musicians at the time, reveals another facet of Christian's
rhythmic daring and resourcefulness. In his other two *Breakfast Feud* solos his phrases fall into entirely different patterns.
These three solos provide rich ground for analysis in that they
demonstrate, independently one to the other (but here placed

in series), the Christian techniques in dealing with basically the same blues derivatives.

Charlie Christian considered no interval "wrong." In his eighth-note phrases, running up and down the basic chords, he extended the chords to include other intervals such as the ninth, flatted ninth, eleventh, augmented eleventh, thirteenth, and flatted thirteenth. In addition, his partiality for the diminished seventh chord, and his superimposition of this chord over basic harmonic progressions, can be heard in any number of his solos.

In the final number of this album, *Solo Flight*, we have the culminating sophistication of Christian's art. With no strain, the voice of the jazz electric guitar fits into a showpiece provided by the big swing band. Christian does not compete with the volume and power of Benny's big band, but easily rides the crests of its waves. With a minimum of effort, he tells his quiet and complex story.

Charlie Christian's long, clean eighth-note phrases consisting of harmonic extensions and alterations, his rhythmic dexterity and drive, his formalistic sense of balance, and his unpredictable yet recognizable treatment of the blues were heard by and strongly influenced the then inchoate movement later called bebop.

This series of articles pointed to a battle and a paradox. With the advent of bebop came a militant kind of journalism that seemed to imply on one side that the style had swept away all that had come before it and on the other that bebop was a dreadful aberration. However, these pieces were published in 1948–49 in The Record Changer, *reputedly a stronghold of reaction. Russell's essays not only have the advantage of being the best critiques of the style before André Hodeir's (*Jazz: Its Evolution and Essence*), but they were directed at people who had a respect and some understanding of the achievements of the past and for whom Russell was able to place the new style in historical perspective. The series appears here (with slight condensations) by permission of* The Record Changer *and Mr. Russell. (The comments on Lester Young have been supplemented by Stanley Dance's appreciation in* Melody Maker, *February 11, 1956.)*

Mr. Russell wrote of bop as of 1948–49, of course, but a part of his reluctance to give more lengthy discussion to the work of the major figure of the bop movement, Charlie Parker, was perhaps modesty. As head of Dial Records, he had been and then still was responsible for some of Parker's most brilliant recordings. Perhaps, too, he underestimated the stature of pianist Bud Powell as a bop soloist, but Powell was active only intermittently both in person and on records. The real maturity of Miles Davis as a soloist came as this series was finished.

ROSS RUSSELL

Bebop

I—BOP RHYTHM

Approximately every decade for the past thirty or forty years the style of American jazz has undergone marked change. In the 1910's jazz style was exemplified by the music of the New Orleans bands and Jelly Roll Morton; successively by the jazz of Armstrong's Hot Five in the 'twenties, of Basie and Elling-

ton in the 'thirties, and in our own time by the bebop jazz of
Charles Parker and Dizzy Gillespie.

This capacity for growth is the cleanest bill of health that our
native music could have. It raises it above the level of a rigidly
styled folk music (hillbilly music, gypsy music) to a music form
which is a challenge to world musical culture.

Any contemporary style, whether that of a James Joyce or an
Arnold Schönberg, remains controversial, and bebop is no exception. The critics and jazz amateurs should bear in mind that
it is not they but the working musicians who create jazz and
authorize style changes.

Nearly ten years ago [1940] the most progressive and able
talents among modern jazzmen began gathering at Minton's
Playhouse to protest the threadbare, aging style of the swing
movement. The history of jazz since then has been largely that
of the Minton insurgents, their militant crusade, and the stub-
born but eventual capitulation of the jazz conservatives to new
ideas.

The 1940's were a period of ferment, in which new and old
ideas clashed and often fused, a period in which the entire
language of jazz was questioned, subtracted from, added to,
purged, and reaffirmed. The emergent style can scarcely be
accepted as a final form, but it is a new level on which the future
growth of jazz must be based.

The two leading voices of the new music, Parker and Gillespie, can be understood in terms of jazz tradition. Dizzy derives
from the trumpet style of Roy Eldridge, who in turn goes back
to the father of modern trumpet, Louis Armstrong. Charlie Parker is an exponent of the Kansas City style in general and Lester
Young in particular. Parker, whose playing is always melodic
and rhythmic and who speaks the language of the blues in a
modern idiom, is the easiest of the contemporaries to understand.

Perhaps the most controversial aspect of bebop jazz is its
rhythmic organization. Bebop rhythmics, or better polyrhythmics, are so revolutionary that they have been largely misunder-

stood and, since no jazz can exist without a solid beat, the new style has been suspect among many uninformed listeners. They say that bebop has no beat, that it is rhythmically incoherent, unrelaxed, meaningless, that it comes from nothing and is directed toward a void.

Nothing could be farther from the truth. The bebop rhythm section is the most functional in jazz history. It scrupulously maintains the basic 4/4 beat upon which all great jazz has been based. Historically it has roots deep in the jazz tradition.

Let us approach bebop rhythm by comparing it with its jazz antecedent, swing rhythm:

Bebop rhythm differs formally from swing rhythm, because it is more complex and places greater emphasis upon polyrhythmics. It differs emotionally from swing rhythm, creating greater tension, thereby reflecting more accurately the spirit and temper of contemporary emotions.

Bebop rhythm also differs radically in mechanics from swing rhythm. Its technique constitutes a new method of playing drums. The swing style perfected by such drummers as Chick Webb, Gene Krupa, Sid Catlett, and Jo Jones used as its rhythmic fundamental four beats to the bar on the bass drum. Bebop drummers no longer keep time with the bass pedal. The swing style made copious use of the high hat cymbal, principally for 2/4 or afterbeat accents. The bebop drummer has abandoned this device. The swing drummer made sparing use of top cymbals, employing them mainly for crash periods. The top cymbal has become the main tool of the bebop drummer. The swing drummer employed a more staccato beat. The bebop drummer strives for a legato sound.

Obviously a foundation-shaking change has taken place in jazz percussion. What then are the positive aspects of bebop drumming? The prime objective of the bebop drummer is to produce a legato sound. To achieve it the drummer makes almost constant use of the top cymbal. On most tempos this cymbal is struck in the Jo Jones manner, or in accented 2/4 time. However, the Jones technique has been so modified that a rhythmic flow is effected. There is no marking-off of accents within the bar. The vibration of the cymbal, once set in motion, is maintained throughout the number, producing a shimmering texture of sound that supports, agitates, and inspires the line men. This is the tonal fabric of bebop jazz.

The top cymbal is also made to carry the rhythmic fundamental, formerly maintained by the bass drum. The fluid cymbal sound is actually a 4/4 pulse. This is the rhythmic base of bebop jazz. The top cymbal thus has a dual role and serves tonal and rhythmic objectives at the same time.

There are variations in the production of the 4/4 fundamental. The right hand (stick) may shift its attack to the high-hat cymbal, which is then damped by pedal action or by the left hand. (Some drummers are skillful enough to play six beats to the bar and damp with the same hand.) The right hand may likewise shift its attack to cymbals of different pitch and timbre. Modern drummers pay particular attention to cymbal sound and dynamics; they prize highly their pet cymbals, which enable them to produce the tonal effects desired. Finally a drier texture may be obtained by using brushes (both hands) on the snare.

It is little wonder that those who rely on records for their contact with new musical ideas should have failed to appreciate the radical change in technique or its objectives, for cymbals record badly. On most records the beautiful shimmering sound produced by a drummer like Max Roach is either lost entirely or mistaken for surface noise. When heard in person these drummers seem to set the air around them in motion and have an exhilarating effect on both listener and fellow musician.

The tremendous step forward achieved by this shift from bass pedal to top cymbal will be appreciated when the reader considers that, in addition to adding tonal dynamics to rhythmic propulsion, the bebop drummer has effected a remarkable economy. His left hand, both feet—not to mention bass drum, high-hat pedal, snares, and tom-toms—are left free for a variety of improvisatory effects never before envisioned! With these devices the various drummers of the new school construct their personal styles, the discussion of which is beyond the scope of this article. However, the secondary object of the drummer remains that of all jazz drummers before him: to inspire the soloist with exciting patterns, and certain general practices are used to produce them.

The bass pedal may be used for accents—readily audible on most records, since bass accents are like muffled explosions. The left hand is used to strike sharp accents on the snare, accents which sound like pistol shots. Occasionally the left foot operates the high-hat pedal to produce a conventional soft "chah" sound as a random accent. Finally, various co-ordinate manual and pedal mechanics of more or less conventional nature are worked into the over-all pattern. Either stick may strike the tom-tom. Various cymbals are struck either by full or glancing blows while not damped and crashing or sharp stinging sounds created. Flams and press rolls are used for accents.

These revelations will no doubt come as a shock to drummers who have spent years developing a solid right foot, a good high-hat, and conventional manual techniques. Bebop is a drastic innovation that demands an entirely fresh approach to the instrument.

To date only a few swing drummers, notably Cozy Cole (*Groovin' High*), Sidney Catlett (*Shaw 'Nuff*), and Harold West (*Red Cross*), have been able to handle bebop assignments with any success, and even their work is not completely within the new tradition. Meanwhile several drummers trying to change styles have ended up by falling hopelessly between the two and now play poorly in both.

It now remains to ask: What are the roots of bebop rhythmics? Stated in the simplest terms, the new rhythm section is a modification of the Count Basie section. There are three important changes: The guitar has been eliminated and the section made leaner. The 4/4 fundamental has been transferred from the bass drum to the cymbals. The section sound has become more vertical and more legato.

Jo Jones, a great drummer by any standards, is also a percussionist of major historical importance. Jones explored the tonal dynamics of his instrument, thereby improving on the dry sound and tight beat of drummers like Kaiser Marshall, who had tried unsuccessfully to adapt the New Orleans small band style to the early jazz orchestra. The first big band to swing solidly and consistently was Basie's, an achievement due in part to Jones's cymbal work, which contributed vertically to the section sound and enabled it to leaven the heavy sonority of ten reed and brass instruments. However, Jones's cymbal accents adhered to the two-four accent pattern, and Jones continued to maintain his four-four fundamental on the bass drum.

The second source of contemporary style is Cozy Cole. Cole's superb technical facility, rapidity of execution, and dry skin sound are very much a part of Kenny Clarke's equipment, not to mention most other bebop drummers.

Clarke is the important link in the style change. He was one of the charter members of the Minton group and the first drummer to abandon the bass pedal. Clarke's early style is preserved by means of the on-the-spot recordings made at Minton's in 1941 by Jerry Newman and released in the Charlie Christian Memorial Album.

One of Clarke's first disciples was Max Roach, a drummer in the Jones manner whose early style is reproduced on *Bu-Dee-Daht* and other sides of the Coleman Hawkins Apollo date. Once indoctrinated, Roach made such rapid progress that he must be credited with important contributions to the new style, especially its cymbal texture. Roach is one of the half-dozen great drummers of jazz.

The drummer remains the key man of the rhythm section. As may be anticipated, the changes in his playing have not been without repercussions on the other rhythm instruments. New emphasis has been placed on the string bass in particular.

Here it would be well to recall that no significant advance in string bass technique or concept has occurred since the remarkable innovations of the late Jimmy Blanton. Only Ray Brown has indicated any ability to explore beyond Blanton. Brown's work on *Dodo's Blues* and *One Bass Hit* reveals a gifted experimenter who may be pointing the way to further advances. However, his tone lacks the incisive and penetrating qualities of Blanton—his model.

For practical purposes the string bass remains the work-horse of the section; its function is to maintain at all times the steady 4/4 beat of bebop jazz. The fault of swing bass men who play bebop is that they lay behind the beat too constantly. They do not lead. In the older swing school the string bass followed the drum pedal by a fraction of a second, augmenting its plangent boom. Now that the pedal has been discarded, the string bass has the responsibility of assuming forceful section leadership.

Modern bass work demands a crisp plunging sound (Oscar Pettiford is exemplary), rapid execution, and a grasp of harmony to match the pianist and line musicians. Furthermore, it is essential that the bass and drums work as a unit. Friction, or absence of one-mindedness, is fatal to the section.

The chief casualty of the new school has been the guitar, for twenty years a section requisite. It is limited by its soft chunking effect, which makes the section sound fat and wheezy. Actually the guitar must be viewed as a victim of the rigorous economy of the bebop rhythm section, which assigns to each instrument a clear function and is an implacable enemy of duplication. Bebop musicians feel that the guitar adds nothing that cannot be obtained more cleanly from the piano, bass, and drums and that its timbre detracts from a clean small band sound.

The irony of the present dubious status of the guitar is that in the hands of its greatest innovator, Charlie Christian, it only recently enjoyed great esteem. The guitar was an important part of the Goodman Sextet and Christian's playing on records like *Till Tom Special* actually foreshadowed bebop line phrasing and harmony. Christian's important role in the Minton laboratory is also well known. Many musicians feel that if Charlie Christian were alive he would have solved the problem of integrating the instrument with the bebop section. However, many of the guitarists who have followed after and been influenced by him play exciting bebop solos.

All admit to the difficulties of reconciling their instrument with the section. Barney Kessel made interesting if insufficiently bold innovations on *Relaxin' at Camarillo,* where he drops the conventional four-four rhythm and plays feed chords. His experiments and those in the harmonic field being made by Billy Bauer may lead to the rehabilitation of this patrician jazz instrument.

The modern piano style is the culmination of a long swing toward spareness and a far cry from the two-handed plenitude of Fats Waller. The new style derives from Count Basie, a swing pianist who would not find himself out of place in the bebop rhythm section.

Basie did not think of the piano as a foundation instrument, as did Ellington and Luis Russell. Nor did he emulate Earl Hines in weaving a hard bright line through brass-reed sonorities. A revolutionary like Jo Jones, Basie used the piano to add dynamics and tone color to the over-all orchestra sound. Basie's technique of lean chords, short runs, off-beat dissonances, and percussive single notes has been adopted and modified by the contemporary pianists. In addition to tonal and rhythmic objectives, their purpose is to unfold the successive chord changes for the solo men and supply them with feed, fill, and echo chords.

Whereas outstanding bass men and drummers are few, there are many excellent pianists for section work. The bebop piano solo entails special considerations which are again beyond the scope of this article. The best soloist is Bud Powell. However, as yet no piano solo talent has appeared whose dimensions may be compared with that of Charlie Parker or Dizzy Gillespie. The shadow of Art Tatum continues to linger over the keyboard of the solo piano.

An effective bebop rhythm section depends upon the lead of a steady bassist, the insight of a skillful pianist, and, above all, the services of an extraordinary drummer. Properly balanced and disciplined, it is productive of a light spare sound and markedly polyrhythmic beat.

The modern rhythm section is the most functional in jazz history. Duplication has been dispensed with and each instrument assigned a basic and essential function. The spirit of bebop jazz, contrary to many opinions, is one of simplification. Jazz has been stripped down to its most functional aspects. Bebop jazz attempts to build complex patterns within a simple structure and with the minimum of materials. Its best performances have been instrumented for trumpet, alto sax, and three rhythm.

II—THE EVOLUTIONARY POSITION OF BOP

The term "progressive jazz" is not always fortunate. The mere fact that a style is contemporary does not mean that it is superior—nor inferior. A great many of the misconceptions regarding jazz forms stem from the lack of historical perspective. Our American music form is the most vital and original in the world today. It has had a magnificent past. It has a robust present. And it will no doubt have a significant future. A true historical perspective will view our music as a living cultural form.

Those who live in the jazz past are tracing in a laudable but sometimes laborious manner the paths already traveled by avant-garde musicians who twenty years ago outgrew the New Orleans style (Armstrong, Hawkins, Hines) and ten years ago outgrew swing (Gillespie, Parker).

The real nature of jazz history is organic. Just as Armstrong, growing out of the great New Orleans tradition, sounds a new style, Roy Eldridge stems from Louis, and Dizzy Gillespie from Eldridge. These are the three great trumpet stylists of the past thirty years. The same trends appear on the other instruments. The contemporaries are products of the past which they have absorbed. The total picture of instrumental change and individual experiment equals a musical language which constantly extends, reaffirms, and replenishes itself. From Jelly Roll Morton to Max Roach, our music is a whole art extended across the time and space of twentieth-century America, and back into the roots of African culture. Those who cannot enjoy the music of Morton and Armstrong are truly as poor as those who are unable to understand the no less wonderful art of Lester Young and Charlie Parker.

This is not the place for a detailed discussion of jazz history. The present series defines as its scope the examination of the new music of the present decade with especial reference to instrumentation and style. In the previous article on the bebop rhythm section, it was contended that the spirit of contemporary jazz was one of simplification.

Since we have already discussed the rhythm instruments, it now remains to examine the chances affecting the line instruments. We can most easily visualize the beginnings of bebop as a simplification of big band instrumentation. Indeed, the new music can best be understood as a revolt against the large, complicated music that reached its peak with Jimmie Lunceford's band. The bebop insurgents were invariably frustrated orchestra sidemen (Gillespie, Parker, Christian, Clarke). For them free expression meant playing in a small combination, and they began gathering together at Minton's after hours and on off nights to exchange ideas and jam. The whole idea of experimentation demanded an absolute minimum number of voices. The embryo bebop band, therefore, substituted the trumpet for the entire brass section of the swing orchestra and the alto sax for the reed section. These two instruments joined the new three-piece rhythm section to set the standard instrumentation for the new small band. The tenor sax was often substituted for the alto or used to augment the early bebop line.

Why did the trumpet and alto emerge as definitive voices, and what happened to the trombone and clarinet? The choice of the trumpet is fairly obvious. Since New Orleans it has been the dominant lead voice of all jazz styles. Jazz had never lacked, nor did it now lack, fine trumpet players, and in Dizzy Gillespie it enjoyed one of the great brass talents of all time. Dizzy Gillespie, followed by such excellent horn men as Fats Navarro, Howard McGhee, Benny Harris, and Miles Davis, became the

high priest of the new style. Of the saxophonists, Charlie Parker, another prodigious talent, set the reed style.

The trombone was left behind chiefly because no musician
possessed the virtuosity required to phrase in the new style;
indeed, this instrument had made little progress since Jimmy
Harrison. It was not until J. J. Johnson appeared in the middle
'forties that bebop found a trombone voice. The clarinet was a
different sort of casualty. In the hands of Benny Goodman it
had become the very symbol of virtuosity. But its inherent lack
of power and articulation made it no match for such instruments as the trumpet and alto sax, especially in the hands of
such formidable musicians as Gillespie and Parker. Generally
speaking, the tenor sax, by reason of its longer wind column,
was slower to adapt itself to the new style than the alto.

Bebop, even in its earliest state, was intricate jazz, requiring
new levels of virtuosity and execution. Psychologically, too, it
was a more complicated art form than New Orleans jazz because it was the expression of a more complex way of life, or a
protest to that way of life. Musically it was more complicated
because it could command jazz skills developed over several
generations of instrumental experimentation. The beboppers
were the cream of the orchestral sidemen, whose virtuosity
enabled them to handle with ease the most complicated scorings
of Sy Oliver, Jimmy Mundy, Eddie Sauter, Fletcher Henderson, and Duke Ellington. Thus, technical skill was a requisite
for those who would free themselves from the bondage of the
moribund swing orchestra and create a new jazz language.

The interesting thing about the new style was that the beboppers were going back to small band music. Virtuosity and
harmonic erudition were merely tools of the revolutionaries—
never, except for the untalented and imitative, ends in themselves. The main emphasis was on a thorough re-examination
of the basic problems of polyrhythmics, collective improvisation and jazz intonation.

Two musicians, Parker and Gillespie, were to play an omnipo-
tent role in the forging of the new style. But again jazz history

was repeating itself. Had not Louis Armstrong been the greatest single influence in jazz twenty years before? Had not Coleman Hawkins almost alone transformed the tenor sax from a supporting instrument into one of the greatest possible range of expression?

The first real bebop band was actually the line combination of Dizzy Gillespie and Charlie Parker, plus a suitable rhythm section. Collaboration between these two contemporaries began at Minton's around 1940 and continued until the end of 1945, when they parted company after an engagement at Billy Berg's in Hollywood. In the intervening years they worked together in the Earl Hines and Billy Eckstine orchestras and fronted a number of combinations on 52nd Street, notably at the Three Deuces in 1943-44-45.

Jazz fans are familiar with the legends of the Creole Jazz Band that electrified Chicago in the 1920's, inspiring every musician who heard Oliver and Louis taking unison breaks. The impact of the Gillespie-Parker combination on the musicians of the 1940's was no less profound. The music was largely lost on the public, but for thousands of musicians it was Messianic. Not a few journeyed across the continent to be in direct communication with the prophets of the new musical order.

The stature of the Creole Band rests upon a handful of rare records on the Gennett and Okeh labels. Due to the recording ban of 1942-44, and the confusion following its termination, not to mention the wartime shellac shortage that created chaos in the record industry, the Gillespie-Parker discography is likewise insufficient.

There are three key sessions on which Gillespie and Parker collaborate to good effect—those for Comet, Guild (later (Musicraft), and Savoy (the *Billie's Bounce/Koko* date only). The Comet date produced great music not entirely within the new idiom, since the rhythm section was essentially a swing section and swing musicians Teddy Wilson, Red Norvo, and Flip Phillips augmented the line. Due to contractual restrictions Gillespie played piano on the Savoy date, contributing the muted trumpet passages between keyboard chores on *Koko* only. The rhythm section for this engagement (Gillespie, Russell, Roach) is superb and Parker is in top form. The *Guild* sides (*Shaw 'Nuff, Salt Peanuts, Groovin' High, Lover Man,* and *Hot House*) are perhaps *the* definitive bebop records. Here there existed the one-mindedness required to play cleanly the haunting unison passages. The solo work is splendid, and the rhythm section, built around that great drummer Sidney Catlett, who is at home in all styles, furnishes excellent support.

All of these sides have played an important part in disseminating the new ideas. Coming upon them, the novice may be struck by their "strangeness" and inclined to reject them. Only by repeated listening and analysis will he be able to overtake the swift course of the players.

The new music will not stand or fall upon this evidence. It has already stood, established itself, and even gone forward. But the evidence at hand raises further questions. The lack of polyphony or counterpoint in bebop is apparent. Manifestly this is the most serious weakness of the new form, and its sole point of inferiority to earlier jazz by commonly accepted standards. Technically bebop unison is more difficult to play than three-part New Orleans ensemble. This, of course, does not mean that it is better. At the present stage of development polyphony would pose insuperable demands upon musician and listener alike. The possibility that the bebopper will reaffirm jazz polyphony is indicated in Parker's recent *Chasin' the Bird.*

In addition to polyphony or counterpoint, the commonly accepted standards of jazz as agreed upon by the consensus of writers is that it be freely improvised, melodic, hotly intoned, and polyrhythmic.

Bebop is improvised jazz. It is seldom written. Ability to read and execute is no substitute for creative and improvising ability among the beboppers. Most of its designs, however intricate, are head arrangements. Of the 100-odd bebop sides the writer has supervised, written music has seldom been in

evidence in the recording studio. In fact it is invariably necessary to secure the services of a skilled music copyist to trans-
cribe the composition from the record in order to apply for
a copyright. This is remarkable when one considers that bebop
is a new form and making a record is more complicated than
merely jamming a tune (*Muskrat Ramble,* for example) with
which everyone is familiar. Such sides as *Billie's Bounce, Shaw
'Nuff, Carvin' the Bird,* and even that monumental big band
side, *Things To Come,* are "heads," worked up and executed
in the recording studio.

Complaints that bebop is not melodic are frequent. These
same complaints greeted Debussy's music at the turn of the
century. Many bebop riffs are dull. So are the less-inspired
riffs of Goodman, Ellington, Basie, Henderson, Armstrong,
Oliver, and Morton. Those who are unable to hear the beautiful melodies of *Hot House, Groovin' High, Ornithology, Relaxin' at Camarillo, Cool Blues,* or *Confirmation* are simply not
listening with open minds. Such melodies have become part of
the same jazz treasury as *High Society, Savoy Blues, Solitude,
Mood Indigo,* and *Till Tom Special.*

The "sound" (intonation) of bebop is certainly unique in
jazz, or for that matter in music. It can be likened to that
profound and delightful change in texture that occurred in
French music with Debussy, and in French painting with
Monet and Renoir. It has a more haunting quality and less
vibrato than earlier jazz intonation. It is at once round and
light, airy and brilliant. It has no relation to any legitimate
or academic concept of intonation. Just as New Orleans and
Chicago jazz have their individual sound and timbre, bebop is
unique.

Several aspects of the new music assert an unmistakable
superiority to what has gone before. In instrumental virtuosity
and technical proficiency bebop brings jazz to a new level.
Bebop harmonics, which have gone beyond the most advanced
concepts of the academically trained arrangers of the late
'thirties, have opened a new vista of vertical possibilities. The
contemporary jazz musician has more harmonic material at

his disposal than a Dodds, Armstrong, Hawkins, or even a Lester Young. Whether the beboppers reached these harmonic levels as the result of pure experiment or whether the new ideas filtered into jazz language through the offices of the swing arrangers remains a controversial subject, although the latter possibility is more likely. To argue that European borrowings (or imitations) are fatal to our native form would be to rule out all jazz, which has borrowed freely and unabashedly from its beginning.

Finally, and without dispute, bebop represents the most advanced development of the rhythmic character of jazz. One must listen carefully to the best records of Armstrong or Roy Eldridge, of Bechet or Hawkins, to find rhythmic accents as rich as those in Dizzy Gillespie's line on *Congo Blues*, or Parker's on *Koko*. Baby Dodds and Jo Jones are two of the greatest drummers of jazz, but the patterns of Kenny Clarke and Max Roach are more complex, and swing as freely.

Of particular interest to the historian are the environmental conditions of the bebop movement. Bebop grew out of the Minton sessions of the early 1940's. It ran a swift course from an esoteric form supported by a handful of innovators to a popular style. From 1942 to 1946, 52nd Street in particular and the industry in general enjoyed a boom the like of which it had not known and which, as a favorable climate for playing uncommercial jazz, can be compared to New Orleans before 1917, Chicago in the early 1920's, and Kansas City in the early 1930's. The Street of the World War II era must rank as one of the four chief milieus of jazz.

During this period The Street supported at least seven major clubs featuring name jazz talent, usually on a continuous (alternate attraction) basis. Talent included almost every important name and certainly every style of playing. New Orleans was represented by Baby Dodds, Sidney Bechet, and Bunk Johnson; Chicago by Art Hodes, Georg Brunis, and Wild Bill Davidson; swing by a galaxy of brilliant names: Ben Webster, Barney Bigard, Art Tatum, Coleman Hawkins, Roy Eldridge, Lester Young, Sid Catlett, Rex Stewart, and Teddy Wilson.

The honest critic must ask himself: Given the opportunity to hear all jazz styles as played by the outstanding exponents of each, why did the generation which was creating a new uncommercial jazz style discard all of the previous models and accept bebop as the contemporary way of playing jazz?

The historical reality is that the beboppers had absorbed consciously or unconsciously from their antecedents the language of earlier jazz and were bent on forging a new idiom which would communicate the ideas and emotions not of the 1920's or the 1930's, but of the 1940's.

The most misleading theory of all remains that which argues that bebop is music fostered by motion picture sound tracks, jazz arrangers, and Tin Pan Alley. Bebop is in violent revolt against all three. It is especially the intransigent opponent of Tin Pan Alley. Indeed the war against the horrible products of the tunesmiths, which began with Fletcher Henderson in the 1920's, has been brought to a successful conclusion only by the beboppers, who take standard melodies at will, stand them on their heads, and create new compositions retaining only a harmonic relationship with the original. Thus, *What Is This Thing Called Love?* becomes *Hot House; How High the Moon* is *Ornithology*, and so on.

Bebop is music of revolt: revolt against big bands, arrangers, vertical harmonies, soggy rhythms, non-playing orchestra leaders, Tin Pan Alley—against commercialized music in general. It reasserts the individuality of the jazz musician as a creative artist, playing spontaneous and melodic music within the framework of jazz, but with new tools, sounds, and concepts.

III—BRASS

The insurgents making up the pioneer bebop group were invariably disillusioned large band sidemen whose creative impulses led them back to small band jazz. It was also emphasized that these revolutionaries gathered at Minton's, during the war period infiltrated 52nd Street and there, during a four-year musical boom when every style had the opportunity to be heard in its pure and uncommercial state, emerged as the leaders of a new style.

The general trend of simplification which had rigorously reorganized the jazz rhythm section meanwhile effected the substitution in the front line instruments of the trumpet for the brass section and the alto sax for the reed section. That the trumpet should assume leadership of the new combination was inevitable. Powerful, forthright, and robust, its range corresponded most nearly to that of the male tenor voice which had supplied the lead in pre-instrumental Afro-American music.

Buddy Bolden, King Oliver, Bunk Johnson, Freddie Keppard, Louis Armstrong had all been aggressive personalities, virile musicians who dominated the musical groups with which they associated. By the mid-1920's Armstrong had become the most imitated musician of the day. As a successful young big-band leader he abandoned the early cornet-ensemble style and, taking up the trumpet, soon expanded its range and flexibility, making it more individual in expression. The Armstrong trumpet style is the foundation style of every trumpet player who has followed him. There are certainly few bebop brass men unfamiliar with Louis' middle-period style.

The "link" musician between Armstrong and the present is Roy Eldridge, a figure of secondary position in jazz, but one whose importance as a stylist is enormous. Between 1936 and 1942, roughly that period which begins with the eclipse of Louis Armstrong and ends with the ascendancy of Dizzy Gillespie, Roy Eldridge was the most listened to, admired, and imitated trumpet player in jazz. Eldridge's records have only occasionally captured the compelling force of his playing (*Heckler's Hop*). Heard in person, especially during the 1937-39 period when he headed his own six-piece band, Roy was the most exciting of musicians.

In effect, Eldridge took as his point of departure the fantastic style of the middle Armstrong period. Roy's trumpet went beyond Louis in range and brilliance, but it had greater

agility, and his style was more nervous. His drive was perhaps
the most intense jazz has ever known. After junking the small
band Eldridge jobbed around as featured trumpet with large
bands and was the "King" until that memorable night in 1941 or
1942 (Kenny Clarke, who tells the story, is not sure exactly
when) that Dizzy Gillespie caught up with him at Minton's.

"Monday night was always a free-for-all at Minton's," Clarke
recalls. "All the young musicians in town would be in the place
with their horns, waiting for a chance to get up on the stand
and blow. Big name stars used to drop in, especially if they
were playing with the band at the Apollo Theatre a few blocks
away—Charlie Christian, Lester Young, and especially Roy
Eldridge. Roy was the king.

"Dizzy Gillespie had started out playing like Roy, but had
gotten on the new kick, working out his ideas with Charlie
Parker, Thelonious Monk, Nick Fenton, and myself. We had
the regular band at Minton's starting in 1941. Dizzy could play,
man, and his ideas were new, but try as he would Dizzy could
never cut Roy. Roy was just too much. Roy had drive and execution and he could keep going chorus after chorus. Every
time Dizzy tried, Roy gave him a lesson, made him pack. But
Dizzy never quit.

"Then one night Dizzy came in and started blowing. He
got it all together that night. He cut Roy to everyone's satisfaction, and that night Roy packed his horn and never came back.
Dizzy was the new king, and the cats were already beginning
to call it bop."

Although ten years Roy Eldridge's junior, Dizzy Gillespie
could hardly be called an upstart. As a high-note trumpet player
in the Eldridge tradition, Gillespie had very early earned himself a reputation with band leaders as one of the most effective
section and solo brass men. Happily, the discographical evidence on this musician, about whom so much of recent history
has been written, is reasonably full. On his earliest records
(*King Porter Stomp* and *Hard Times* with Teddy Hill) it is
difficult to say the soloist is not Eldridge himself—Eldridge
with perhaps a touch of the early uncommercial Harry James.

Hot Mallets with a Hampton pick-up group already showcases
a talent of high potential. The two short solo passages are too
fleet and graceful for Eldridge. With the prophetic *Pickin' the
Cabbage* with Cab Calloway, which Gillespie composed and
arranged, using revolutionary rhythmic ideas, and on which he
plays a long solo utilizing whole-tone scales, it is plain that a
large new talent has arrived. Sometime later Dizzy overtook
his teacher at Minton's. Thereafter he was the idol of the
younger generation and shortly the prophet of the new style.
Once established, Gillespie's talent increased in breadth and
depth, and indeed has yet to find its limit, for Dizzy has not
only played the role of high priest of bebop but displayed unusual powers as writer, arranger, band leader, entertainer,
and popularizer of its new idiom.

Of all the beboppers, Dizzy is perhaps the most solidly entrenched in jazz tradition. Oliver, Armstrong, Eldridge, and
Gillespie are securely in linear contact with one another. Gillespie's trumpet remains a lead jazz voice, masculine and lusty
(*Salt Peanuts*). It is also capable of brilliant solo flights (*I Can't
Get Started, Confirmation*). His range and agility are greater
than those of the earlier masters. His tone deliberately has
less vibrato, being lighter, airier. Its virtuosity is often fabulous. It can sing and it can punch.

The technical ability possessed by Gillespie has worked a
hardship on his imitators, who are prone to lose sight of the
fact that Dizzy was among the two or three ablest trumpet
players in jazz as early as ten years ago and that his later innovations are grounded on a thoroughgoing craftsmanship. Gillespie can move with facility through most of three octaves on
his horn, and his intonation everywhere in the register is controlled. It is reasonable to predict that at least five years must
elapse before any considerable body of jazz trumpet players
acquire facility in the new style.

There are many Gillespie followers, three of major importance: Howard McGhee, Fats Navarro, and Miles Davis. Mc-
Ghee belongs to the Gillespie generation and is in fact a musician whose first inspiration was Armstrong, and who turned

toward Eldridge sometime around 1938. McGhee's early solo with the Andy Kirk band *(McGhee Special)* evinces a style influenced by both Louis and Roy. A favorite of Coleman Hawkins, McGhee began to listen closely to the new ideas emerging from the bebop experiments and especially to Gillespie. At the beginning of the present decade McGhee's style changed with the times, and on his Asch [now Stinson] date with Coleman Hawkins we can hear the new ideas incorporated into the solos.

Fats Navarro lacks McGhee's brilliance and Gillespie's stature. He is a quieter and more subtle musician, a very delightful and badly underrated one. His tone is superb—veiled and haunting, yet light and highly personal. Navarro plays with a more relaxed beat than Gillespie and McGhee. His phrasing is faultless. Much in the manner of Lester Young, Navarro constructs long phrases in which staccato multi-note passages are balanced against shorter statements where the notes are more hoarsely intoned and dramatically placed.

Unfortunately Fats Navarro has been heard little outside of New York, and his recording performances have seldom done him justice. A native of Key West, of mixed Cuban-Negro-Chinese parentage, Navarro's music presents a fascinating blend of flavors, predominantly those of the jazz and Afro-Cuban tradition.

Barely twenty-two at this date (1948), Miles Davis may be said to belong to the new generation of musicians. There is now a mounting body of evidence that Davis is leading the way to or even founding the next school of trumpet playing.

Nothing could be further from the Eldridge-Gillespie school than the Miles Davis trumpet. Miles plays a "soft" horn. He has consistently been overlooked by critics because he lacks the virtuosity of his contemporaries. Davis seldom uses the upper register, preferring to play almost wholly "'within the staff." His tone is broad and warm.

Davis's sound, and his sense of chord changes and rhythm suspensions, are very close to the Charlie Parker alto style—he has played much with Parker in the past three years. As an idea man and influence Miles Davis has just come into his full powers. If his grasp of the instrument still leaves something to be desired, he has shown considerable improvement *(Barbados, The Hymn)* since his first record *(Billie's Bounce)*, and is certainly the trumpet to watch.

Trumpet players like Charlie Shavers, Al Killian, Peanuts Holland, Cat Anderson, and Snookie Young are often lumped with the bebop brass men but usually by reason of their high-note work or pyrotechnical delivery, which per se has nothing to do with the new idiom. These musicians do not phrase in the contemporary style. They are essentially swing musicians.

Bebop brass men constitute a school as well established as the new form itself. The range of the instrument has been further extended by them. They have added to its virtuosity, speed of execution, and brilliance. Their trumpet tone is lighter, rounder, and more transparent.

IV–THE PARENT STYLE AND LESTER YOUNG

The shadows of three great jazz musicians lie heavily over the contemporary scene—Dizzy Gillespie, Lester Young, and Charlie Parker. In our examination of bebop brass instrumentation it was shown how the modern style had evolved along a line of great trumpet players from Louis Armstrong to Roy Eldridge, emerging in the bebop idiom with the ascendancy of Dizzy Gillespie. In that article certain references were made to Lester Young, whose tone and phrasing, even though on saxophone, were studied and adapted to brass instruments by the earlier boppers.

When we come to examine bebop reed instrumentation we find the influence of Lester Young even more dominant. In fact, modern reed playing stems almost solely from "Pres," the most revered of the swing musicians.

The new individual voices of swing—Goodman, Wilson, Eldridge—had brought about an improvement of technique, sophistication, refinement, and involvement of line. Teddy Wilson had refined the punching orchestral piano of Earl Hines; Eldridge elaborated the fantastic style of the later Armstrong period. Benny Goodman was a clarinetist who phrased in the Chicago tradition of Jimmy Noone and Frank Teschemacher, but he went far beyond his models in musicianship.

Great changes had come to be associated with these musicians, but they had not actually introduced a new way of playing jazz. The challenge sounded by Lester Young marks a division point in jazz history. Most of the critics and musicians of the past fifteen years fall into two groups: the traditionalists who hold with the old models—the classic jazz of Armstrong, Hawkins, and Goodman; and the "moderns" who have followed the path of Lester Young, Dizzy Gillespie, and Charlie Parker. An understanding of this schism will simplify the appraisal not only of music but of jazz criticism since 1935.

Like Wilson and Eldridge, Lester Young represents virtuosity, harmonic maturity, delicacy, and complexity. But these qualities are not acquisitions with Young—they are integral in his playing. He is the first to make a break with the past and create a style which is actually unique. With Morton, Armstrong, and Parker, figures that loom in their respective eras, Lester Young is one of the four chief innovators of jazz. A musician of less stature than Armstrong, Young is none the less comparable to Louis in historical importance.

Lester was the first to junk the machine-gun style of Coleman Hawkins, with its reliance on eighth note-dotted sixteenth-note patterns. This is the phrasing method of Chu Berry, Ben Webster, and Young's Basie section mate, Herschel Evans. Lester used both more notes and less notes than his predecessors, for abundances were balanced against bareness within the structure of his solos.

In his solo on *Lady Be Good* (small band version), Young employs a bare ten notes for the first four-bar section. A classic stylist would have doubled the amount. These ten notes are set with lapidarian skill in the rhythmic and melodic framework. The opening phrase, so succinctly stated, leads to longer and complex improvisations upon the melody, the whole of which is a masterpiece of economy, subtlety, and logic.

Lester's musical thought flowed, not within the accepted confines of two- or four-bar sections, but more freely. He thought in terms of a new melodic line that submitted only to the harmony of the original as it reworked the melody into something fresh and personal.

Harmonic sense that enables a jazzman to improvise readily is a talent. Melodic vision of Young's quality is a mark of genius. His example and that of the Basie band restored to the jazz language a tool which had been dulled by improper usage.

Lester Young's chord and bar changes are arranged with such adroitness that the listener is frequently not aware of them until after they have fallen. Lester's method is to phrase ahead—to prepare for and gracefully lead into the next change several beats before its arrival. To be able to move so freely in and out of the harmonies with an ear so keen and a step so sure, always to come out on the right note and the right beat—this is a mark of genius. Jazz had known nothing like it since the first daring improvisations of Louis Armstrong.

As an innovator of harmonic change, Lester employed the light polychrome orchestral palette of the Debussyians. Lester's spirit was pleased by the sound of the sixth and ninth intervals which lie adjacent to the dominant and tonic notes. It was typical of his subtle and inquiring nature to play just off what the ear expected and thereby extend musical structure on a horizontal plane.

Lester added variety to the melodic line, but he knew well how to balance the parts. He is complex but never complicated. Wild crescendoes are contrasted with hammering repetitions, iridescent multi-note passages with sections where notes are massed like blocks. Short statements lead to long flowing sentences. Lester's solos are replete with dips and soaring flights, surprises, twists, hoarse shouts, and bubbling laughter. The holes—and, like Basie, Lester leaves many—are deliberate and meaningful. The dry bite of the attacking notes, the fatness of the slurs and periods—all are parts of the deliberate style of a master virtuoso of the tenor saxophone.

Like all of the giants, Lester possesses a tremendous beat. He is one of those rare musicians who can swing an entire band. The massive swing of the Basie orchestra became even more exciting when Lester soloed. Very often, when he had the first solo, as on *Taxi War Dance,* Young would divest the opening statements of all but their rhythmic elements. Here Lester underlines the first and third beats, giving greater emphasis to Jo Jones's high hat accents, which fall on two and four. In rhythmic language this solo develops a four-four, a two-four, and a one-three pattern simultaneously and results in rhythmic complexity that goes beyond that of any contemporary. No one before him—neither Armstrong, nor Morton, nor Hawkins—had created melodic line as rich in rhythmic interest as did Lester Young.

New Orleans bands achieved this rhythmic complexity collectively. The quality deteriorated during the following period when jazz emphasized romantic and individualistic tendencies. Lester Young, the arch-romantic, re-creates this quality in an individual style.

Lester's insistence on the rhythmic priorities of jazz came as a tonic to a music which was drifting away from the drive of early New Orleans music. Lester did more than reaffirm these priorities. He replenished the stream polluted by the arrangers and thus made possible the even more complex rhythmic developments of the bebop style.

Lester Young's work falls into two periods; first, 1935–40, when he was featured with Basie and recorded with the parent band and with Teddy Wilson, Benny Goodman, and Billie Holiday; second, 1940 to the present [1948–49], during which time he has concentrated mainly on concert and small band work.

During the first period Lester's playing is notable for its freshness and abandon. Lack of inhibition does not mean that

Lester was nervous or frenzied. He is the most relaxed of musicians. His notes flowed like water out of a tap and the source showed no signs of depletion.

Lester's detachment was unshakable. He always seemed to be in a world of his own. Heard in person, in the midst of the happy jungle of Basie's orchestral sound, or on record, Lester gave the impression of impassioned absorption. On records his solos glow with a radiance like the light from another planet. In the parlance of the times, he was "out of this world."

The Lester Young style is essentially romantic. It is uninhibited and relaxed, sensitive, imaginative, deeply subjective. It is the very intimate communication of an artist who was voicing the ideas of the day in the language of the next decade.

Lester always sounds spontaneous. Less disciplined than Hawkins, he is nonetheless a musician whose product is orderly and structural. But these qualities—balance and unity of parts, clarity of concept—lie beneath the surface, under the luminous texture of notes.

When Lester first appeared on the jazz scene he had command of a completely integrated style which has undergone little or no basic change since 1935. It was as if he had been planning a frontal attack on orthodoxy for years.

The roots of Lester's style extend in many directions. On one side they are indisputably in the reed tradition of the early clarinetists, who emphasized the melodic and lyrical qualities of jazz and thought in terms of the blues scale. Indeed, the Kansas City style speaks the language of the New Orleans clarinetists, and such link figures as Eddie Barefield show how the reed style shifted from clarinet to alto or tenor saxophone during the 'twenties. Barefield's feeling for phrasing contrasts and his fluid quality are to be heard consistently in Lester Young's style.

But Lester draws equally from sources of a much different nature—Debussyian harmony, light intonation, and the spiritual qualities which are attached to the white jazz tradition of Bix Beiderbecke and Bud Freeman, both of whom Young listened

to during his early period. Beiderbecke's search for the springs
of hidden beauty, hypersensitivity, and Bohemianism are reflected in Lester's music. Like Bud Freeman, a healthier exponent of Chicago jazz, Young uses clean technique, lightness
of tone, and a sense of chromatics. Occasionally Freeman's
work suggests the flights of exuberance that we find so frequently in Lester.

It is this synthesis of opposing attitudes and ideologies—the
profound tradition of the blues combined with the infusions of
European harmony and white romanticism—that gives Lester
Young's music its special appeal. The various materials are combined in a style which has no eclectic qualities, but is fused,
integrated, and intensely personal.

From a historical point of view Lester Young's influence was
most effective during his Basie period. It affected less his own
generation than those young musicians learning their instruments and developing a style, upon whom his influence was
transcendant. From the date of his very first record release with
Basie, young musicians in all parts of the country began listening to jazz with a new attitude. Basie records were sedulously
collected, the Young solos replayed, hummed, whistled, imitated. Appearances of the Basie band were *de rigueur* functions
for the growing number of fans who sat at his feet on such occasions, "digging" every phrase played by the master.

As Dexter Gordon describes it: "Hawk was the master of the
horn, a musician who did everything possible with it, the right
way. But when Pres appeared, we all started listening to him
alone. Pres had an entirely new sound, one that we seemed to
be waiting for. Pres was the first to tell a story on the horn."

Of course, Coleman Hawkins and other saxophonists of the
Hawkins school had "told a story," and an important one, on
their horns. Dexter Gordon is saying in clear language that the
art of the older school, the jazz classicists if we like, no longer
held valid for the insurgents of his generation. They were in revolt against the orthodoxy of the older school of jazz, with its

powerful vibrato, emphatic periods, lusty intonation, rigid harmonies, and severe solo architecture.

What they admired in Lester Young was his lighter and purer tone, his broader harmonic concepts, his greater extension of the solo line—with the resultant freedom from its bar divisions—his dreamier and more lyrical style. And, of course, like all who appreciate great jazz of any kind, they recognized his transcendant qualities: his melodic gift, inventiveness, and, above all, his tremendous swing.

Pres became a cult in the late 'thirties and his camp followers numbered dozens of musicians who were to take part in the changes of the next decade: Dizzy Gillespie, Charlie Parker, Bud Powell, Thelonious Monk, Dexter Gordon, Wardell Gray, Stan Getz, Allen Eager, Sonny Stitt, Max Roach, Kenny Clarke, Miles Davis, Leo Parker, J. J. Johnson, Serge Chaloff, Charlie Christian, Benny Harris, Fats Navarro. Practically every important new musician of the 'forties learned from Lester Young.

RECORD NOTE

Savoy 12020 collects the Parker-Gillespie Guild masters *Salt Peanuts, Groovin' High, Hot House*, etc., but omits *Shaw 'Nuff* and *Lover Man*. The Red Norvo sides featuring Parker and Gillespie, originally issued on Comet, were last available on Dial 903 and Jazztone J–1204.

Columbia CL–652 contains the recordings of Charlie Christian with the Benny Goodman small groups and includes *Till Tom Special*. Two sessions recorded at Minton's Playhouse in 1941, featuring Christian, Kenny Clarke, and Thelonious Monk, are now available on Esoteric 548.

Charlie Parker's *Red Cross* appears on Savoy 12001. His *Relaxin' at Camarillo* was last available on Concert Hall CHJ–1004. Other Parker recordings made for Ross Russell's Dial label have been issued on Roost 2210. Savoy 12070 collects the entire *Koko, Billie's Bounce, Now's the Time* recording date, including warm-ups, alternate versions, etc. Different takes of *Chasin' the Bird*, featuring Parker and Miles Davis, have been reissued on Savoy 12001, 12009 (which also has Davis's solo on *Barbados*), and 12014.

Coleman Hawkins's Apollo recording date with Dizzy Gillespie, which included *Woody'n' You* and *Bu-Dee-Daht*, was last available on Grand Award 33–316. Gillespie's *Hot Mallets* solo with Lionel Hampton was on Victor LJM–1000. His *I Can't Get Started* is part of the Columbia anthology CL–1036, while *Confirmation* was last issued on Jazztone J–1204. The Gillespie big-band version of *Things To Come* appears on Savoy 12020. Roy Eldridge's *Heckler's Hop* is on Epic LG–3252.

Lester Young's solos with Count Basie on *Lady Be Good* and *Taxi War Dance* are currently on Epic LG–3107.

Again we have some enduring comments on the jazz of the mid-'forties originally appearing in The Record Changer. *Paul Bacon was perhaps the only American critic of that time to see Thelonious Monk's music for what it was. His 1948 review of Monk's recordings of* 'Round Midnight *and* Well You Needn't *(now on Blue Note 1510) contained points which many others have caught up to only recently.*

In his 1949 review of The Skunk *and* Boperation *(now on Blue Note 1532) by trumpeters Howard McGhee and Fats Navarro, he was not only incidentally prophetic (a year later, Navarro was dead, an apparently disillusioned man, and McGhee has remained relatively inactive in jazz circles), but he stated the perpetual dilemma of the intuitive improviser who has neither a mastery of orchestral form nor is a potential leader but has only himself to offer. A few giants (an Armstrong, a Hawkins) survive—but not even all the giants necessarily. What does a man of integrity do when he is an expert soloist—and that alone?*

PAUL BACON

Two Notes on Modern Jazzmen

There's something about the confidence and dash with which Howard McGhee and Fats Navarro go about their work that makes me wonder where they're going to be two years from now (I may wonder idly where I'll be two years from now, too, but it's not the same thing), because the possibilities are pretty limited; the fact that, right now, McGhee plays specialties in front of the Machito band may be the handwriting on the wall. Fats took a fling at a big band (Goodman), which was hardly a triumphant experience for him, and he has gone about as far as he can go with what's around him; it must be a bit disconcerting to stand on top of a heap and not find God waiting for you with outstretched hand.

I don't think either one has the instinctive savvy to make a
go of his own group, as Dizzy did—neither is salesman enough to
do it right. Maybe Bop City* will give fellowships some day.

It's useless to pick out special bits of rare value in this record
of *'Round About Midnight* and *Well You Needn't* and describe
them at length; it is a remarkable thing. Thelonious Monk may
well be the man finally to straighten out people about modern
informal music, besides having had a great deal to do with its
present direction. His kind of playing isn't something that occurred to him whole—beyond its undoubted originality, it has
the most tremendously expressive and personal feeling I can
find in any musician playing now. It has cost Monk something
to play as he does—not recognition so much, because he's always
had that from the people he wanted to find it in; jobs and
money, certainly, although his personality has had a little to do
with that (he is best described as a dour pixie); and still more: I
believe his style and approach cost him 50 per cent of his technique. He relies so much on absolute musical reflex that Horowitz's skill might be unequal to the job.

That isn't to say that the music is formless. Taken as a whole,
it has a very satisfying feeling of solidity. And Monk has a beat
like the ocean waves—no matter how sudden, spasmodic, or
obscure his little inventions, he rocks irresistibly on.

What he has done, in part, is quite simple. He hasn't invented
a new scheme of things, but he has—for years, too—looked with
an unjaundiced eye at music and seen a little something else. He
plays riffs that are older than Bunk Johnson—but they don't
sound the same; his beat is familiar but he does something
strange there, too—he can make a rhythm seem almost separate,
so that what he does is inside it, or outside it. He may play for a
space in nothing but smooth phrases and then suddenly jump
on a part and repeat it with an intensity beyond description.
His left hand is not constant—it wanders shrewdly around, sometimes playing only a couple of notes, sometimes powerfully on

* A nightclub—Ed.

the beat, usually increasing it in variety, and occasionally silent.

At any rate, Monk is really making use of all the unused space around jazz, and he makes you feel that there are plenty of unopened doors.

As to the record, *'Round About Midnight* is a beautiful melody, played with great feeling and charm. The band is for background only, setting the stage for Monk, and the background is good. The trumpet and alto switch parts now and then for variance in sound. Dizzy recorded this tune for Dial a while ago, but there isn't much comparison.

Well You Needn't is an intriguing number, with Gene Ramey on bass and Art Blakey on drums. Blakey deserves a column of his own—he can steal a record with his drumming—and if I may quote Ike Quebec, "Other drummers say 'thump'—Art says 'POW.'"

The major event after bop was "cool" jazz. Innately conservative, the cool was something simply "in the air" in the late 'forties and early 'fifties in the work of several tenor saxophonists whose basic inspiration was Lester Young, in the work of pianist Lennie Tristano and some of his pupils, and in a series of records led by Miles Davis (now collected on Capitol T–762). For the most comprehensive comment on those latter, again see M. Hodeir's Jazz: Its Evolution and Essence. *The progeny of the cool is large and includes subsequent work by Gerry Mulligan, J. J. Johnson, Lee Konitz—and, indeed, a whole "West Coast" jazz "movement." But the most enduring will undoubtedly be the work of the Modern Jazz Quartet.*

Mr. Harrison's essay appeared in Jazz Monthly *for April 1958, after the Quartet's British tour, and is included by permission of the author and of the editor, Albert McCarthy.*

MAX HARRISON

Looking Back at the Modern Jazz Quartet

No matter how long they continue to visit us, we shall probably always expect overmuch of the legendary figures of jazz. Two years ago our expectations were artificially high because the Musicians' Union had not *allowed* us to hear any of them in person for about twenty-two years.

But now, with several U.S.-British band exchanges behind us, we have at least learned not to be over-optimistic. Few who were present are likely to forget the monumental disappointment of Louis Armstrong's debut at the Empress Hall nearly two years ago or the hooliganism of Lionel Hampton's opening concert there a few months later. After working for several years as a prop for very inferior French bands Sidney Bechet came to us with his unique vitality at last diminished and sounding like a carbon copy of his own mannerisms. Gerry Mulligan's appearances here added nothing to what we already knew from his recordings, and Eddie Condon's attitude of openly bored indifference was displeasing to at least some of his audiences. The Basie machine gave wonderful ensemble performances but appeared to have no creative spark, for apart from the leader's piano there was little individuality of expression in the solos. Perhaps of all our visitors only Earl Hines and Cozy Cole were not content to rest on the laurels of past achievement and left us with enlarged, not diminished, reputations.

One approached the renowned but not yet legendary Modern Jazz Quartet with some caution. In spite of the originality and apparent seriousness of their records and a recent appearance at the Donaueschingen Festival of Contemporary Music, they had been described as "the most commercial act today and certainly rival Bill Haley . . . in this respect." What could really be expected of them?

With a very few exceptions—like the Ellington orchestra—most groups have a limited creative period, after which they either break up or go on repeating themselves. Viewing as a whole those of their records available at the time it seemed at least possible the Quartet had reached this stage and a stalemate was imminent. In this case there were two alternatives: to play stereotyped versions of their recorded successes, or to present new material that showed no advance on what had gone before. The former was unlikely on account of John Lewis's integrity and of Milt Jackson's inventive powers on vibraharp. More probable was the latter, especially in view of the dangers and potential blind alleys that had always seemed latent in the group's work and which would fully reveal themselves only when the period of real creativity was over. One of the foremost weaknesses implicit in many of the Quartet's scores is Lewis's penchant for overly delicate effects of color and texture. If allowed to develop too far this could lead to a general over-subtilization of style and a consequent inability to produce work of real musical and emotional power. (Elling-

ton faced a similar danger in the 'thirties when he was forging his very personal harmonic idiom. Some of his recordings
at that time have unduly sweet harmonies that suggest he was
a little uncertain of his direction. Perhaps the four sides of *Reminiscing in Tempo* are the best examples of this, if only because
the harmonic weaknesses are made all the more acute by the
additional problem of an extended form. These weak harmonic
sequences were one of the growing pains of his waxing powers
of composition, and Ellington emerged from this difficult phase
to produce finer work than ever.)

Although continuing to perform a variety of ballads and
other standards, the MJQ has evolved increasingly elaborate
textures and adopted a number of the devices of classical composition. The obvious danger of this is that, in spite of the
presence of a soloist of Jackson's caliber, improvisation could
be gradually strangled and have no further vital part in the
group's performances. Over-elaboration of texture could easily
lead to lack of swing, and any great use of straight musical
forms would seemingly result in a loss of contact with the blues.
The result of all this would supposedly be just one more un-
happy potpourri of distorted jazz and straight music of the
kind that has been offered to us several times before in the
name of progress. The Quartet's instrumentation, with its
limited dynamic range and small tonal palette, would appear
to be another limiting factor on Lewis's achieving much more
with the group.

One concert proved that fear was unjustified on any of the
above points, and after two it was clear that most past problems had been solved, potential blind alleys negotiated, and
that the Quartet had gone on to new and more remarkable
achievements. There can be no question of the jazz credentials
of a group that swings as do the MJQ on *I'll Remember April*
and plays such convincing blues as their versions of *Now's the
Time* or *Bags' Groove,* but doubt may still be felt on the increasing use of contrapuntal devices adapted from classical
models. Although it is no kind of justification in itself, it may
be noted that straight composers have conducted rather un-

comprehending flirtations with jazz for about forty years now, and it was to be expected that jazz musicians should return the compliment in due course. However undesirable this may seem to be, MJQ bassist Percy Heath was probably correct in pointing out to the present writer that the influence of straight music on jazz is now unavoidable. Gone are the days when a Mezzrow could dismiss a Beiderbecke's enthusiasm for Debussy and Stravinsky with "A lot of the music he tried to sell us seemed like something second grade—and some of it was really corny." Jazzmen no longer live in such an enclosed world of their own as in the 'twenties, and many of the modernists have at least some acquaintance with straight music. Musical experience tends to be all of a piece—one cannot separate playing, writing, and listening into entirely separate compartments—and if a creative musician hears sufficient of a particular kind of music, be it modern straight compositions or anything else, he will eventually be influenced by it. It would be unfortunate if jazz lost its unique qualities through the excessive influence of an alien form of expression, but it is unlikely that the MJQ's work is part of any such process. The increasing contrapuntal element in their work and most of the other innovations are the natural and inevitable result of the fruition of Lewis's particular gifts and of the remarkable versatility of Jackson, Heath, and drummer Connie Kay that enables them to meet the unprecedented and ever-widening demands made on them.

Many small jazz groups are collections of separate egos, rather than communal musical bodies. Their music, particularly in a series of solos, tends to be the work of men who, as it were, merely happen to be gathered together and have no fundamental creative unity. Among exceptions to this were the best of the Ellington small band recordings. The success of these is not explained by their being great collections of talent "on paper"—many all-star groups have made very dull records—but by the chief participants sharing, apart from their long-term membership to a great orchestra, a common musical viewpoint developed through playing together over the years. Such a unity is also very much a characteristic of the

MJQ, even though its members have not been together so long. In spite of the frequent and lengthy solos, theirs is essentially *group* music in which everything is subservient to the production of work perfectly integrated both in content and performance. Each item in their repertoire is not merely an arrangement or a sequence of solos but is a *composition* in the fullest sense of the term. This applies not only to Lewis's own pieces but to such standards as *But Not for Me* and *Over the Rainbow*, which may be said to have been recomposed by the Quartet on a higher level than that of their Tin Pan Alley origin. Thus, nearly all their recordings convey an impression of shape, balance, and proportion that is only consistently found in the best recordings of the great jazz composers, Morton and Ellington.

The main point to be remembered in the face of any difficulties the MJQ's work may at first impose on the listener is that Lewis, too, is that rarest of musicians, a jazz composer. In the same way that Morton's and Ellington's singular creative powers placed their music somewhat apart from the category into which it would otherwise fall, so Lewis's gifts account for many of the Quartet's unique qualities. There have been countless men able to produce facile "originals" that are adequate bases for improvisation, and some few, like the composers of such tunes as *Royal Garden Blues* or *'Round About Midnight* and the superior ballad standards, have done better. Yet so far only Morton, Ellington, and now John Lewis have consistently been able to regard a performance as a unit of musical architecture, to see part in relation to whole and to develop an intimate relationship between improvised solos, predetermined ensembles, and general structure. Lewis might paraphrase Strayhorn's remark about Ellington and say, "I play the piano but my real instrument is the Quartet."

There is a parallel between the way Duke has molded his bands to suit many diverse compositions, using the great soloists as vehicles for his own ideas yet not trespassing on the individuality of their own expression, and Lewis developing his compositional gifts through the more limited medium of the

MJQ without confining Jackson's freedom in solos or compromising the basic jazz qualities of the group. Although this parallel is striking, it should be emphasized that while both are well rooted in the soil of jazz, Lewis's gifts, though similar in nature, are different in kind to Ellington's. However diversified his compositions may be, Ellington is an impressionist, and his work has been ably discussed in this light in several articles by Vic Bellerby and Burnett James in past issues of this magazine. In spite of a few delicate tone-poems like *Autumn in New York,* it has become increasingly clear that, as far as composition is concerned, Lewis has a basically contrapuntal outlook. This may be disputed in view of the impressionistic cast of his harmony and the mildly programmatic titles he sometimes employs. The present writer considers, however, that counterpoint occurs so frequently in Lewis's compositions and arrangements and is handled with such feeling that it indicates a consistent approach that is conditioned by the nature of his gifts.

The contrapuntal bent was not apparent in his earliest work with Gillespie's second big band but became evident soon afterwards, if only in the simplest terms at first. His composition *Afternoon in Paris,* recorded in 1949 by J. J. Johnson, is an early example. Johnson's trombone and Sonny Stitt's tenor commence the theme statement in unison, then break off into separate but mutually dependent lines. It is soon evident that counterpoint has not been added as a decorative element, but that the theme has an intrinsically contrapuntal character. Other instances could be quoted, but they are not frequent, as Lewis could not often indulge in this kind of writing while working as a free-lance musician. Once established, however, with a group with the potentialities of the MJQ, it was natural he should become more ambitious.

The use of classical contrapuntal devices, even of fugal form itself, is not an innovation on the Quartet's part, for jazz fugues can be found on records by Dave Brubeck, Shelly Manne, and Stan Kenton. But whereas these musicians have used contrapuntal devices perhaps once or twice in search of novelty,

Lewis has done so consistently. It may at this point be asked why it was necessary—even for Lewis—to turn to classical models, particularly in view of the apparent incompatibility of improvisation and the strictness of fugal form. New Orleans jazz was rich in counterpoint, but later styles have been very conspicuously less so. The New Orleans style would have no personal validity for Lewis or the other members of his group and, being drawn to contrapuntal composition, there was no jazz method of counterpoint on which he could base his work. It was therefore necessary to go further back. With his classical training it was easy for Lewis to go back to Bach, the supreme master of contrapuntal composition, and the fugue, the form of which counterpoint is the essence.

The objection may now be raised that, if the New Orleans style had no practical validity to Lewis, the much remoter music of the eighteenth century could have even less. But, although a *style* will date and lose its contemporary validity, the technical *devices* it incorporates need not. There is no device of melody, rhythm, harmony, orchestration, or counterpoint, however stale, that cannot be revivified by a musician of vision. Certain other jazz musicians may have been overwhelmed by classical influences, but Lewis's gifts are such that he has been able to come into contact with them freely without forfeiting his individuality. It is his achievement that he has succeeded where all others have failed in grafting a number of classical devices into the technique of jazz without doing violence to the spirit of the music. Whereas the self-styled progressive will vainly attempt to force the raw material of jazz into *soi-disant* classical textbook molds, Lewis never takes over a formal device as it stands but makes it his own by adapting it to his and the Quartet's expressive and stylistic needs.

A steady line of progress—that is to say, a line of increasing technical mastery—can be traced through those of the group's recordings that employ much counterpoint. *Vendôme*, although a striking piece, was dangerously near to being a Bach pastiche. *Concorde*, the first full fugue they recorded, is a much more confidently handled work, in which the contrapuntal development is allowed to run its course without interruption. The interweaving of piano and vibes in *Versailles* shows greater contrapuntal plasticity, which makes it one of the finest performances of any kind they have recorded. *Three Windows,* which they performed at many of their concerts here last year, is a triple fugue and must be one of the most formally elaborate pieces of jazz yet produced. It has three distinct subjects that are announced and developed in turn.

The influence and example of Bach is undeniable in the earlier pieces, but his name has been too glibly invoked in discussion of the more recent compositions and arrangements. Classical methods are likely to remain the parental root of all the Quartet's contrapuntal work, but it is essential to recognize that Lewis has developed a personal style of counterpoint that is synthesized with the other elements of his technique and has moved out of Bach's shadow. He is on his own now. *Vendôme* frequently reminds one of Bach; *Versailles, Three Windows,* and the opening and closing sequences of *The Rose Truc* do not. Similar remarks may be made about the Quartet's other recordings in which counterpoint is only used intermittently, for here, too, is much evidence of growing technical mastery.

The criticism has several times been made that, whatever the merits of the more traditional jazz elements of the Quartet's work, Lewis's contrapuntal scores are really quite unremarkable and "could for the most part have been supplied off-the-peg by any moderately gifted music-school graduate." This is an excellent criticism of most of the self-styled progressives, but when applied to Lewis it reveals considerable insensitivity. It is certain that no conservatory man could write pieces imbued with the jazz feeling that characterizes *all* Lewis's work. Further, counterpoint is an extremely difficult art that very few people really master, and the fluency displayed in Lewis's compositions could be matched by few people and is—aside from his other accomplishments—conclusive evidence of altogether exceptional gifts. Fairly elaborate counterpoint, generally in two parts, occurs frequently in the Quartet's simpler performances, which is an obvious sign that contrapuntal texture has become a normal part of their style and approach. A particularly felicitous example, among many others, is in *Love Walked In*—part of the Gershwin ballad medley. Here the piano's second voice sets off to perfection the melody stated on the vibes. Further evidence in this direction is that there is no stylistic divergence between the elaborately contrapuntal scores and the simpler treatments of ballads and blues.

Although it is not surprising that criticism of the group has centered on the formal quality of a number of their originals, reflection suggests that the contrapuntal style is in fact the basis of much of their success. However freely it is used and however much improvisation is present, counterpoint imposes a certain discipline on musical texture and in the case of the MJQ has probably acted as an antidote to Lewis's weakness for coloristic *chi-chi* mentioned earlier. The astonishing integration of the group's performances—which must surely be unique in jazz and enables them to work without microphones and to create, in pieces like *God Rest Ye Merry, Gentlemen,* the quietest jazz yet heard—is due mainly to sheer mastery of ensemble playing but may also be helped by the contrapuntal textures. This ensemble cohesion—which can only be fully appreciated in live performances—is most noticeable in long fugues like *Three Windows*; a good contrapuntal piece tends to be better-knit than a good homophonic one.

In all the MJQ's fugues the episodes are improvised and are based on predetermined harmonic sequences. A considerable part of the counterpoint in the group's other pieces would seem to be improvised too. Thus the Quartet has brought about a rebirth of the collective improvisation that, although one of the glories of the New Orleans school, has been conspicuously absent from later phases, with the exception of the isolated and inconclusive experiments of Lennie Tristano and Charlie Mingus. The word "rebirth" is used, because the work of men like George Lewis represents a preservation of the old original patterns, while that of the MJQ is a rebirth of the same concept into newer surroundings. It is to be hoped other musicians will follow their example.

All these aspects of the Quartet's contrapuntal approach are of importance, but what may prove to be the most significant has not yet been mentioned. In an article published in this magazine about a year ago I suggested that jazz needed to develop beyond the limits of the twelve- and thirty-two-bar chorus structures and get away from the usual theme and variations formula. Such a development was only likely to come about through a close co-operation between the composer or arranger and the improvising soloist, such as occurs in the MJQ. It seems that Lewis, with his additions and modifications to the language of modern jazz, has, for the small group at least, succeeded in utilizing more elaborate forms while preserving the soloist's freedom. The innovations have been proved valid, and form and content, improvisation and composition, have in his hands entered into a closer, more complex relationship.

The above rather cheerful reflections were prompted mainly by hearing the MJQ in person and not by a study of their records. It is clearly impossible to determine from recorded performances, particularly those of a restrained and intimate ensemble like the Quartet, just how much improvisation is present. As was suggested earlier, the elaborate textures the group produces lead one to suspect extemporization is minimal. It was both surprising and encouraging to learn from hearing the group in person that, although their jazz is at times the most complex on the contemporary scene, it is also among the most spontaneous. To hear them play pieces like *Django* and *Now's the Time* twice in one day with largely different solos on each occasion, to hear a *Queen's Fancy* that recalled the familiar recording in theme and framework but was quite different in pace, mood, and detail, was to realize that the group is very far from stagnation. The MJQ presented more improvisation per concert than any other group that has visited us, and this increased one's admiration for their innovations in other directions all the more.

The concerts last year made it clear how much one was underestimating Lewis by assuming the instrumental limitations of the MJQ would act as a brake on his creative development. A fixed and apparently immutable instrumentation may lead minor figures like George Shearing into stagnation, but not the genuine composer of jazz. Fairly recent additions to the repertoire like *God Rest Ye Merry, Gentlemen* and *The Rose Truc* emphasize that even in the field of tone color the group's resources are not yet exhausted. In view of the greater knowledge one acquired of the group during their visit it does not seem surprising that Lewis does not wish to enlarge the ensemble. One is reminded of the classical string quartet, the combination of two violins, viola, and 'cello for which straight composers have been writing for about two hundred years. In spite of two centuries' exploitation by a succession of great and original minds, the medium is not regarded as exhausted yet. Lewis probably feels the same about the combination of vibes, piano, bass, and percussion.

Aside from the quality of the improvisations and compositions presented by the Quartet, any feeling of monotony induced in the listener by the limited instrumentation is more than balanced by the breadth of their repertoire. Besides standard blues and ballads like *Now's the Time* and *Over the Rainbow* and the expected fugal pieces like *Versailles,* their programs include some very welcome bop classics such as *Confirmation* and *Yardbird Suite,* a number of pieces based on a film score, like *The Golden Striker* and *Venice,* and a few unexpected items like *Bess, Oh Where's My Bess?* and the already mentioned carol *God Rest Ye Merry, Gentlemen.* Avowed sources of inspiration appear to be equally varied and range from the Renaissance Commedia dell' Arte *(Fontessa)* to the Hopi dancers of New Mexico *(Sun Dance)* to virginal composers of the time of Elizabeth I such as Giles Farnaby *(The Queen's Fancy).* Again, this is surely unique in jazz.

Although this article is far from being in any sense a concert review, two points arising from the actual performance last November may be mentioned. The effect may have varied according to the hall in which the group was heard, but many readers will have noticed that Jackson dominated the ensemble much less than on the records. This was not an acoustical phenomenon but was because he was playing a softer-toned instrument than usual. Neither he nor Lewis liked it very much. Lewis's piano playing was criticized on various unjustified grounds. It is true he is no virtuoso, but no pianist would agree that his technique is poor. Perhaps the most mysterious criticism ever made of the Quartet is that "Lewis goes about his piano work as if he would be much happier for that instrument to be a harpsichord." Really his treatment of the instrument is perfectly attuned to its genius. His touch is exceptionally sensitive, and it may be that he prefers his solos to be simple in outline to contrast with the elaborate ensembles.

There remains the phenomena of the group's great popularity and material success. This is remarkable even when the utmost allowance is made for publicity and the boom jazz is enjoying at the present time. Some part of the boom may be due to Tin Pan Alley merchandise having reached such a level of offensive vulgarity that many listeners have turned to jazz who might in other circumstances have been content with reasonably tasteful dance music and ballads. Even so, the MJQ would seem to be the last type of group to benefit from such a reaction. Perhaps the unlimited popularity of Elvis Presley and the more restricted success of the MJQ are parts of a larger general picture to which we are still too close to be able to see as a whole. It may be that one of the Quartet's attractions is its unbending approach. Success has not been achieved by abandoning early ideals or even by compromise; on the contrary, as the group's following has grown so has its repertoire included more complex items. Their aloof demeanor on the stage is the greatest possible contrast to that of older musicians like Armstrong and Hines. Equally unusual in a jazz context is the hushed and respectful silence they are accorded at concerts. Jazz is always changing—perhaps the audience is beginning to change with it. Whether these modifications are for better or for worse is a matter the individual must always decide for himself.

RECORD NOTE

Most of the pieces referred to in the article are currently available in recordings by the Modern Jazz Quartet. To deal with their recording career chronologically, *Django, The Queen's Fancy, Autumn in New York,* and *But Not for Me* appear on Prestige 7057; *Vendôme* on Prestige 7059; *Love Walked In, I'll Remember April,* and *Concorde* on Prestige 7005; *Fontessa, Versailles,* and *Over the Rainbow* on Atlantic 1231; *Sun Dance, Oh Bess, Where Is My Bess?,* and *God Rest Ye Merry, Gentlemen* on Atlantic 1247; *Bags' Groove* on Atlantic 1265 (as well as an earlier version on Blue Note 1509); *Now's the Time* from a concert performance, Verve 8269; the film score *One Never Knows* (called *No Sun in Venice* in the United States), which includes *The Rose Truc, Three Windows,* and *The Golden Striker,* on Atlantic 1284; and a version of *Yardbird Suite,* plus performances of *Bags' Groove* and *A Night in Tunisia* with tenor saxophonist Sonny Rollins added, on Atlantic 1299.

. .*The original version of this essay appeared in* Music '58, *the* Down
Beat *yearbook, and it is used here by permission. For this version I have
made some additions and expansions.*

*Behind my effort to sift what seemed to me the important events in
jazz since the mid-'fifties is the assumption (or, perhaps, metaphor) that
an art has a kind of extra-human autonomy which leads it to its own
destiny, a kind of "the times make the man" theory perhaps. I hope I
have not overstated it in those terms, but I did feel that if a rather
shocking reversal of tendencies like the current reaction to cool jazz does
take place, one had best look at it for larger reasons which may go even
beyond the talents of individual artists involved in bringing it about.*

MARTIN WILLIAMS

The Funky-Hard Bop Regression

The gradual dominance of the Eastern and then national
scene in jazz by the so-called "hard bop" and "funky" schools
has shocked many commentators and listeners. The movement
has been called regressive, self-conscious, monotonous, and even
contrived.

It was Horace Silver as musical director of Art Blakey's Jazz
Messengers who first announced it, of course, and obviously he
and the rest had turned to church and gospel music and the
blues as sources of renewed inspiration. If these men were re-
luctant to listen to King Oliver and Bessie Smith, they heard
Ray Charles and Mahalia Jackson with a kind of reverence.

I think that this almost wholesale "return to the roots" has already had significance and has been made with good reason.
First, it has saved both the emotional heart of jazz and its very
substance from a preciocity, contrivance, and emptiness that

certain tendencies in "cool" jazz might have led to. Current "hard" jazz has produced its share of failures, to be sure, and a lot of what passes for "funk" and "soul" is more on the surface than in the depths, but such failures are inherent in any artistic movement.

Second, this "hard bop" jazz of the middle 'fifties is far from regressive because it is taking up certain pressing problems where they were left in the middle 'forties and is working out the solution. Musicians often debate the point, but I don't see how there can be any doubt that since the bop revolution the rhythmic lead in jazz has been carried by the bass. Bop also released the drummer's right foot and left hand, the pianist's left hand, and did away with rhythm guitar. At the same time, both drums and piano began to take on a polyrhythmic-melodic function which swing percussion had largely minimized and simplified over that of previous jazz.

There are two recent recordings which I think best illustrate further developments. The first is Lucky Thompson's ABC-Paramount LP (or rather half of it); the second is Thelonious Monk's *Brilliant Corners* with Max Roach.

The trio selections on the Thompson record are the most successful drumless records since the Armstrong Hot Fives. A guitar is present, but usually its role is that of a piano, hardly a rhythm instrument. The instrument which states the beat is Oscar Pettiford's bass—and it is the only one which needs to. It is to Jimmy Giuffre's great credit that, although his intentions are in many ways opposed to those of the hard school, he, too, has recognized this pressing fact in jazz in forming a drum-less ensemble.

The most important track in *Brilliant Corners* from a rhythmic point of view is *Bemsha Swing*. The fact that there were kettle drums in the studio and Roach and Monk decided to use them did not determine what happened on that record, it only served to dramatize something which is inevitable: the basic beat in future jazz will be carried by the bass; the drummer, if he is used (and he will be) will be free to provide a separate percussive line, a complex counter-rhythmic pattern.

The germ of this has been in modern drumming since Kenny

Clarke took it up from Jo Jones and passed it on to Roach, but the crisis has obviously been coming in Art Blakey's work. When such drumming as Blakey's ceases to be a "push" behind the soloist and slips into the role of a parallel voice, I think we will hear a release both in the horns and in percussion, but whether Blakey himself will make that slight but crucial shift or the final break will be made by another remains to be seen. *

The bassist is obviously going to have a heavier burden to carry. But imagine the release in the music! Those who complain that even the most varied jazz drumming is monotonous are difficult to answer. But when the basic rhythm is passed to an instrument that is both melodic and rhythmic in one, and the drummer released, the problem will be solved.

There are two further hints, I think, about the future role of the bass. These are found in the development of orthodox playing which Charlie Mingus has made, and in the heterodox style of the still-developing Wilbur Ware. Mingus can be a virtuoso soloist, but perhaps more important is his striking ability to maintain a beat firmly and clearly while providing a polyphonic line behind soloists as well. Ware's style is deceptively simple on the surface, but the technical, percussive, and harmonic freedom with which he plays shows that, with discipline, he may not only become an excellent rhythm bassist but one with a unique melodic approach to the role of his instrument both in ensemble and in solo.

Obviously such changes are going to mean other reshuffling in the rhythm section, and I think that Monk's style may give hints about them. One might say of Count Basie that he stripped jazz piano to its essentials, cut the chain which tied it to stating the beat, and shifted its function. Since then, various men have rebuilt it in imitation of horn styles and past styles. Monk's playing sometimes seems to say that the piano is not to be re-

---

* Tenor saxophonist-flutist Bobby Jaspar has pointed out in an excellent essay in *Jazz-Hot* (republished in translation in *The Jazz Review* for February 1959) that the work of "Philly Joe" Jones and Elvin Jones carries the style of Blakey a step further, introducing a greater polyrhythmic complexity, but still basically in the role of inspirational accompaniment.

built into a kind of virtuoso's "horn" because the experiments with rhythm, meter, and harmonies haven't yet scratched the surface.

Thus, on the one hand, we have Monk's approach to the ballad, freeing jazz of its dependency on the harmonic variations of most modern playing and returning it to an almost classic conception of variations *on theme,* and, on the other hand, the Monk who on his originals lays down percussive and harmonic patterns from which drummers, bassists, pianists, and hornmen all may draw. Already some of the developments we hear in Monk's style have an avant-garde in the piano playing of Cecil Taylor, Bill Evans, and Martial Solal.

What about the hornmen? I think two problems are pressing for them, and I think tenor-saxophonist Sonny Rollins is working on both of them. The first is that of continuity within a long solo passage. Many jazz musicians—many of them very celebrated—meet the problem of extended solos today simply by stringing together as many licks as they can beg, borrow, steal, and commit to memory, with as little repetition as possible. Even those who are more original are sometimes more concerned with not repeating themselves than with structure.

Some soloists have managed to come to terms with the problem excellently, but I think that at his best Rollins meets the problem head on, with a great awareness of just what it means to solo for chorus after chorus. His lines can show a gradual, relaxed building and a developing of continuity and structure that is unique. Rollins, under inspiration from Monk, bases improvisations on the theme. He may also structure his solos by a gradual revelation and diminishing of technical virtuosity. But behind it all is a fluent imagination which can keep his longest solo interesting even when he is relying on more conventional harmonic variation alone.

Rollins's other contribution has to do with the attack on bar lines, a problem he inherited from Gillespie and Parker (and not, I think, from Lennie Tristano). Rollins has the sound aesthetic intuition not to exploit his ability to create continuous lines. He has no fear of following a long line with phrases as short as one or two bars. Another tenor player, John Coltrane, has already shown a striking facility with lines, a superior harmonic freedom, and has at times implied that he wants the eighth-note rhythmic style of bebop further subdivided into even sixteenths; his problems as a soloist are not problems of such techniques. The respect of both these men for Monk is not without reason.

Probably the rediscovery of Thelonious Monk is the most significant of recent events in jazz. It now becomes clear that, whatever his contributions to bop, Monk has been working on something else all along. In the course of it, Monk has revealed himself as a great virtuoso of rhythm, meter, space, time. Also, especially recently, he has shown through the use of thematic variation and the elaboration of motival phrases that he is, together with John Lewis, the first master of form that modern jazz has had, and a major jazz composer. Monk is what no jazzman has ever been before him: still a legitimate innovator and experimenter, after over fifteen years, working directly with the materials of jazz and extending them along the way their own inner nature implies they should go. And he is what any major jazzman must be, a uniquely expressive player.

There may be a certain amount of divination involved in such an analysis, of course. But it is not as if I were to declare in the early 'twenties that jazz would soon become a soloist's style after hearing Louis Armstrong on a riverboat, or predicted bop after dropping in at Minton's in early 1941. I believe such things as I have discussed are happening now.

RECORD NOTE

Recordings reflecting contemporary "New York" jazz are listed in Category 9 of the "basic library" immediately following. The number of Lucky Thompson's ABC-Paramount is 111, *Brilliant Corners* on Riverside 12–226. Bill Evans is on Riverside 12–223, 12–291, and Coral CRL 57230. Cecil Taylor can be heard on Transition 19 (to be reissued by Blue Note), United Artists 4014, and Contemporary M–3562. Martial Solal's best American release is probably Epic LN–3376, with Kenny Clarke.

A BASIC LIBRARY OF JAZZ ON LP

The inadequacies of the catalogue and the unevenness of some long playing collections being granted, a beginner's library might include:

1. "FOLK" BACKGROUNDS AND BASIC BLUES

An Anthology	FOLKWAYS 2801
Blind Lemon Jefferson	RIVERSIDE 12–125
Big Bill Broonzy	FOLKWAYS 3586
Leadbelly	FOLKWAYS 2004

2. RAGTIME

Collections transcribed from piano rolls RIVERSIDE 12–110, 12–126

3. NEW ORLEANS ENSEMBLE AND SOLO STYLES

King Oliver's Creole Jazz Band	RIVERSIDE 12–122, EPIC 3208
Jelly Roll Morton, piano	RIVERSIDE 12–111
Jelly Roll Morton's Red Hot Peppers	RCA VICTOR LPM–1649
Johnny Dodds/Kid Ory	EPIC 3207
Bunk Johnson	COLUMBIA CL–829, AMERICAN MUSIC 643
Louis Armstrong	COLUMBIA CL–851–854
Sidney Bechet	BLUE NOTE 1201, COLUMBIA CL–836

4. SOLOISTS OF THE 'TWENTIES AND 'THIRTIES

Bix Beiderbecke	COLUMBIA CL–844–5
Fats Waller	RCA VICTOR LPM–1502
Earl Hines/James P. Johnson/Art Tatum	EPIC 3295
Jimmy Yancey	LABEL "X" LX–3000
Meade "Lux" Lewis	BLUE NOTE 7019
Louis Armstrong	DECCA DL–8327

5. BIG BANDS

Anthology	FOLKWAYS 2808
Fletcher Henderson	DECCA DL–6025
Duke Ellington	RCA VICTOR LPM–1364, LPM–1715
Count Basie	DECCA DL–8049, BRUNSWICK 54012
Jimmie Lunceford	COLUMBIA CL–634

6. SMALL GROUP AND SOLO SWING

Red Allen/Roy Eldridge, etc.	EPIC 3252
Art Tatum	VERVE 8118
Lester Young/Buck Clayton	COMMODORE 30014
Johnny Hodges/Cootie Williams	EPIC 3108
Lionel Hampton (Coleman Hawkins, Benny Carter, etc.)	JAZZTONE J–1246
Ben Webster	CLEF MGC–717
Charlie Christian (with Benny Goodman)	COLUMBIA CL–652
Erroll Garner	COLUMBIA CL–883

7. TRANSITION, BEBOP, AND MODERN

Christian-Monk-Clarke/Gillespie-Byas	ESOTERIC 548
Dizzy Gillespie-Charlie Parker	SAVOY 12007
Charlie Parker	SAVOY 12000, ROOST 2210
Bud Powell	BLUE NOTE 1503
Thelonious Monk	BLUE NOTE 1509, 1510

8. COOL

Miles Davis	CAPITOL T–762
Modern Jazz Quartet	PRESTIGE 7005, ATLANTIC 1231
Gerry Mulligan	PACIFIC JAZZ 1207

9. CONTEMPORARY EASTERN

Horace Silver-Art Blakey	BLUE NOTE 1518
Miles Davis	PRESTIGE 7076, 7109
Thelonious Monk	RIVERSIDE 12–209, 12–226
Sonny Rollins	PRESTIGE 7079, CONTEMPORARY 3530
Charlie Mingus	ATLANTIC 1237

10. SOME ADDITIONAL SINGERS

Ma Rainey	RIVERSIDE 1016
Bessie Smith	COLUMBIA CL–855–8
Billie Holiday	COLUMBIA CL–627, COMMODORE 30006
Ella Fitzgerald	DECCA DL–8149
Mahalia Jackson	COLUMBIA CL–1244
Sarah Vaughan	COLUMBIA CL–745
Joe Turner	ATLANTIC 1234
Jack Teagarden	CAPITOL T–692
Ray Charles	ATLANTIC 8025

In one of his first pieces of criticism, Gunther Schuller reviewed
The Art of Jazz *in the March-April, 1960 issue of* The Jazz Review. *Mr. Schuller comments today (1981) that he finds the
article a trifle opinionated and hard-edged in its tone, but stands
by its basic judgments.*

The Art of Jazz is one of the finest books ever compiled on
the subject of jazz and perhaps in some ways the most important, for it represents an anthology of jazz criticism and writing
on jazz at the highest level, and contains essays that are not
only edifying in their perceptiveness, but even inspiring.

Both qualities are rare in jazz writing. The articles selected
by the editor are not the kind of glib journalism that, by and
large, plagues jazz year in-year out. One has the feeling, on the
contrary, that the writers of these articles wrote them because
they had to; they had something original and important to
express. In fact, in most of the writing, there is the same kind
of creative urgency that distinguishes the music and musicians
discussed in the anthology. *The Art of Jazz,* therefore, gives us
not only a collection of illuminating essays, but indirectly also
a history of intelligent jazz criticism of the last twenty years.

Having said that, I feel free to add that, in the individual
parts, the book occasionally does not measure up to its quality
as a whole. Obviously it would be hard to point to an anthology
about which such a criticism could not be made. But whatever
weaknesses some of the articles may disclose, they are more
than outweighed by the definitive quality of nearly half of the
essays in the collection.

The best pieces, in my opinion, are Larry Gushee's on the
King Oliver band and Glenn Coulter's on Billie Holiday. They

combine intelligent analysis with a deep love and respect for their subject. They are the kind of articles that make an indelible impression, and make you run right out and buy the recordings discussed. Moreover, both essays are written with excellent literary style, which, for me, raises the content to an expressive level rarely encountered in jazz writing.

Several contributions are almost as good. Max Harrison's is certainly the most thoughtful critique of the Modern Jazz Quartet to date. Ross Russell's four articles on "be-bop," written in the late forties when this music was still controversial—at a time, in other words, when very few people (including most musicians) were able to say anything articulate about the music—stand up very well after ten years, and are, in addition, of considerable historical importance. Paul Bacon's perceptive words on Thelonious Monk, at a time when Monk was still totally unrecognized by laymen and musicians alike, fall in the same category.

William Russell's studies on three Boogie Woogie pianists (Lofton, Yancey, and Meade Lux Lewis) set new standards of jazz criticism back in 1939. They combine historical fact with a certain amount of unpedantic analysis in a judicious blend. Occasional musical examples illustrate Russell's points succinctly.

Guy Waterman's otherwise fine piece on ragtime fails precisely in the area of musical analysis. Two pages of analysis of Joplin's "Euphonic Sounds" are not only full of errors, but are confusing and amateurishly stated even when correct.* I think Mr. Waterman should have been advised to leave the analyzing on this level to a competent musician, or at least he or the editor should have checked his results with one. Fortunately, musical analysis is not the most convincing method with which to appraise either ragtime or Joplin's simple music (simple in the best sense); therefore not much damage is done. And Waterman's two-part article is otherwise very commendable.

*The accidentals omitted in the original are herein restored for the Da Capo edition.

There is also Martin Williams' excellent summation of recent stylistic changes (1958) in jazz, and his perceptive statements on Monk, Rollins, Wilbur Ware, John Lewis, and the changing role of jazz drumming constitute rare present-day examples of real jazz criticism.

The Art of Jazz also contains a number of solid pieces that make a good start but in various ways do not go quite far enough. The best of these are George Avakian's superior liner notes on Bix Beiderbecke and Bessie Smith, and Ross Russell's fine study of James P. Johnson—all three excellent in their own way. William Russell's article on Jelly Roll Morton's "Frog-i-more Rag" is good, aside from an occasional touch of overstatement. But I kept wishing that the article had dealt with Morton's Hot Peppers recordings, surely his greatest claim to fame.

Charles Fox's piece on Ellington in the thirties fills a serious gap, I suppose, but again does not say nearly enough about this crucial period in the development of the Ellington band. I have no particular opinions about Paul Oliver's piece on Big Maceo, mainly because I don't know enough about Maceo. But perhaps that's just the joint. I had hoped to know more about this blues singer after reading the article than I now know. Off hand it seems to me, this is the kind of "personal opinion" piece that doesn't really tell you very much, and of which jazz has had an over-abundance. Vic Bellerby's piece on various aspects of Ellington's music I found similarly "impressionistic" and unfortunately most annoying in its hyperbolic and inaccurate use of adjectives. Somehow words like "spectral," "macabre," "occult," "fierce," "raging," are words that seem out of place and far-fetched in speaking of Ellington, especially in the context of the recordings so described.

André Hodeir's controversial study of Tatum is weakened by a far too personal and subjectively polemical approach. Although some of his points contain a basis of truth, one is inclined to think, after reading some of Hodeir's more naïvely brandishing statements and in view of Tatum's absolutely unique abilities, "So what!" The music of Tatum—even despite some of the weaknesses Hodeir ascribes to it—somehow still is more important than Hodeir's criticism of it. And if Hodeir demands "toughness, ruthlessness and cruelty" in his jazz geniuses, one is tempted to ask where he finds these characteristics in the music of Gil Evans, whom Hodeir admires so unequivocally.

Marshall Stearns' note on Sonny Terry is, for my taste, a little vague at crucial moments, and I can't help feeling that a better example by Dr. Stearns might have been chosen, especially on the early sources of jazz. One other minor point that bothered me was that the original dates of publication were not given for many of the articles.† In view of the constantly shifting nature of jazz, and out of consideration for the writers involved, I think it is mandatory in an anthology that covers such a span of years to give these dates.

In conclusion I should like to emphasize that this is a book not only for fellow jazz writers and aficionados. I recommend its best sections to musicians as well. Musicians are notoriously

---

†Dates for this Da Capo edition were provided by Martin Williams:
Prologue: Sidney Bechet in Europe, 1919 *by Ernest Ansermet (1919)*
Sonny Terry and His Blues *by Marshall Stearns (1954)*
Ragtime *by Guy Waterman (1956)*
Jelly Roll Morton and the Frog-i-more Rag *by William Russell (1944)*
King Oliver's Creole Jazz Band *by Larry Gushee (1958)*
James P. Johnson *by Ross Russell (1941)*
Dixieland *by Orrin Keepnews (1954)*
Bix Beiderbecke *by George Avakian (1952)*
Bessie Smith *by George Avakian (1952)*
Recording Limits and Blues Form *by Martin Williams (1953)*
Three Boogie-Woogie Blues Pianists *by William Russell (1939-40)*
Big Maceo *by Paul Oliver (1957)*
Duke Ellington in the Nineteen-thirties *by Charles Fox (1958)*
Duke Ellington *by Vic Bellerby (1959)*
Billie Holiday *by Glenn Coulter (1956)*
The Genius of Art Tatum *by André Hodeir (1955)*
Charles Christian *by Al Avakian and Bob Prince (1954)*
Bebop *by Ross Russell (1948-49)*
Two Notes on Modern Jazzman *by Paul Bacon (1949)*
Looking Back at the Modern Jazz Quartet *by Max Harrison (1958)*
The Funky-Hard Bop Regression *by Martin Williams (1957)*

ill-informed about their own musical tradition. And while I would agree that, as a rule, writing on jazz does not exactly inspire confidence in the genre, several pieces in this collection are definitely a welcome exception to the rule.

—GUNTHER SCHULLER

Related Quality Paperback Books from Da Capo Press

RAISE UP OFF ME
A Portrait of
Hampton Hawes
by Hampton Hawes
and Don Asher
Introduction by Gary Giddins

THE WORLD OF
DUKE ELLINGTON
by Stanley Dance

LOUIS ARMSTRONG
by Hugues Panassié

IN SEARCH OF
BUDDY BOLDEN
First Man of Jazz
by Donald M. Marquis

BIRD
The Legend of
Charlie Parker
Edited by Robert Reisner

TREAT IT GENTLE
An Autobiography
by Sidney Bechet

MUSIC ON MY MIND
The Memoirs of an
American Pianist
by Willie the Lion Smith
and George Hoefer

JAZZ MASTERS OF
NEW ORLEANS
by Martin Williams

. . . available at your bookstore